BLACK HOMELAND / BLACK DIASPORA

BLACK HOMELAND
BLACK DIASP RA

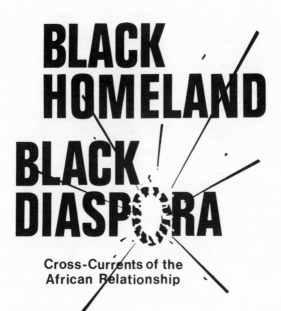

Cross-Currents of the African Relationship

PREFATORY ESSAY BY **BONIFACE I. OBICHERE**
Director of African Studies Center, University of California, Los Angeles

Edited by JACOB DRACHLER

National University Publications
Kennikat Press ● 1975
Port Washington, N. Y. ● London

Acknowledgment is gratefully made to the following authors, agents, and publishers:

James Baldwin, "Black Colloquium in Paris" from the book, *Nobody Knows My Name* by James
Baldwin. Copyright © 1961 by James Baldwin. Reprinted by permission of the publisher, The Dial
Press. Originally published in *Encounter.*

Horace Mann Bond, "Forming African Youth at Lincoln University" from *Africa Seen By American
Negroes*, edited by John A. Davis, published by the American Society of African Culture, 1958. By
permission of Mrs. Julia Bond and the Estate of Horace Mann Bond.

John Pepper Clark, "The Garment of Damnation" from *America, Their America* by John Pepper Clark,
published by Andre Deutsch Ltd.

W.E.B. Du Bois, "An Official Visit to Liberia" from *Dusk of Dawn* by W.E.B. Du Bois, copyright ©
1940, by Harcourt Brace Jovanovich, Inc.; copyright © 1968, by Shirley Graham Du Bois. Reprinted
by permission of the publisher.

Ernest Dunbar, "Bill Sutherland: Pacifist Expatriate" from the book, *The Black Expatriates* by Ernest
Dunbar. Copyright © 1968 by Ernest Dunbar. Published by E.P. Dutton & Co., Inc. and used with
their permission.

Ralph Ellison, "Negro Culture: Some Questions and Some Answers" from *Preuves*, No. 87, May 1958,
pp. 33–38, published and copyright © by the International Association for Cultural Freedom, Paris,
and reprinted by their permission.

E.U. Essien-Udom, "In Search of a Saving Identity" from *Black Nationalism* by E.U. Essien-Udom,
copyright© 1962, by the University of Chicago Press, and reprinted by permission of the author and
the University of Chicago Press.

Langston Hughes, "Looking In On West Africa" from *The Big Sea* by Langston Hughes, copyright ©
1940 by Langston Hughes. Reprinted by permission of Hill and Wang, a division of Farrar, Straus &
Giroux, Inc.

Leslie A. Lacy, "Black Bodies in Exile" from *The Rise and Fall of a Proper Negro* by Leslie A. Lacy.
Copyright © 1970 by Leslie A. Lacy. Reprinted by permission of Macmillan Publishing Co., Inc.

Taban lo Liyong, "Negroes Are Not Africans," from *The Last Word* by Taban lo Liyong. Copyright ©
by Taban lo Liyong 1969. Reprinted by permission of East African Publishing House, Nairobi.

Malcolm X, "After the African Visits" from *Malcolm X Speaks* published by Merit Publishers.
Copyright © by Merit Publishers and Mrs. Betty Shabazz. Reprinted by permission of Pathfinder
Press, Inc.

Ali A. Mazrui, "New-World Roots of Pan-Africanism" from the essay, "Borrowed Theory and Original
Practice in African Politics" in *Patterns of African Development: Five Comparisons*, Herbert J. Spiro,
Ed., copyright © 1967. Reprinted by permission of Prentice-Hall, Inc., Englewood Cliffs, N.J.

Tom Mboya, "Africa and Afro-America" from *The Challenge of Nationhood* by Tom Mboya. Copyright © 1970, Estate of Tom Mboya. Reprinted by permission of Andre Deutsch and Praeger Publishers.

Albert Murray, "The Role of the Pre-American Past" from *The Omni-Americans* by Albert Murray.
Copyright © 1970 by Albert Murray. Published by E.P. Dutton & Co., Inc. (Outerbridge & Dienst-
frey) and used with their permission.

Kwame Nkrumah, "Hard Times in America" from *The Autobiography of Kwame Nkrumah*, first
published in 1957, Panaf Books Ltd., 243 Regent Street, London, W1R 8PN.

Richard Wright, "On Tour in the Gold Coast" from *Black Power* by Richard Wright, published by
Harper & Row, 1954. Copyright © 1954 by Richard Wright. Reprinted by permission of Paul R.
Reynolds, Inc., 599 Fifth Avenue, New York, N.Y. 10017.

Library of Congress Cataloging in Publication Data

Drachler, Jacob, comp.
  Black homeland/Black diaspora.

  (National university publications)
  Includes bibliographical references.
  1. Negro race — Addresses, essays, lectures.
I. Title.
GN645.D73   301.45'19'6   74-80066
ISBN 0-8046-9077-4

In Memory of
JULIAN F. JAFFE
Teacher — Scholar — Generous Spirit

CONTENTS

BLACK HOMELAND /
BLACK DIASPORA

JACOB DRACHLER

Introduction

In 1898 Edward W. Blyden—the father of black nationalist ideology—published a pamphlet, *The Jewish Question,* praising "that marvelous movement called Zionism." He had been deeply impressed by Theodor Herzl's *Der Judenstaat* (*The Jewish State,* 1896) and apparently saw a striking and inspiring parallel between Herzl's ideal and his own labors to build in Liberia a Negro state and center of African renaissance.

A half century later Ralph Ellison was one of those black intellectuals who challenged the concept of Africa as a black Zion, saying that if everyone had to have "some place to be proud of . . . I am proud of Abbeville, South Carolina, and Oklahoma City. That is enough for me." He was concerned, he said, that "by raising the possibility of Africa as a 'homeland', we give Africa an importance on the symbolic level that it does not have in the actual thinking of people."[1]

For more than a century ideas about the relationship between Africa and its diaspora have been debated by black thinkers and leaders, and tested in the crucible of events. The polar opposites represented by such views as those of Blyden and Ellison define the limits between which these ideas have oscillated, but barely suggest the variety of experiences and concepts through which Negroes here and abroad have struggled to achieve a viable

---

[1] *Daedalus,* winter 1966, vol. 95, no. 1.

relationship that would satisfy desires for both symbolism and actuality, that would fill the needs for both pride and power.

The present collection of Afro-American and African writings is designed to explore this tortuous historic relationship, which, in the present generation, has had so momentous a rebirth. Both sides of the relationship are examined: on the one hand, how Afro-Americans have experienced Africa and conceived their connection with it, and on the other hand, how Africans have responded to the Afro-American world and its growing interest in Africa. Most of the selections have a markedly personal dimension, whether the writer appears as a pilgrim or sojourner, observer or activist, advocate or critic. The contributors—as men of letters, scholars, political leaders, and educators—have all played some part in shaping the relationship which is the subject of this book, and with the exception of Robert Campbell and Edward Blyden, are all of the twentieth century.

For generations the consciousness of Africa flickered uncertainly in the mind of the American Negro, sometimes flaring up in gusts of pride and hope, as happened most spectacularly in Marcus Garvey's "Back to Africa" movement of the 1920s. However, no previous generation of Afro-Americans has experienced so wide and steady an interest in Africa as the present one, a development directly connected with the dramatic rise of some thirty independent black states in Africa during the fifties and sixties. During the same period Negro Americans forged ahead in civil rights, political power, and economic gains. These events in the two hemispheres were significantly related. Over the years many Africans had prepared themselves for leadership by living and studying in Afro-American settings. Black Americans, for their part, had drawn inspiration from African contacts and achievements. Enfolded in these events of the mid-twentieth century lay the promise that a great historic trauma was beginning to be healed.

The original phase of this trauma had been the cruel alienations of the slave trade, the folk memories of being sold by other black men to the white slave-traders, of being torn away from kith and kin, native customs, language and traditions. Under slavery, locked in by the white master's racist ideas and practices, the Negro would come to think of Africa as a dangerous place, its people as brutish pagans whose best hope was to be made Christian. And this negative view of Africa and Africans was later purveyed by the Negro churches themselves, where the people would hear Negro missionaries, in self-justification, give distorted impressions of African life. Even Frederick Douglass, an indomitable defender of the Negro, spoke disparagingly of Africa. George Washington Williams, a black historian, who had been a Union soldier in the Civil War, wrote *A History of the Negro Race in America* (1883), a very influential book, which characterized Africans as abject and degraded. There were other leading Afro-American editors and spokesmen who expressed strong aversion to any association with Africa. Thus, for most black Americans the idea of being bracketed with Africans became tainted with embarrassment and shame. School textbooks, newspapers, and other popular media tended merely to proliferate and reinforce such feelings.

But there were other streams of opinion, other outlooks, among Negroes. As early as 1787 a group of free Negroes in Newport, Rhode Island, organized a "Free African Society" to urge that Negroes be repatriated to Africa. In 1815 Paul Cuffee, a wealthy Negro ship owner, took a group of freedmen to Africa at his own expense. However, as Walter L. Williams has pointed out, emigrationists tended to regard themselves as missionaries for European values; they "wished to establish a Westernized Afro-American nation in the midst of African darkness."[2] Many Negro organizations took African names like Sons of Africa or African Methodist Episcopal Church. There were important black leaders with a pro-African orientation like Bishop H. M. Turner, Martin R. Delany and Edward W. Blyden. Blyden, in an address at Hampton Institute, warned students not to believe disparagements of African civilization.

Plans for mass repatriation of blacks to Africa seem to have been far more popular with whites than with blacks. In 1818 the American Colonization Society—a creation primarily of white leaders and statesmen—succeeded in establishing a tiny colony of freedmen at Monrovia on the west coast of Africa, which was later to develop into the republic of Liberia. Some sponsors of the Colonization Society were slave owners who thought their grip on their human property would be safer if the free Negroes

---

[2] Walter L. Williams, "Black American Attitudes toward Africa 1877–1900", *Pan African Journal* (Spring, 1971, Vol. 4, No. 2).

were shipped out of the country. But the overwhelming majority of freedmen, numbering close to half a million, rejected ideas of African nationality and emigration. Typically, a convention of free Negroes meeting in New York in 1831 preferred to look toward the realization of democracy in America, declaring "God hasten that time. This is our home and this is our country. Beneath its sod lies the bones of our fathers; for it, some of them fought, bled, and died. Here we were borne and here we will die."[3]

Two nineteenth-century Afro-Americans, Edward W. Blyden and Robert Campbell (both born in the West Indies), were interested in founding settlements of freedmen on African soil. Blyden emigrated to Liberia and became a significant leader in its development. Campbell sought to pioneer a settlement of black immigrants in the Niger delta in what is now Nigeria. However, Campbell and his colleague Dr. Martin R. Delany failed to establish a colony. No emigration followed the expedition. It was only in the 1920s after emancipation and reconstruction had failed to bring equal citizenship to blacks, and their oppression and misery continued, that a separatist, emigrationist appeal, under the flamboyant leadership of Marcus Garvey, was able to garner significant mass support. But this movement soon collapsed, not only because of Garvey's wild mismanagement, imprisonment for fraud, and subsequent deportation. The underlying reason was summed up by the Negro historian John Hope Franklin in this way: "Regardless of how dissatisfied Negroes were with conditions in the United States, they were unwilling in the 20s, as their forebears had been a century earlier, to undertake the uncertain task of redeeming Africa."[4] The use of the word "redeeming" here is an echo of the theory of "providential design" popular among mission-minded Christians in the nineteenth century, which taught that God allowed Africans to be enslaved and civilized so they could then redeem their benighted brethren. As it turned out, however, another kind of redemption was undertaken by the Africans themselves. It is quite a different situation today, when

---

[3] Herbert Aptheker (ed.), *A Documentary History of the Negro People in the United States* (New York, 1951), I, 109.

[4] John Hope Franklin, *From Slavery to Freedom* (New York, 1952) p. 483.

Afro-Americans as volunteers, tourists, or settlers, swarm to the homeland in order, as they often feel, to redeem themselves.[5]

Marcus Garvey's movement, with its emotional and ritualistic appeal, drew masses of uneducated and poor people together in a dream of Africa as justification, solace, and salvation, but it failed utterly with the educated classes. However, for the latter, an African orientation began to be offered by such black scholars as Carter G. Woodson and W. E. B. Du Bois. Woodson founded in 1915 the Association for the Study of Negro Life and History, and was its director, as well as the editor of its organ the *Journal of Negro History,* for thirty-five years until his death in 1950. The influence of this association and the work of the Negro colleges led by Atlanta, Fisk, Howard, and Lincoln universities generated increased scholarly activity on African subjects.

W. E. B. Du Bois had a large influence in spreading respect for the African heritage through his long editorship of *The Crisis* and his many eloquent books, at least one of which, *The World and Africa* (1947) was entirely devoted to a massive marshaling of materials pointing to Africa as a source of world civilization from most ancient times.

An important breakthrough was the landmark publication of a collection of essays, *Africa from the Point of View of American Negro Scholars* (1958). This richly informative volume was initially sponsored by the Paris-based Society of African Culture (SAC), an international movement launched by black intellectuals from the French colonies in Africa and the Caribbean. The volume was edited by John A. Davis, the director of the affiliated American Society of African Culture (AMSAC).[6] From this book we have excerpted Horace Mann Bond's essay "Forming African Youth at Lincoln University" as an example of the fruitful interactions between Afro-Americans and Africans. A historic conference of SAC in 1956 is reviewed with brilliant commentary by James Baldwin in "Black Colloquium in Paris." AMSAC itself is

---

[5] At a convention of black American travel agents held at Abidjan, Ivory Coast, in October, 1972, Earl Kennedy, the president of their organization declared, "The black thrust toward Africa is real—you find black groups of the elderly, the professionals, the civil servants and even students are all trying to book a trip to Africa, back home to their source" (*New York Times,* October 22, 1972).

[6] This was followed by another significant AMSAC publication, *Pan-Africanism Reconsidered* (University of California Press, 1962) edited by Samuel W. Allen.

etched in acid by the controversial Nigerian poet-playwright J. P. Clark, in a selection from his book *America, Their America* (1964). These cross-references indicate some of the dialogue on cultural issues that has taken place between African and Afro-American intellectuals.

Almost all the African and Afro-American contributors to this volume have lived, studied, worked, or at least visited in the overseas black communities. The currents of the relationship which they portray obviously run deeper than print; they flow from historic sources and recent experiences in which these authors have shared.

In addition to the two nineteenth-century figures Campbell and Blyden, at least five twentieth-century contributors may be considered under the heading of "journeys to Africa," although each is rather different from the others. Langston Hughes's youthful account of a visit to the west coast of Africa as a member of a ship's crew is the least political or ideological, the most personal. The pages from Du Bois are political in a double sense: first, in that he is on an official mission, representing the United States at the inauguration of a Liberian president, and second, in that he employs the occasion, in keeping with his role as a Negro ideologist, to exalt the African character and culture. William Sutherland's choice of expatriation to Africa and his work for various African governments or committees are based more on his radical pacifist philosophy and his alienation from American society than on a sense of racial identity. Leslie Lacy's two-year stay in Ghana begins with a very ardent commitment to the politics of his two heroes Du Bois and Nkrumah, progresses through an intense ideological involvement with the large colony of Afro-Americans and with his Ghanaian students, and ends with the confusions and soul-searchings attending Nkrumah's decline and fall. The responses of Malcolm X to his six months of travels in Africa are on a more professional political plane, since, as an ambitious organizer of a new Afro-American movement after his break with Elijah Muhammad, he has to take into account old constituencies among Muslim-oriented blacks, while trying to build new ones on a secular nationalist base.

To Negroes suffering deprivations and indignities, searching for an identity of wholeness and pride, a number of disparate ideologies and strategies have offered themselves, pointing toward Africa as the ancestral homeland. With reference to the writings gathered in this volume, we can distinguish the following as main tendencies:

1. *Mass emigration.* Edward W. Blyden devoted his life to the upbuilding of the republic of Liberia, founded on white-sponsored Negro emigration.[7] Robert Campbell, together with his colleague Martin R. Delany, hoped to colonize the Niger valley. Most freedmen in America resisted all such projects. When Marcus Garvey roused his thousands of messianic followers, mostly poor West Indians, no emigration followed. Even quite recently, as we learn from Tom Mboya's article, a faction of American black separatists demanded automatic citizenship rights for emigrants to Kenya. This was, of course, denied by Kenya, as it probably would be by the other African regimes. From the point of view of most black Americans, as well as of African states, mass emigration is not a very promising option. However, the advocacy of emigration has from time to time helped in restoring and building pride and morale among many black Americans, while remaining at the same time an expression of frustrated hope for full integration into American society.

2. *Pan-Africanism.* In addition to doing a great deal of research and writing about Africa, W. E. B. Du Bois was the founder and guiding spirit of the Pan-African movement which sought to link black independence forces in Africa with leaders of Negro rights struggles in the diaspora. Du Bois had originated the slogan of this movement: "The problem of the twentieth century is the problem of the color line," had organized four Pan-African conferences between 1919 and 1927, and a fifth in 1945, before leaving in advanced old age to become a citizen of Ghana.

Today the term "Pan-Africanism" connotes at least three distinct approaches: first, efforts to increase areas of cooperation among the Negro nations in Africa, and on a continental scale as well; second, cultural and scholarly contacts between Africa and the diaspora communities (such as those conducted by the

---

[7] But even Blyden, who so ardently advocated a black exodus to Africa, said, "That exodus may never come for all; but the feeling and aspiration on the part of the exile must ever be towards the Fatherland, as the Jew, wherever he is, looks to Palestine. . . ."

above-mentioned organizations SAC and AMSAC);[8] third, a pragmatic, issue-oriented politics on both sides of the Atlantic; e.g., declarations on African topics by black American leaders, and statements made by the Organization of African Unity on problems of blacks in America. The excerpts from Malcolm X and Tom Mboya in this book suggest further examples of this approach.

Kwame Nkrumah's drive for a kind of preemptive Pan-Africanism seems to have been impelled by a characteristically grandiose ambition to put himself at the head of some sort of continental superstate before the individual African governments had a chance to settle into their separate sovereign establishments. This project might better be called Nkrumahism than Pan-Africanism.

3. *Expatriation.* Of course, some Negro Americans, like certain white compatriots, have chosen to become expatriates—as individuals—in various corners of the globe. Well-known cases are those of Richard Wright and James Baldwin, both of whom lived for many years in Paris. Ernest Dunbar, in his book *The Black Expatriates,* reports on a number of others. In the present context those Negro Americans who chose to settle in Africa are the relevant cases. Mr. Dunbar's very interesting interview with Bill Sutherland in Tanzania is included here, along with Leslie Lacy's fascinating account of the Afro-American expatriate community in Ghana, of which he was a part. Many individuals, according to their talents and interests, and their discontent with their life in the United States, will undoubtedly exercise this option in one African country or another. Thus, conceivably, individual expatriation—including families or groups of friends—could become a sizable trend.

4. *Separatist nationalism.* The Black Muslims discussed by Dr. Essien-Udom in the selection "In Search of a Saving Identity" are an ambiguous example of this particular orientation, because they are more likely to refer to the Arabic-speaking countries of Africa and the Middle East as their homeland, and to treat prospects of an "exodus" as a distant, if ultimate, goal. Possibly

---

[8] Dialogues on the cultural plane have, since independence, continued in such events as the Negro Arts Festival held in Dakar in 1966, and the Black and African Culture Festival scheduled to be held in Lagos in 1975.

Garvey's movement also fits under this "separatism-without-emigration" rubric if we are to believe Garvey's widow Amy Jacques Garvey when she states, "There was no Back-to-Africa movement except in a spiritual sense."[9] Several other separatist nationalist groups exist or have existed for a time, but none as successful as the Muslims or the Garveyites.

5. *Pluralist integration.* "The point of our struggles," says Ralph Ellison, "is to be both Negro and American and to bring about that condition in American society in which this would be possible." This statement may serve as a definition of pluralist integration. It is a point of view shared, with varying nuances by the largest number of contributors to this anthology: the Afro-Americans Richard Wright, James Baldwin, Ralph Ellison, and Albert Murray; the Africans Taban lo Liyong, E. U. Essien-Udom, and Tom Mboya—and probably others, too, in both sections.

It is a striking fact that the three great contemporary Afro-American novelists, Wright, Ellison, and Baldwin have all expressed skepticism about the importance of African cultural survivals in American Negro life. All three are distrustful of the Negritude mystique, or of any ideology which attempts—as they see it—to blunt their very keen sense of the particularities of the black experience in America, out of which they write.[10]

Again and again writers of this tendency on both sides of the Atlantic maintain (1) that the past of Negro Americans is most significantly an American rather than an African past, and (2) that present tasks should be faced with an eye to exploiting the viable resources of world cultures rather than to nostalgic preservation of cultural relics. Not that the African heritage is to be summarily dismissed. "This remote heritage," says the Nigerian sociologist Essien-Udom, speaking of the American Negro, "no

---

[9] "The Ghost of Marcus Garvey", *Ebony,* March, 1960. The redoubtable Mrs. Garvey, interviewed more recently, at the age of 77, repeated this idea with a riposte entirely in the tradition of her husband's antagonism to middle-class, educated blacks: "He never meant there should be mass migration of black people from the United States to Africa. A lot of intellectual niggers wrote a lot of hooey about Garvey" (*Miami Herald Magazine,* May 6, 1973).

[10] Langston Hughes was also of this orientation when he wrote, "I was only an American Negro—who had loved the surface of Africa and the rhythms of Africa—but I was not Africa. I was Chicago and Kansas City and Broadway and Harlem" (*The Big Sea,* New York, 1940).

matter how insignificant its content may be, is part and parcel of the Negro's being. This, too, like his Americanism, should be understood."

In recent decades an assimilationist "melting-pot" model of America has been replaced by the pluralist concept. In this framework, Negro ethnicity takes its natural place in the cultural orchestra of America. In fact, it has been there for a long time, whether recognized or not. In his book *The Omni-Americans* Albert Murray speaks of "a process of Americanization that has now equipped and disposed [Afro-Americans] not only to reclaim and update the heritage of black Africa but also to utilize the multicolored heritage of all mankind of all the ages."

On the African side, the Uganda-born writer Taban lo Liyong believes that "African culture is to be a synthesis and a metamorphosis—the order of things to come," and he winds up his essay "Negritude: Crying over Spilt Milk" with this exuberant peroration:

This is the crossroad and cross-breeding place. No mules are born. Trespassers will not be prosecuted. Indeed, New York (and Paris, and Moscow, and Peking) 'let the black blood flow into your blood'; let it flow uncontrolled. A racially and culturally mixed person is the universal man; all is in him; he identifies with all; he is kith and kin to all other Homo sapiens. This leads us to a super-Brazil. He will have slant eyes, kinky hair, Roman nose, Red Indian knight-errantry, democratic folly, dictatorial changeability, Maori tattoos, use English as a tool for rebuilding Babel Tower. All these (and more) will make him the hundred per cent African; the descendant of Zinjanthropus, the culturally and racially mixed man of the future.[11]

Of course, this vision of a miscegenetic utopia does not tell us what has actually been happening in Mr. lo Liyong's East Africa, where thousands of long-settled Asiatic and other non-African residents were forced to leave for the economic and political convenience of the new regimes, and where many thousands of Hutu and Tutsi succumbed to mutual genocidal pogroms. Such events indicate some of the realities that stand in the way of the cultural assimilation which Mr. lo Liyong envisions.

And as for the United States—whether or not it may become a "super-Brazil" at some future time, the present scene suggests that a strong mood of separation, of drawing in and consolidating the inner resources of the Negro people, has accompanied

---

11 Taban lo Liyong, *The Last Word* (Nairobi, 1969), p. 206.

their economic and political advances, and that this is very much a part of the pluralistic tenor of the country. In this ethnic consolidation the sense of a proud relationship with Africa has been a very considerable factor. As always, the relationship is akin, in unresting changefulness and continuity, to the ocean which separates the black homeland and its diaspora. The intellectual exchanges and living interactions, exemplified in the present collection, reflect both the promise and the problems of a many-dimensioned mutuality. It is not difficult to read in the record of this relationship a growing power.

This record is expertly brought up to date in the special prefatory essay, "Afro-Americans in Africa: Recent Experiences" by Professor Boniface I. Obichere, director of the African Studies Center at UCLA and editor of the *Journal of African Studies.* Dr. Obichere brings to bear both scholarly resources and personal experiences in illuminating the many fruitful interactions between Afro-Americans and Africa. He suggests that the significance of this relationship should not be measured merely in terms of the numbers of black Americans present in Africa at any given time:

In looking at the whole picture, one can posit the theory of the critical mass. What we see in this case is a small number of highly skilled and well-educated Afro-Americans interacting with African societies in the new African states. The important thing is that they have produced lasting results in his interaction.

But the numbers are also there, he adds:

The most important facet of the present relations between Africa and Afro-Americans is the astronomic increase in the number of short-term visitors and tourists who pour into all parts of Africa every year. These black Americans are keenly interested in Africa and its peoples. There is a touch of messianism in the pilgrimage of Afro-Americans to contemporary Africa.

His paper documents several interesting cases of long-term settlers who have taken up permanent residency in Africa as business entrepreneurs, technologists or professionals.

On a more controversial plane, Dr. Obichere is concerned to challenge what he considers inadequate or tendentious reports by certain white as well as black writers on the African relationship. Among the blacks, he singles out Leslie Lacy, author of *The Rise and Fall of a Proper Negro,* as a disputed source of information as to what went on in the very large Afro-American colony in Nkrumah's Ghana. Dr. Obichere says, "Many of Mr.

Lacy's friends and acquaintances dispute his recollection of most of the events, as well as his interpretation of Ghanian affairs." This should be of particular interest in connection with the long excerpt from Mr. Lacy's book which is reprinted here. Conflicting versions of events are not surprising in any political context, but even less so in the super-heated atmosphere of intrigue generated by a dictatorship on Leninist lines. The confusion in the hearts and minds of Afro-Americans who tried to function in such a milieu is vividly portrayed by Mr. Lacy. Independent scholarly analysis, as exemplified in the brilliant studies of the East African political scientist, Ali A. Mazrui, who is an admirer of Nkrumah's continental pan-Africanism, point to Leninism as the basic model for Nkrumah's career and regime. The Ghanaians were caught in the debacle of that regime, and so, inevitably, were the Afro-Americans who went there. But Mr. Lacy also describes the tremendous elation and satisfactions experienced by these black Americans who went to Ghana determined to establish their identity as scions of Africa, and to be part of an actual black power base.

Since neither Africa nor Afro-America is a quiescent monolith, it is safe to predict only that there will continue to be a great variety of cross-currents in the African relationship. However, Dr. Obichere's summary sentences seem well grounded:

Afro-Americans can derive a lot of psychological and racial pride from the progress of Africa. Africa can derive a lot of productive and beneficial inputs from the vast technological skills possessed by Afro-Americans.

BONIFACE I. OBICHERE

Afro-Americans in Africa: Recent Experiences

One of the most striking changes in the configuration of the international system in the second half of the twentieth century is the presence of several new African states.[1]* This African presence in international affairs has been asserted by a small but dynamic and forceful number of African leaders and statesmen. The Euro-American world has been impressed by the political and cultural thrust of the new African states in international affairs.[2] As a young Black student in Atlanta University put it, "What's happening man, is Africa and the Black Revolution. Africa is the source, dig, and there ain't nothing that the Black Revolution can do if it left out Africa." This folk appraisal of the emergence of Africa appears to have a more general and widespread support all through the Afro-American world in the United States.[3]

One of the significant factors in contemporary Africa is the ever-growing interest and active presence of Afro-Americans in various parts of the continent. Afro-Americans can be seen in the independent states in Africa; they can also be seen in those territories still struggling to achieve their independence. They have come to the new Africa as diplomats, businessmen, investors, cultural ambassadors, missionaries, Peace Corps volunteers, teachers, housewives, ideologues and militant radicals in search of a base of

---

* Notes appear at the end of this essay.

15

operation. These recent experiences have increasingly brought hundreds of thousands of blacks in the diaspora back to the homeland. How has this come about?

The historical roots of the "Back to Africa Movement" in the United States go back to the earliest years of the slave trade. Individual freemen yearned to return to Africa as the ultimate assertion of their freedom and independence.[4] As time went on, groups and structures were created to enable those free blacks who wished to return to Africa to do so. Furthermore, some blacks who were slaves were promised manumission on the condition that they return to Africa. The historical strands of the "back to Africa movements" have been recently synthesized by Professor Edwin S. Redkey in *Black Exodus*. Marcus Garvey gave a new fillip to the "back to Africa movement" by the formation of his Universal Negro Improvement Association (U.N.I.A.) and his economic plans to make the return to Africa meaningful. His career galvanized thousands of Afro-Americans into conscious political and cultural activities connected directly or indirectly with Africa.[5] Had his plan worked out in its entirety, he might have succeeded in returning more blacks to Africa than the American Colonial Society ever did.[6] Garveyism, the Pan-Africanism that followed World War II and the achievement of political independence by over forty African states since 1957 all combined to pave the way for the active participation of many Afro-Americans in contemporary African affairs.[7]

The mass media in the United States played a very significant role in introducing independent and modern Africa to the American people in general and to the Afro-Americans in particular. It appears that the newspapers, news magazines, monthly journals and television have been in the forefront in this regard. Television coverage of African news and events has meant the transmission of these events into the homes of millions of Afro-Americans. The inquiries which I conducted in Marshall, Texas and Shreveport, Louisiana in the summer of 1960 confirmed the important role played by the mass media in bringing a knowledge of independent Africa to the masses of Afro-Americans. Most of my respondents recounted with enthusiasm and warmth what an experience it was when they saw Dr. Kwame Nkrumah of Ghana on their television sets when he addressed the General Assembly of the United Nations in 1957.

Several news magazines, such as *Time, Newsweek, U.S. News and World Report, Sepia, The New Yorker, Ebony, Life, Jet* and *Saturday Evening Post* had feature articles and photographs of the events that accompanied the emergence of independent Africa. Some of the articles were favorable and some were unfavorable comments on African affairs. What was impressive was the crescendo of the volume of news material on Africa, and not the partiality or impartiality of the articles themselves. For instance, Stewart Alsop's serial on Africa in the *Saturday Evening Post* reached millions of Americans and kept the subject of Africa alive in thousands of Afro-American homes.

Afro-American newspapers, news magazines, and scholarly journals carried several publications and features on Africa. The *Pittsburgh Courier, Amsterdam News, Muhammed Speaks, Los Angeles Sentinel, Chicago Defender*, the *Herald Dispatch, Atlanta Daily World, Baltimore Afro-American, Louisiana Weekly*, and many other Afro-American-owned newspapers carried abundant coverage of African affairs after the emergence of the new African states in 1960. However, it should be pointed out that some of these newspapers had been paying attention to African affairs for many years before 1960. Several of these newspapers maintained black correspondents in Africa. *Muhammed Speaks* was represented in Africa by Joseph Walker, and the *Amsterdam News* was served by James Hicks. Black Americans were also sent to Africa as correspondents for some of the leading U.S. newspapers: the *New York Times* was represented by Tom Johnson and the *Washington Post* was represented by Jim Hoogard. The majority of the correspondents of the major U.S. newspapers who lived in Africa were white, but it must be said that through their reporting and articles, African affairs were kept alive in the columns of these newspapers. Mr. Ira Bell Thompson was the African correspondent of *Ebony*. Several other Afro-Americans functioned as freelance journalists in Africa and their articles were published in some of the thousands of newspapers and magazines in the United States.

The magic of the radio was brought to bear on the development of the recent experiences of the Afro-American in Africa. Reporters for the major national networks were present in Africa and covered the events that unfolded all over the continent for the American audience. Of special importance here was the Congo crisis (1960-1965), which followed the wake of the independence of the Congo Republic (Zaire) from Belgium in 1960 under the leadership of Patrice Lumumba. On the other hand, there is the powerful Voice of America which broadcasts daily to Africa. The broadcasts of the Voice of America provide valuable information to Africans about life and people in the United States. Through these broadcasts, the details of the Civil Rights Movement in the U.S. were made available to African listeners. One must mention the popular program entitled *Music U.S.A.* which featured several Afro-American artists. Furthermore, the Voice of America carried the special jazz program which was hosted by Mr. Louis Cannova, whose encyclopedic knowledge of jazz and of jazz musicians was appreciated by his listeners all over the world. This type of radio program paved the way for the tour of Mr. Louis "Satchmo" Armstrong and his jazz band to Africa.

The most important element in the recent experiences of Afro-Americans in Africa is the human factor. The physical movement of Afro-Americans into Africa since 1957 is indeed one of the most striking phenomena of the second half of the twentieth century. Because of this movement, this return to the homeland even for a temporary period, the total picture of the relations between blacks in the diaspora and blacks in Africa has acquired a different hue. This movement to Africa has involved the interaction of persons, personalities and powers. It has resulted in the juxtaposition of blacks from the mainstream of Western culture to blacks from the quintessence of African culture. This movement can be seen as a continuing process which has built up its own dynamics and which defines its own parameters and scenario. The contact between Afro-Americans and Africans in our times has not involved millions from the New World but the test of its impact cannot be judged by numbers. In looking at the whole picture, one can posit the theory of the critical mass. What we see in this case is a small number of highly skilled and well-educated Afro-Americans interacting with African societies in the new African states. The important thing is that they have produced lasting results in this interaction.

There has been a lot of discussion about whether Afro-Americans and Africans have anything in common and whether they could get along with each other. This philosophical discussion has gone on for many years in the United States.[8] The protagonists in this debate have been Jewish and Anglo-Saxon exclusively. Harold R. Isaacs, Russell Warren Howe, Stewart Alsop and a few others have been in the forefront of the argumentation. In addition to his provocative article in the *New Yorker* in 1961, Harold R. Isaacs has published a volume entitled *The New World of Negro Americans* (1963). In it he purported to examine "the impact of world affairs on the race problems in the United States and particularly on the Negro, his view of himself, his country and of Africa." Despite his extensive interviews with many prominent Afro-Americans of the time, he missed the point about the place of Africa in the life and struggle of Afro-Americans generally. It might be of interest to note that hundreds of Afro-Americans have emigrated to Africa since Harold R. Isaacs became interested in this question. However, this does not include any of his respondents. One can simply say that Mr. Isaacs interviewed the wrong people and that he labored under the misconception that the relations between Africa and Afro-Americans can be adequately measured through the opinions and experiences of the most successful Afro-Americans. He had committed a capital error by neglecting the masses of Afro-Americans who were not in the limelight of American economic and social success but who firmly believe in Africa as the homeland. To these Afro-Americans a return to Africa is the ultimate vindication and realization of their freedom.

The problem that emerges from a study of the works of Harold R. Isaacs, Russell Warren Howe, Stewart Alsop, Edwin S. Redkey and others is that the focus of their analysis is misplaced and the result is not only blurred vision but also warped conclusions. They conceptualized the question as "the Negro problem" and not as "the white problem." It may be said that this stems from the nineteenth century orientation of American society towards the emancipation of black slaves. For instance, in 1867 a Southern gentleman named Hinton Rowan Helper published a book entitled, *Nojoque: A Question for a Continent,* in which he advocated the total extermination of blacks from the face of the earth as the only and final solution to the problem of racial pluralism in the United States.[9] Other racist writers like Thomas Carlyle, Thomas R. Dew, Eric L. McKitrick, Henry Hughes, George Fitzhugh, David Christy, Thornton Stringfellow and Nehemiah Adams set the pace for these latter-day analysts.[10] It can be said that since the legal abolition of the slave trade and slavery in the United States, the white man's reaction to the presence of Afro-Americans around him has involved organized colonization of blacks in Africa,[11] Mexico or other parts of tropical Latin America.[12] Even as these solutions were being discussed, several voices of opposition were raised against the shipment of Afro-Americans back to Africa. Frederick Douglass was very vehement in his opposition to the sending of free blacks back to Africa. The most eloquent statement of the anti-colonization and emigration proposal was by the Reverend Peter Williams, Pastor of St. Philip's Episcopal Church, New York. In an impassioned 4th of July speech, he inveighed against those who sought a return to Africa. He gave vent to his patriotic sentiments for the United States, the land of light and Christianity. He attacked the American Colonization Society for supporting the return of Afro-Americans to Africa.[13] The point that I am pressing here is that some prominent Afro-Americans have always opposed the efforts of whites to move free blacks back to Africa or to move them outside of the United States. In the 1920's and 1930's some prominent blacks opposed the designs and plans of Marcus Garvey and his Universal Negro Improvement Association which advocated a return to Africa.[14] Garvey was forced to clarify his position and to state that he did not mean that every Afro-American should return to Africa. He encouraged only the few who wished to do so to return to Africa so that they would form the dynamic nucleus for the new state which Garvey envisioned.[15]

Paul Cuffee, who landed thirty-eight Afro-Americans in Freetown in 1816, was a pioneer in black emigration organized by Afro-Americans. As stated above, Marcus Garvey was the foremost member of this school of thought in the years between World War I and World War II. However, it was through black evangelism that several important and prominent Afro-Americans went back to Africa.[16] Henry McNeal Turner, Thomas Birch Freeman, and Alexander Crummell were leaders among the many black missionaries who labored in Africa in the nineteenth century.[17] The traditions that these men established have been kept alive by a steady flow of Afro-American missionaries of the various Christian sects who can still be seen at work in various parts of Africa. Evangelism and education have been strong forces that have motivated several Afro-Americans to go back to Africa.[18]

As one African politician put it recently, "Africa has too many people already. What we do not need is more people, more black people. We need black people with skills who will contribute to the development of Africa." This reaction to the recent phenomenon of the return of Afro-Americans to Africa is symptomatic of the thinking of millions of Africans. Immigrants who have technological or bureaucratic skills are preferred to those who are unskilled and without substance. The types of Afro-Americans who have returned to Africa in recent years have a wide variety of backgrounds and training. Several Afro-Americans have gone back to Africa as wives of Africans who studied in the U.S. (It should be pointed out here that several American whites have also gone to live in Africa as a result of their marriage to Africans who have studied or worked in the United States). These wives have in most cases been very well educated. Some of them are scientists, some are doctors and some are teachers, professors, nurses or librarians.

Radical militants and black nationalists are to be found among the Afro-Americans who have returned to Africa in recent years. These have included Stokely Carmichael, Eldridge Cleaver, Robert Williams, Leslie Lacy, Julian Mayfield and Julia Wright. The stock in trade of these radical militants, black nationalists and cultural nationalists has been the rhetoric of the revolution that is to come. These merchants of ideas and "hot air" have been significant in the politicization of Afro-American youth in the United States rather than in Africa, where their impact has been almost zero.

Incidentally, one of these self-styled militant and radical reformers, Leslie Lacy, has chronicled his African experience in Ghana and a few other nations in his book, *The Rise and Fall of the Proper Negro* (1972). The experiences recounted in this book have been the subject of continuing controversy. Many of Mr. Lacy's friends and acquaintances dispute his recollection of most of the events, as well as his interpretation of Ghanaian affairs.

Furthermore, this group of Afro-Americans elicited the most scathing criticisms from the African middle class. They were seen as boisterous and impolite. They were adjudged as idle ideologues who were supported by state funds and who were not engaged in gainful and productive employment. This criticism was not justified in all of the cases because some of these militant ideologists were productively employed. For instance, Julian Mayfield was the editor of the *African Review* in Ghana. Tom Feelings was employed as an artist for the *Africa Review* and *The Spark*. Some others were employed in the Kwame Nkrumah Ideological Institute, Winneba. A few others were employed in the University of Ghana as lecturers. Tanzania is the only other country where a similar situation has arisen, but it can be said that the Afro-Americans in both Ghana and Tanzania were not all militant Black nationalists who were supported by government funds.

The most important facet of the present relations between Africa and Afro-Americans is the astronomic increase in the number of short-term visitors and tourists who pour into all parts of Africa every year. These black Americans are keenly interested in Africa and its peoples. There is a touch of messianism in the pilgrimage of Afro-Americans to contemporary Africa. The ever-increasing volume of Afro-American tourists and visitors to Africa refutes the stale assertion of Russell Warren Howe and his ilk that Afro-Americans and Africans have nothing in common. In his book, *The African Revolution,* Mr. Howe deplored the fact that the United States Government had assigned Afro-American officials to positions of importance in the new African states.[19] His argument is fallacious because the United States Government does not and has not made it a policy to send only Afro-Americans to fill diplomatic and consular positions in Africa. Perhaps Mr. Howe was unable to deal with the fact that these Afro-Americans were appointed to high offices as representatives of the United States in the new African states. His analogy about the U.S. Government and business corporations automatically sending "the Vandenbergs to Holland, the Murphys to Ireland or the Lipschultzes to Germany," is not only far-fetched but completely inappropriate and erroneous.

What is striking about the impact of the short-term visits of Afro-Americans to the new African states is the openness with which they are received in Africa.[20] In the context of the Caribbean and the New World, there has been great receptivity in Africa to the constructive inputs and suggestions of those Afro-Americans and Afro-Caribbeans who have shown interest in Africa. These visits may last for a few weeks, a few months or a few years depending on the needs of the African countries concerned and the availability of the Afro-Americans involved. A spinoff from the short-term visits is the number of Afro-Americans who decided to naturalize and live in Africa. There have been very many of these since World War II. There are also the cases of long-term settlers who have left the United States bag and baggage and who have taken up permanent residency in countries like Ghana, Nigeria, Tanzania, Kenya, Algeria, Egypt, Ethiopia and other states. A large number of Afro-Americans who have taken up permanent residency in Africa are doctors, engineers, teachers and businessmen. Those cases that I have studied, especially in Ghana, have been very successful in their business undertakings. There are a large number of these permanent settlers or repatriates who hold important positions in the civil service of the countries in which they live. They are contributing their skills as technocrats and as bureaucrats in the service of the African state in which they live. Two striking examples of entrepreneurship may be mentioned here. These are the business corporations of Caramafra Ltd. and All-Afra Electric Company, The founder and managing director of Caramafra Ltd., which specializes in air conditioning and allied services is Mr. Thomas Brown. The founder and managing director of the All-Afra Electric Company is Mr. Carlos Alston, who has been a very successful leader in his field.

In Nigeria, we have several examples of Afro-American entrepreneurship. One of the most striking is the poultry farm which was opened by an Afro-American repatriate from Mississippi. He set the example for many Nigerians, and in fact helped several people open their own poultry farms. Analogous to this is the enterprise and industry of Mrs. Laura Plange and her husband, who are graduates of Tuskegee Institute, Alabama. They opened a poultry farm near Accra, and it was such a success that they added a beautiful and scenic restaurant to it called The Point. Some Afro-Americans initiated the bakery industry in some parts of Nigeria and Ghana.

Worthy of honorable mention among the list of Afro-American entrepreneurs in Ghana is Mrs. Inez A. Pabi.[21] She began a meat and produce marketing and distributing business which is still going strong. The meat importing and distributing business was the exclusive reserve of the multi-national European corporations, such as the United Africa Company, the United Trading Company and the Compagnie Francaise de l'Afrique Occidentale. Mrs. Pabi entered into this field of endeavor with courage and made a success of it. Here I should mention the energy, drive and initiative of another Afro-American, Mrs. Christine Benjamin Davis who operated a very successful beauty salon in Accra before she moved to Nigeria, where she now lives with her husband who is in the electric industry. Mr. Davis is a white American.

In the professions, Afro-American doctors, dentists, pediatricians and gynecologists have been the most prominent in Africa. The most notable example is Dr. Robert E. Lee and his wife Dr. Sara Lee who moved to Ghana in the early 50's and have since become Ghanaian citizens.[22] They operate a very significant clinic in Accra. Dr. Carlton B. Goodlett of San Francisco, California, has also shown great interest in Africa and African affairs. He has been to Africa several times and was one of the notable participants in the Accra Disarmament and Ban the Bomb Conference in the early days of President Kwame Nkrumah's administration. However, Dr. Goodlett has not set up any practices in Ghana or elsewhere in Africa. It should be mentioned here that Dr. Goodlett has rendered an outstanding service to African and Afro-American relations in recent years in various ways, especially through the pages of his influential weekly newspaper, *The Sun Reporter*. This newspaper has carried news items, features and comments on African affairs. One may argue cogently that Dr. Goodlett and *The Sun Reporter* were instrumental in the decision of many young men and women in the San Francisco Bay Area to go to Africa to settle or to visit. The second source of inspiration for the Afro-Americans in the San Francisco Bay Area with regards to Africa is Attorney Donald Warden, who founded the Afro-American Association in 1961. Mr. Warden was not only a good sidewalk preacher and college campus orator, but also a good organizer and businessman. He formed the African Chamber of Commerce of San Francisco and has made several business trips to Africa. It was at the Afro-American Association's Annual Conference organized by Donald Warden in October 1962 that I met Malcolm X, who spoke on the same platform with me,[23] and we became very well acquainted until his death in 1965.

I have often wondered why Ghana attracted more Afro-Americans than any other African state. Certain factors come to mind when one thinks about Ghana and Afro-Americans. The commanding presence, nationalist militancy, the persuasive rhetoric and charisma of Dr. Kwame Nkrumah appear to be the magnets that drew many Afro-Americans to Ghana.[24] Secondly, Ghana was the first black African colony to gain its independence from Britain on March 6, 1957. As such, it became a shining example of success against white domination. It became a symbol and an ideal for emulation in the civil rights struggle that was shaping up and gathering gale force and whirlwind momentum in the United States. Dr. Kwame Nkrumah's commitment to Pan-Africanism was definitely a crucial feature in attracting Afro-American attention to Ghana. Furthermore, Dr. Nkrumah appeared to support Marxist-socialist ideas of social reform and reconstruction in the Third World. This aspect of Nkrumah's intellectual life appealed to a certain segment of Afro-Americans who visualized the new state of Ghana as a *tabula rasa* on which socialism was to be imprinted without obstacles and with the near utopian perfection described by Saint Simon and Francois Fourier before Karl Marx.[25]

President Nkrumah actively sought the support of Afro-Americans in his gargantuan task of reconstructing Ghana. I have already mentioned the impact his TV appearances had on Americans generally and on Afro-Americans in particular when he came to take up Ghana's membership in the United Nations in 1957. During another trip to the United States in July 1958, he made a public appearance in Harlem, where he spoke at the Armory. The late Dr. Ralph Bunche presided at this meeting which was attended by over 10,000 people. At this meeting, Nkrumah made an appeal to teachers and technicians to come to Ghana to take up jobs to help him in the reconstruction of his newly independent state.[26] This was given wide publicity throughout the United States and several people, both black and white, began to go to Ghana in response to this appeal. Earlier in 1951, Kwame Nkrumah had visited Lincoln University, where he received an honorary doctorate degree. That was also a moving occasion. Nkrumah delivered the commencement address at his alma mater. Professor Hill of the English Department at Lincoln read the citation for Nkrumah's degree and said, "To the British, Nkrumah may be the Leader of Government Business but to us he's the Prime Minister of Ghana."[27] This memorable occasion not only renewed the bonds between Nkrumah and Lincoln University, but it cemented the ties between Dr. Horace Mann Bond, the then President of Lincoln, and Dr. Kwame Nkrumah. This relationship was going to involve Dr. Bond in Ghanaian and African affairs for many years to come. Max Bond, a relative of Dr. Bond, was soon invited to Ghana as a government architect. Gene Bond, Richard Wright, Alphaeus Hunton, Bayard Rustin, Bill Sutherland, Lawrence D. Reddick, Frank Pinder, James Mosely and Beverly Carter all came to Ghana because of Nkrumah and what they believed he stood for. In 1961 W. E. B. DuBois repeated the sonorous call that Kwame Nkrumah had issued earlier to Afro-Americans to come back to the homeland in his famous poem entitled, "Ghana Calls." This appeal was reinforced by the poetry of Georgia Douglas Johnson, especially, "To Africa," and "A Song of Courage," published in 1961.[28] Such appeals from highly respected Afro-Americans and from Dr. Nkrumah himself were re-echoed in the mass media and in the black student organizations that were active in the Civil Rights Movement, such as Congress of Racial Equality, the Student Non-violent Coordinating Committee and the Afro-America Association. It appears that the result was the influx of several Afro-Americans into the newly independent state of Ghana. They went to Ghana in waves, some at the express invitation of President Nkrumah, and others on their own volition as the ultimate fulfillment of their commitment to total freedom and racial equality.

Though Afro-Americans have gone to other African states, Ghana, Nigeria and Tanzania, in a descending order of magnitude, have attracted the largest number. The French-speaking African countries have attracted some Afro-Americans as well, but the language barrier has been a serious handicap. Moreover, many Afro-Americans complain openly about how neo-colonial most of the French-speaking African states are, with the obvious exception of Guinea, under the leadership of Sékou Touré. The movement of Afro-Americans to Africa still continues in spurts and trickles. Some organizations have arisen to channel the flow of Afro-Americans into various parts of Africa. The most prominent among these is the African Descendants Association Foundation, with its headquarters in Accra. The president of this foundation is Dr. Robert E. Lee. Ambassador Franklin Williams, now of the Phelps-Stokes Fund, New York, is the vice-president. The board of directors includes Dr. Carlton B. Goodlett of San Francisco, Dr. Henry Mitchell of Claremont, California and Mr. Ernest N. Morial of New Orleans. There is also the Pan-African Skills Project with its headquarters in New York and its African headquarters in Dar es Salaam. The objective of this organization is to supply skilled Afro-American technicians and technologists to the various African states. Its avowed goals include the utilization of Black skills for Black development. It is under the directorship of Mr. Irving Davis. The Pan-African Skills Project was launched in January 1970. Since then, it has recruited over five hundred skilled Afro-Americans for important jobs in the various African states. In conformity with its policy of "loyal and efficient service to Africa," the recruits are given a three-day orientation course in New York prior to their departure to Africa, and a three-week orientation program "upon arrival in the Motherland." Candidates and recruits who participate in this project are expected to learn the language of the African country involved. "Our objective has been quite clear from the beginning; to actively recruit those Afro-Americans who have knowledge, technical skills and the commitment needed to assist in the building of truly independent African nations. We believe that all Black people must become masters of their own fate and directors of their own destiny—and African liberation and development is the first step toward that destiny." The brochure of the Pan-African Skills Project states:

We are committed to a free and independent Africa; our spirit is that of Ujama. All developing countries are struggling to meet their manpower needs more adequately and are recruiting people with technical skills from foreign countries. Until now the supply of technical and professional manpower has been the exclusive monopoly of white, Anglo-Saxon countries. The militant, revolutionary struggles of the 60's revealed that while each developing country has the responsibility to raise itself up by its own abilities, oppressed people the world over have similar experiences which form a common basis for unity. We can band together in this struggle against capitalism and imperialism by assisting one another with the skills we possess, or we can continue on our present separate courses, which most certainly will lead to our continued exploitation and impoverishment.

It can be seen from the above that there is planning and organization, as well as an ideological thrust, in the efforts of the Pan-African Skills Project.

A few other organizations have been formed recently in the U.S. whose aims are largely geared to practical action in Africa. Among these one may mention Relief for Africans In Need in the Sahel (R.A.I.N.S.), which is committed to relief services in the Sahel and other drought-affected areas of Africa, such as

Ethiopia, Northeast Kenya and Botswana. The co-presidents of R.A.I.N.S. are Professor Elliott P. Skinner of Columbia University, who was the U.S. Ambassador to Upper Volta, and Congressman Charles Diggs, Jr., Chairman of the House Sub-Committee on Africa. This organization works through the African governments and collaborates with the Interstate Committee of Seven, established by the African states directly affected by the drought in the Sahel. Upper Volta's Ambassador to the United States, Honorable Telesphore Yaguibou is the liaison man between this relief organization and the African states.

It appears that the natural disaster of the drought that has hit Africa hard since 1972 has united several Afro-American organizations for the first time in common action involving Africa. Not even the Biafra-Nigeria War, which in itself was a tragedy, could bring these disparate groups together in concerted action. Among the organizations that are cooperating with R.A.I.N.S. to provide relief to the Sahel are the Washington Task Force on Africa, headed by Mr. Daniel Mathews of the African Bibliographic Center, the National Black Theater of New York, under the leadership of Barbara Ann Teer, the National Conference of Black Lawyers, the Pan-African Liberation Committee, the National Committee of Black Church Ministers, the National Association of Black Social Workers, the National Association for the Advancement of Colored Peoples, the African Liberation Support Committee, the Youth Organization of Black Unity, the African Heritage Studies Association, the Congress of African Peoples, the African Information Service, Afri-Care, Inc., Afram Association and People United to Save Humanity (PUSH), which is led by the Reverend Jessie Jackson. Reverend Jackson has appeared on national television in the U.S. several times with appeals for relief to the Sahel. He has visited Africa several times and I remember vividly his pleasant experience in Ghana in March 1971 during the Soul-to-Soul Festival which was held in Black Star Square, Accra. It should be pointed out here that by April 1974, R.A.I.N.S. had collected and delivered over $100,000 for relief to the Africans affected by the Sahel drought.[29]

Africans and African political leaders have shown great awareness of Afro-Americans and the contemporary problems faced by these Americans of African origin in the United States. In the Second Conference of African Journalists held in Accra on November 11, 1963, the ties between Africans in the diaspora and those in the homeland were underscored by Dr. Kwame Nkrumah. He cited the example of George Padmore, whose journalistic writings and contributions to the press in Africa have been as valuable and effective as those to the Black press in the West Indies and in the United States.[30] Mr. R. Annoh-Oprensem, Senior Lecturer in Political Science at the Kwame Nkrumah Ideological Instiute, Winneba, commented that "over one hundred million Africans were shipped to the plantations in America during the Atlantic Slave Trade." He then went on to praise Richard Wright, whom he called a courageous journalist and writer. Wright was his hero because of the perspicacity with which he pointed out the negative attitudes that have been created in the minds of former colonial and oppressed peoples in Africa and the United States.[31]

The Ghanaian press gave ample publicity to Afro-American affairs. *The Evening News* of April 3, 1961 carried an article by Dr. Lester B. Granger, Executive Director of the National Urban League, U.S.A., on "The Changing Image of the American Negro." On April 6, 1961, it was announced in *The Evenings News* that the Afro-American Association of Industrial Development was to be formed in New York. This would serve as a clearinghouse of investment and development programs for the new African countries. Ghana was represented in the inaugural meeting of this association in New York by R. S. Amegashie, M. K. Amoh-Awuah and K. O. A. Appiah. There were constant news items in the Ghanaian and other African papers about Afro-Americans of prominence, especially in the entertainment and educational business. For instance, photographs of Leontyne Price, the talented soprano, Paul Robeson, Eartha Kitt, Martin Luther King, Jr., and W. E. B. Du Bois appeared in *The Evening News, L'Entincelle* and *The Spark* in Ghana and in the *West African Pilot* and the *Daily Times* in Nigeria. On April 10, 1961, Dr. Linden Leslie, leader of a West Indies group from Jamaica, published an article in *The Evenings News* entitled "They Want to Return to Africa." This front-page article spoke about the surplus of experienced agricultural workers who could come to work in Africa from the West Indies. Dr. Leslie supported the return of Blacks in the diaspora to the Motherland, especially to Ghana, Liberia, Nigeria and Sierra Leone. Even the first U.S. Ambassador to Ghana, Mr. Donald W. Lamm, underlined the ties between Africa and the

U.S. in pure genetic terms. When he presented his credentials to Dr. Nkrumah, he stated that the United States was glad that Dr. Nkrumah was educated in America. "We are proud that many of our leading citizens had their ancestry in your country," added Mr. Lamm.[32]

Dr. James Robinson, theologian and founder of Operation Crossroads Africa in 1958, was a constant visitor to Ghana. As a prominent Afro-American, he believed in the interaction of both Black and white Americans and Africans. It was for this reason that he founded Operation Crossroads Africa, which since its inception has made it possible for thousands of Americans to spend short periods of time in African communities. Dr. Robinson is also remembered for his assertion that "Afro-Americans look to the new Ghana and Africa with hope and they are proud of their African heritage."[33]

According to Professor J. G. St. Clair Drake, a distinction can be made between racial Pan-Africanism and continental Pan-Africanism.[34] The former addresses itself to Africans in the homeland and in the diaspora. The latter involves the Africans resident on the African continent. What is important is the fact stated by Locksley Edmondson that "historically, strivings for emancipation in various parts of the Black world have been characterized by measures of cooperative tactical endeavors and/or ideological exchanges between Africans in the diaspora and those on the continent."[35] Henry Winston, in his recent book entitled *Strategy for A Black Agenda,* examined with scrutiny the nuances of meaning and the diversity of opinion that existed among the various proponents of Pan-Africanism. He lumps the contemporary intellectual and ideological approaches to Pan-Africanism into his new category of Neo-Pan-Africanism.[36]

The liberation movements in Southern and Central Africa and in Guinea-Bissau have attracted the attention of Afro-Americans, as well as their support. Afro-Americans have been involved in the liberation struggles in Angola, Mozambique, Zimbabwe and Guinea-Bissau. They have been active as party bureaucrats, combat troops and members of the Auxiliary and Supply Corps. On the other hand, several Afro-Americans in the United States have organized to provide relief in the way of food and clothing to the areas affected by the liberation struggles. The Liberation Support Movement Information Center is very active in disseminating information about the successes and hopes of the guerrilla movements in white-dominated Southern Africa.[37] It should be pointed out here that the position of militant Afro-Americans with reference to the liberation movements in Africa was clearly defined by Stokely Carmichael. In an interview published in the *Sun News* of Dar es Salaam, on November 5, 1967, he let it be known that Blacks would burn the United States to the ground if its government intervened on the side of Southern Africa in a conflict with the rest of Africa.[38]

Congressman Charles Diggs, Jr. and his House Sub-Committee on Africa have shown great interest in the involvement of the United States Government and United States corporations in Southern Africa. Black Americans in Congress and in the Senate have also shown some interest in the question of sanctions against Rhodesia. Afro-Americans have lobbied the United Nations to put the heat on Rhodesia in the way of economic sanctions. They have also joined Africans in demanding that Great Britain use military force to bring an end to the white-minority rule in Southern Rhodesia.[39]

Among the Afro-Americans who have been very active in the liberation movements is Mr. Robert Van Lierop. Mr. Van Lierop was among those invited by F.R.E.L.I.M.O. in 1971 to tour the liberated areas in Mozambique. The result of this tour has been the widely circulated film, "A Luta Continua," produced and narrated by Mr. Van Lierop. Another Afro-American who has been dangerously involved in the liberation movements is Mr. Leon Dash, a correspondent of the *Washington Post,* who traveled in June 1973 through the liberated sections of Angola at the invitation of the National Union for the Total Independence of Angola (U.N.I.T.A.). Mr. Dash and his colleagues traveled eight hundred miles across Angola, taking photographs, observing the guerrilas in action and interviewing the leadership of U.N.I.T.A. This trip originated from an invitation in May 1973, which Mr. Dash received "from a Harvard University graduate student, Connie Hilliard, who was recruiting Black American journalists to attend U.N.I.T.A.'s Third World Congress," which was held in the guerrilla-occupied area of Angola in August 1973. Mr. Dash has given a detailed account of this marathon effort in the *Washington Post* of December 21-26, 1973. The realities described by Leon Dash put into serious question the conclusion and generalizations which have been offered by Mr. Henry Winston, National Chairman of the Communist Party, USA, in his *Strategy for a Black Agenda: A Critique of New Theories of Liberation in the United States and Africa.*

The Soul-to-Soul Music Festival in Accra brought several Afro-Americans to Ghana. Most of the entertainers and musicians who participated in this interface and trans-national experience had never visited Africa before. I talked to Les McCann in the airy terrace of the Continental Hotel in Accra about his first visit to Ghana. He summarized his feelings and reaction to Africa artistically and in his unique pithy style: "Africa is too much, man. I dig it." The musicians who were in Ghana for the Soul-to-Soul Festival included Roberta Flack, Willie Bobo, The Staple Singers The Jackson Five, Wilson Pickett, and Ike and Tina Turner. Thousands of Ghanaians and other people turned out to enjoy the variety of Afro-American talent that was represented at the festival. Of course, James Brown's visit to Nigeria in 1971 was a landmark in the history of soul music in Africa. There was a clamor in Ghana about the failure of the social leaders in Accra to invite James Brown to perform in their capital. These events are reminiscent of the visits of Eartha Kitt, Harry Belafonte and Sidney Poitier to Nigeria in 1956, at the invitation of Dr. Nnamdi Azikiwe, then Premier of Eastern Nigeria.

Of special significance in the recent experiences of Afro-Americans in Africa is the meteoric career of Malcolm X, that firebrand and orator whose vehement venom was not spared against the colonialists and oppressors of Black people in the United States and Africa. Leroy Clark, in his article in *Freedomways,* in 1968, entitled "Leadership Crisis: A New Look at the Black Bourgeoisie," asserted that Malcolm X was the real catalyst to the current Black Power thinking of the 1960's and 1970's. This is an important statement because it brings into view the central position of Africa in the philosophy of Malcolm X. Malcolm in his lifetime used Africa as a symbol in his speeches and in his exegesis of the social, political and economic situation in the United States. He always referred to Africa as home. He dealt with Africa in real terms. The reality of Africa can be differentiated from the symbolic meaning of Africa in the thought of Malcolm X. His trips to Africa and the warmth and enthusiasm with which he was received are eloquent demonstrations of his fraternity with

Africans. In a very short time, Malcolm X became involved with various social and political groups in Ghana, Nigeria, Algeria, Egypt and Ethiopia. He even gained the recognition of the Organization of African Unity, which recognized him as a veritable leader of a liberation movement worthy of the support of the Organization of African Unity. It was a result of this recognition which led Malcolm X to found the Organization of Afro-American Unity shortly before his death.

Malcolm X believed strongly in the liberating role of a thorough knowledge of the African heritage. It was this belief that led him to read as much about African history and culture as he could. He was of the opinion that a knowledge of African history was a pivotal factor in the struggle for the liberation of Black people in both Africa and the United States. Malcolm X was virulently anti-colonialist. He always compared European colonialism in Africa with the situation of Afro-Americans in twentieth century U.S.A. He made a subtle distinction between colonialism and slavery, even though he inveighed against the evil and deleterious effects of both on the Black man in Africa and in America. He stated that the Black ghettos of the United States were analogous to the colonial territories in Africa. The exploitation and oppression perpetrated in both places were similar if not identical. These had debilitating effects on both Afro-Americans and Africans, and had an adverse effect on the struggle for Black liberation in Africa and in the Third World. The legacy of Malcolm X to Africa and to the Blacks of America is as important as his legacy to the Third World in general. Malcolm was perhaps instrumental in getting a young Black Muslim to volunteer for Peace Corps service in Ghana. This young man, Elijah Muhammad Sprigs, served in Takoradi. Especially important in any consideration of the legacy of Malcolm X is the question of Islam. His visits to Africa and Mecca brought him into contact with the leading Muslims in both North and East Africa and Arabia. His pilgrimage to Mecca put him right in the center of world Islam. It was after this pilgrimage that he began to reevaluate the doctrine of the Black Muslims of America and those of world Islam.[40]

The recent experiences of Afro-Americans in Africa include service in the United States Diplomatic and Consular Corps in Africa since 1957. It is true that the United States had exchanged ambassadors with Liberia prior to 1957. However, the emergence of several new African states led to the appointment of more ambassadors to Africa. Naturally, several prominent Black American citizens of outstanding ability were appointed ambassadors to the various African states. These ambassadors include: Mercer Cook, Clinton Everett Knox, Elliott P. Skinner, C. Clyde Ferguson, Jr., Franklin Williams, Charles Nelson, Rudolph Aggrey, John Morrow, Beverly Carter, Samuel Westerfield and Samuel Adams. In the foreign service and consular corps, we have many Afro-Americans serving in Africa. In Nigeria alone in recent times Mr. P. D. Peters, Cultural Attaché, Mr. Robert Watkins and Ms. Charmaine Keyes served in the U. S. Consulate. The Agency for International Development has sent several Afro-Americans to serve in the various African countries. Mr. William Green has been the Director of A.I.D.'s programs in Tanzania. Recently, Ambassador Charles Nelson has been appointed the Director of A.I.D. in Nairobi. In the United States Information Service there are several Afro-Americans. A notable Afro-American with the U.S.I.S. in West Africa is Mr. William Petty, who has served in Nigeria, Senegal and Togo. Janet Hall served in the U. S. Consulate in Dakar and Sara Lee Owen served in Lagos and Nairobi.[41] Several Afro-Americans also served in the labor movement in Africa in the heydey of the Cold War competition between Russia and the U. S. to gain control of African labor unions. Mr. George McCray of the State, County and Municipal Employees Union of the U. S. was prominent in the African Labor College in Kampala, Uganda. He also worked with the labor union in Lagos, Nigeria, where the competition between the U. S. and Russia was very intense.[42]

In conclusion, it can be demonstrated that the recent experiences of Afro-Americans in Africa have involved a great variety of endeavors and activities. They range from the mundane to the esoteric, from rock music groups to opera singers and progressive jazz. Afro-Americans have gone to Africa in recent times motivated by a multiplicity of factors. It cannot be asserted that one factor is more important than the other, but it can be said that several of them working in convergent conjunction have produced the ever-increasing flow of Afro-Americans to Africa. They have gone as tourists, adventurers, short-term settlers and permanent residents. Their fields of endeavor have ranged from engineering, medicine, education, industry to diplomatic service. Some of them found fulfillment in Africa; others have met with disappointment. Many have settled in Africa for good; others have returned to the United States, as restless as they were when they first went to Africa. Africa is no panacea for the social problems foisted on Afro-Americans by the peculiar social conditions under which they have lived in the United States. Afro-Americans who wish to go to Africa must come to terms with the fact that Africa is very different from the United States. Their disappointment will be compounded if they expect to find a little America in Africa.

The Sixth Pan-African Congress in Dar es Salaam (June 19-June 26, 1974) is a landmark in the recent experiences of Afro-Americans in Africa. The theme of this conference centered around Black labor and technology. It was taken from the thoughts and philosophy of President Julius K. Nyerere. The conference has been spurred by Afro-Americans and thousands of them are expected to benefit from the discussions and deliberations of this conference. Its recommendations will mark a new point of departure in African-Afro-American relations and cooperation in the economic, political and ideological spheres.

The commitment of Afro-Americans to African liberation is a very healthy thing. Since 1962, I have been asserting the fact that Afro-Americans should look to Africa as their homeland and they should get involved in African affairs just like the Jews, the Irish, the Germans and other groups in the United States show concern and get involved in the affairs of their European or Middle-Eastern homeland. Afro-Americans can derive a lot of psychological and racial pride from the progress of Africa. Africa can derive a lot of productive and beneficial imputs from the vast technological skills possessed by Afro-Americans. What is needed overall and what will result from the continued interface and interaction and international cooperation between the two groups is a better understanding of each other.

1   Mazrui, Ali A. and Hasu Patel, eds., *Africa In World Affairs: The Next Thirty Years* (New York, 1973). George E. Haynes, "Americans Look At Africa," *Journal of Negro Education* (Winter, 1958).

2   Spiro, Herbert J., "The American Response to Africa's Participation in the International System," *Issue*, Vol. III, No. 1 (Spring, 1973) pp. 20-23. James Mayall, *Africa: The Cold War and After* (1971). Jack Wooddis, *Africa: The Lion Awakes* (New York, 1961). Louis Lomax, *The Reluctant African* (1959). Thomas R. Adam, *Government and Politics in Africa South of the Sahara* (New York, 1962). Thomas Hovet, *Africa in the United Nations* (Evanston, 1962). *United States Foreign Policy, Africa,* a study directed by Melville J. Herskovits for the Senate Committee on Foreign Relations of the U.S. 86th Congress, First Session (Washington, D.C., 1959).

3   Davis, John A., ed., *Africa From the Point of View of American Negro Scholars* (Paris, 1958)—(Special issue of the Journal *Présence Africaine*). George Shepperson, "Notes on Negro American Influence on the Emergence of African Nationalism," *Journal of African History*, Vol. I (1960), pp. 299-312. Herbert Aptheker, "Consciousness of Negro Nationality: An Historical Survey," *Political Affairs* (June, 1949).

4   Bell, Howard H., "Negro Emigration Movement, 1849-1854: A Phase of Negro Nationalism," Phylon, No. 2 (1959), J.W.E. Bowen, "Who are We? Africans, Afro-Americans, Colored People, Negroes or American Negroes?", *The Voice of the Negro* (Jan., 1906).

5   Frazier, E. Franklin, "Garvey: A Mass Leader," *Nation* (August, 1926). Birgit Aron, "The Garvey Movement: Shadow and Substance," *Phylon* (1947).

6   DuBois, W.E.B., "On Migrating to Africa," *Crisis* (June, 1924). ————, "Reconstruction and Africa," *Crisis* (February, 1919). Edmund D. Cronon, *Black Moses* (Wisconsin, 1962). Amy Jacques-Garvey, *The Philosophy and Opinions of Marcus Garvey* (New York, 1925)

7   Emerson, Kupert and Martin Kilson, "The American Dilemma in a Changing World: The Rise of Africa and the Negro American," *Daedalus* (Fall, 1965), pp. 1055-1084.

8   Skinner, Elliott P., *Afro-Americans and Africa: The Continuing Dialectic—A Minority Report* (The Urban Center, Columbia University, New York, 1973), pp. 4-30. Louis Lomax, *The Reluctant African* (New York, 1960). Harold R. Isaacs, "Back to Africa," *New Yorker* (1961). Charles V. Hamilton, "Pan-Africanism and the Black Struggle in the U.S.," *The Black Scholar*, Vol. 2, No. 7 (March, 1971).

9   Helper, Hinton Rowan, *Nojoque: A Question for a Continent* (New York, 1867). Bell I. Wiley, *Southern Negroes, 1861-1865* (New Haven, 1969). H.R. Helper, *The Negroes in Negroland, the Negroes Generally. Also the Several Races of White Men, Considered as the Involuntary and Predestined Supplanters of the Black Races* (New York, 1868).

10 McKitrick, Eric L., ed., *Slavery Defended: The Views of the Old South* (Englewood Cliffs, 1963).

11 Redkey, Edwin S., *Black Exodus: Black Nationalist and Back-to-Africa Movements, 1890-1910* (New Haven, 1969). Martin R. Delany, *The Condition, Elevation, Emigration and Destiny of the Colored People of the United States Politically Considered* (Philadelphia, 1852). Delay, *The Official Report of the Exploring Party* (New York 1861).

12 Bell I. Wiley, *Southern Negroes* (New Haven, 1969). Redkey, *Black*

Exodus (New Haven, 1969), pp. 15-23. Philip J. Staudenraus, *The African Colonization Movement, 1816-1865* (New York, 1961), pp. 1-17; 32-33.

13 Woodson, Carter G., *Negro Orators and Their Orations* (Washington, D.C., 1925) pp. 79-81. Leslie Fishel and Benjamin Quarles, *The Black American: A Documentary History* (Glenview, Ill., 1969) pp. 145-147.

14 Logan, Rayford W., "The American Negro's View of Africa," in *Africa Seen By American Negroes,* edited by John A. Davis (Paris, 1958). Julian Mayfield, *The Grand Parade* (New York, 1961). Louis R. Mehlinger, "The Attitude of the Free Negro to African Colonization,'" *Journal of Negro History* (July, 1916). George Shepperson, "Notes on Negro American Influences on the Emergence of African Nationalism," *Journal of African History,* Vol. I, No. 2 (1960).

15 Cronon, E., *Black Moses,* pp. 15-19; 203 Frank Chalk, "DuBois and Garvey Confront Liberia: Two Incidents of the Coolidge Years," Paper delivered at the 52nd Annual Meeting of the Association for the Study of Negro Life and History (13 to 17, October 1967, Greensboro, North Carolina).

16 Harr, Wilber Christian, "The Negro As An American Protestant Missionary in Africa," Unpublished thesis, University of Chicago Divinity School, 1945. *Africa and the American Negro: Addresses and Proceedings of the Congress on Africa, December 13-15, 1895,* Gammon Theological Seminary, Atlanta, Georgia (1896). Alexander Crummell, *Africa and America: Addresses and Discourses* (Suringfield, Massachusetts, 1891).

17 Turner, Henry McNeal, "The American Negro and the Fatherland," *Addresses and Proceedings of the Congress on Africa, December 13-15, 1895.* M. M. Ponton, *Life and Times of Henry M. Turner* (Atlanta, Georgia, 1971).

18 Harr, Wilber C., "The Negro As An American Protestant Missionary in Africa," Unpublished thesis, University of Chicago Divinity School (1945). E.S. Redkey, *Black Exodus* (pp. 195-218).

19 Howe, Russell Warren, *The African Revolution* (pp. 262-263).

20 John Hendrick Clarke of New York confirmed this view in a discussion I had with him in Accra in July, 1971 at the Annual Conference of the Association of African Universities.

21 I met Mrs. Inez A. Pabi March 1971 and I have interviewed her several times since then. Taped interview, August, 1973, Accra, Ghana.

22 Interview, Accra, Ghana, August, 1973.

23 "Global Zeal Urged On Negroes," *San Francisco Chronicle* (November 25, 1962) pp. 1 and 26.

24 Padmore, George, "Pan-Africanism and Ghana," *United Asia: Magazine of Asian Affairs,* Special African Edition, (1957). Alpheus Hunton, *Decision in Africa* (New York, 1957). John Phillips, *Kwame Nkrumah and the Future of Africa* (New York, 1961). James R. Hooker, *Black Revolutionary: George Padmore's Path From Communism to Pan-Africanism* (New York, 1970) pp. 109-140. "Padmore and the Struggle," *Evening News* (Accra, March 11, 1957) p. 2.

25 Nelkin, Dorothy, "Socialist Sources of Pan-African Ideology," in *African Socialism,* edited by W. Friedland and Carl Rosberg (Stanford, 1964). Timothy Bankole, *Kwame Nkrumah: His Rise to Power* (London, 1955).

26 *Amsterdam News,* July, 1958. Interview with Professor J.G. St. Clair Drake, Stanford University, California, June 23, 1973.

27 Interview with Professor J.G. St. Clair Drake, Stanford University, California, June 22 and 23, 1973.

28 *Presence Africaine,* October 1960—January 1961, pp. 156-160.

29 I am indebted to Professor Elliott P. Skinner for this information concerning R.A.I.N.S.

30 National Archives of Ghana, ADM.16/55. *The African Journalist* edited by W.M. Sulemanu-Sibidow, p. 3.

31 N.A.G. ADM.16/55, "Looking Forward," p. 67.

32 Thompson, Era Bell, *Africa, Land of My Fathers* (New York, 1954). *Evening News,* March 22, 1957, p. 1.

33 *Evening News,* March 22, 1957, p. 1 Harold R. Isaacs, *Emergent Americans: A Report on Crossroads Africa* (New York, 1961).

34 St. Clair Drake, J.G., "Negro Americans and the African Interest," in *The American Negro Reference Book,* edited by John P. Davis (Englewood Cliffs, New Jersey, 1966) pp. 691-700. Mercer Cook, "The Aspirations of Négritude," *New Leader* (October 24, 1960).

35 Thorpe, Earl E., "Africa in the Thought of Negro Americans," *Negro History Bulletin* (October 1959). Locksley Edmundson, "Africa and the African Diaspora: Interactions, Linkages and Racial Challenges in the Future World Order," *Africa in World Affairs: The Next Thirty Years,* edited by Ali A. Mazrui and Hasu Patel (New York, 1973) pp. 1-21; p. 10 Léopold Sedar Senghor, "La Négritude et l'Amerique Latine," *La Nouvelle Revue Des Deux Mondes* (February 1974) pp. 351-356; p. 354.

36 Winston, Henry, *Strategy for a Black Agenda: A Critique of New Theories of Liberation in the United States and Africa* (New York, 1973) pp. 45-69. Wilson Record, *The Negro and the Communist Party* (Chapel Hill, North Carolina, 1951). Wilson Record, "The Negro Intellectual and Negro Nationalism," *Social Forces* (October 1954-May 1955).

37 *LSM Information Center 1974 Catalogue* (Richmond, British Columbia, Canada, 1974) pp. 1-24.

38 Bell, Inge Powell, *CORE and the Strategy of Nonviolence* (New York, 1968). Benjamin Muse, *The American Negro Revolution: From Nonviolence to Black Power, 1963-1967* (Bloomington, Indiana, 1968). Howard Zinn, *SNCC: The New Abolitionists* (Boston, 1964). Stokely Carmichael and Charles V. Hamilton, *Black Power: The Politics of Liberation in America* (New York, 1967).

39 *U.S. Business Involvement in Southern Africa,* Hearings before the Subcommittee on Africa of the Committee on Foreign Affairs, House of Representatives, Ninety-second Congress, First Session, Part 2, September 27, November 12, December 6 and 7, 1971. Ian Brownlie, *Basic Documents on African Affairs* (Oxford, 1971) pp. 365-453. Al J. Venter, *The Terror Fighters: A Profile of Guerrilla Warfare in Southern Africa* (1969)

40 Little, Malcolm X and Alex Haley, *Autobiography of Malcolm X* (Grove Press, New York, 1965). Alvin D. Zalinger, "The West African Student and American Race Relations," Paper Presented at the 2nd Annual Conference of the American Society of African Culture (June, 1959). Joseph C. Kennedy, "The American Negro's Key Role in Africa," *The New York Times Magazine* (February 4, 1962).

41 Among those Afro-Americans who have worked in Africa for the U.S.I.S., State Department and AID are William Davis (Addis Ababa), Horace Dawson (Nigeria), William Lewis, Fletcher Martin,

William Jones, and Mr. Baker who recently served in Johannesburg, South Africa.

42 Cohen, Robin, *Labour and Politics in Nigeria, 1945-1971* (London, 1974) pp. 85; 230. Russell Warren Howe, *The African Revolution* (Croydon, London, 1969) p. 262. James Mayall, *Africa: The Cold War and After* (London, 1971).

I

The
Afro-American
Experience of Africa

ROBERT CAMPBELL

Robert Campbell, a well-traveled, well-educated Jamaican chemist, was teaching at the Institute for Colored Youth in Philadelphia shortly before the Civil War, when he was chosen by Dr. Martin R. Delany, the forceful black separatist leader, as an associate in a projected exploration of the Niger valley. The aim of the expedition would be to prepare the way for a voluntary emigration and settlement of black freedmen from the United States. The majority of freedmen had always resisted such projects as the American Colonization Society's settlement of Liberia, even after Liberia became a black republic in 1847. Their feeling was that emigration was desertion of the struggle for freedom of enslaved black brothers and abdication of their right to live in the America that they had helped to build.

On the other hand, there were those who strongly advocated emigration (not just to Africa, but to such places as Canada, Haiti, British West Indies, Central and South America.) Men like Delany were seeking to set up black colonies overseas in order to demonstrate in action the blacks' equality or superiority to whites in the arts of agriculture, commerce, and government. They felt, also, that the establishment of such autonomous Negro colonies would have a powerful effect toward undermining the slavery system. Out of such motives Delany and Campbell were eager to try more colonization in Africa.

In mid-1859 the two men started their journey, but separately.

Campbell traveled as a representative of the white-supported African Civilization Society. Since Delany was adamantly opposed to accepting money from whites, he traveled independently. However, they later joined up in the Egba-Yoruba country of what is now Western Nigeria, and spent the latter half of their year abroad together. Before they left Africa, they were joint signatories on an agreement with the native chiefs in Abbeokuta permitting settlement on unoccupied lands of the region. No groups of emigrants followed the Delany-Campbell expedition: the African rulers had thought better of, and canceled, their agreement.

Each man wrote his own report, but it was Robert Campbell's book, *A Pilgrimage to My Motherland,* which was the more readable account of the African experience. In his preface Campbell stated, "I have determined, with my wife and children, to go to Africa to live." And he was reported in 1863 to be running a publication called the *Anglo-African* in the city of Lagos. Campbell's book is the work of a keen, well-organized, and objective reporter. Such an achievement was not easy, since he found it necessary to explain to Africans wherever he went that he was of African descent. (Actually, as he states in the book, he was three-quarters white.)

As the following pages reveal, Campbell, while a generally objective observer, also states his own feelings and opinions about what he sees. He obviously has a warm and defensive attitude toward the Aku people who practice the traditional African religion, although he is staunchly Christian in his views. He praises the affability and courtesy of the people, and although he holds polygamy to be a "sister evil" to slavery, he perceives that it is practiced within a moral order and decorum. He points out the significant differences in the ways slavery is practiced by Christian Americans, by the Mohammedans in Ilorin (a northern Nigerian town which he visited), and by the heathen Africans, crediting the last with a more humane system, but finally urging the overthrow of all slavery, even the most benign.

A Pilgrimage to My Motherland*

There is not a more affable people found anywhere than are the Akus. Not even Frenchmen are more scrupulous in their attention to politeness than they. Two persons, even utter strangers, hardly ever pass each other without exchanging salutations, and the greatest attention is paid to the relative social position of each in their salutations. Equals meeting will simply say, *acu;* but one addressing a superior affixes some word to *acu,* thus, *acabo,* (*acu abo,* one vowel dropped for euphony) *acuni,* etc. The superior usually salutes first, and when the disparity of position is great, the inferior prostrates. The young always prostrate to the aged. Women kneel, but never prostrate. Sons, without reference to age or rank, prostrate to their mothers or senior female relatives. They never suffer anything to interfere with the observance of these courtesies. There is an appropriate salutation for every occasion for instance: *acuaro,* good morning; *acuale,* good evening; *acushe,* for being industrious; *acabo,* or *acuabo,* (*ua* as diphthong,) for returning from a journey; *acatijo,* for long absence; *acujoco,* for sitting or resting; *acudaro,* for standing or walking; *acuraju,* expressive of sympathy, in distress or sickness; *acueru,* for bearing a burden; *acualejo,* for entertaining a stranger. So rich is the language in salutations, that the above list could have been increased indefinitely.

At Oyo, the capital of the Yoruba nation, there is an old man, apparently in a very humble position, for no one is more condescending and courteous than he. He is, nevertheless, no less a personage than the Onoshoko, or "Father of the King," an officer of state so called. In the event of the king's demise, the privilege of choosing a successor devolves on him, hence his position is really very exalted; besides, he is the party with whom the king is bound to advise on all important affairs. It is customary for men in high positions, the king's relatives, chief Balaguns, and so forth, to construct in front of their houses certain turret-like contrivances, called by them *akabi.* The king allowed Onoshoko to construct *akabis* in front of his house, as

---

* From *A Pilgrimage to My Motherland: An Account of a Journey Among the Egbas and the Yorubas of Central Africa in 1859–1860* (New York, 1861).

his position and rank demanded them. "No," said the old man, "Onoshoko is well enough without *akabis*. Let not any one be able to say, from my example, that he too must have *akabis*: honor belongs to the king only." He is the only man in the kingdom who is privileged to approach the king without prostrating, nevertheless he insists on doing so, explaining his conduct always by the remark that he, in his respect to the king, would ever be an example for others to copy. The king himself, determining not to be outdone, whenever Onoshoko enters the palace yard, prostrates to the old man; and it is common for those about the palace to see one of them stealthily approaching the other, in order first to assume this position of respect.

Except with the few Africans who have been brought under the influence of Christianity, polygamy is universal. A man's position in society is estimated either by his bravery in war, or his wealth; and he can only manifest the latter by the number of his wives, children and slaves. From this circumstance men are frequently reported wealthy, and yet in emergencies can not raise ten bags of cowries (about $40). Wives are commonly engaged at an early age, frequently before six or seven years old. This is done by paying to the parents a stipulated sum, and occasionally making presents both to them and the betrothed. When the engagement is concluded, a bracelet is placed about the wrist to signify the new relation she sustains. She remains with the parents until of proper age to be taken home to her husband. If she comes with honor, two or three days after, adorned with costly cloths and jewels, and with music, she marches with a large company of maidens through the city, to receive the congratulations and presents of her friends, which are generally on such an occasion very liberally bestowed. Otherwise, the parents are made to refund the whole amount advanced in engaging her, and the guilty partner to her infidelity, if known, is prosecuted for adultery. If the intended husband is a youth, never before married, his mother, or less frequently his father, makes the engagement for him, and the parties are respectively kept in ignorance of each other until they are both of suitable age to live together.

A less troublesome way of procuring a wife, with many, is to resort to the slave-marts of Ilorin at once, money in hand, and make their choice. The latter, of course, are slaves, as well as their children, between whom, however, and other slaves, there is some distinction. Wives procured according to the first of these methods, although not regarded as slaves, are practically as much so as the others, for like them, at the death of their lord they become nominally, and often really, the wives of his eldest son, except, of course, his own mother. They have, however, the privilege of choosing the next elder son, or of observing ever after a state of celibacy, which but few women would choose, as it is regarded reproachfully.

According to their means of procuring them, men possess from a single wife to two or three hundred. Except the chiefs there are few, however, who have more than about twenty. The Yoruba king of Oyo, Adelu, who is reported the wealthiest man of the Akus, maintains about three hundred wives.* They are never suffered to leave the palace yard, except on certain days, when they march in procession through the town in charge of eunuchs, of whom the king has a large number. Men are not suffered to approach them in these excursions. The King of Ilorin and other great personages of his court also keep their wives always confined. In this case, however, they are supported. In Abbeokuta, where even the wives of the king must support themselves, they are permitted to go abroad, and are generally among the most industrious traders of the place.

Inquiry is sometimes made as to whether wives agree among themselves. I answer, they do as well as a number of women living in the same house can under other circumstances: at any rate, their disputes do not arise from the fact that they are all the wives of the same husband. There is always one, only one, who is intrusted with the domestic affairs of her lord, and to her all the others pay the greatest deference, and they expect the recently married to receive more favor than others: making this philosophic calculation, they are saved much of what, under a different and purer system of morals, would be highly irritating and disgusting.

After polygamy it may be appropriate to make a few remarks respecting its sister evil, slavery, which exists all through this section of Africa. Although the term "slavery" is the only word by which the institution can be properly designated, it is certainly not of the same character as the American institution, there

---

* Including the surviving wives of his father, who as already mentioned, are all nominally his, he is said to have about one thousand.

being but little disparity between the condition of the master and that of his slave, since the one possesses almost every advantage accessible to the other. Slaves are often found filling the most exalted positions, thus at Abbeokuta all the king's chief officers are his slaves, and they are among his most confidential advisers. On certain state occasions, one or other of these slaves is often permitted to assume in public the position of the king, and command and receive in his own person the homage and respect due to his master. So in Ilorin, Dungari, the prime minister of the king, daily sits in the market place to receive the homage of the populace intended for the king, and yet Dungari, really the most important personage of the kingdom, and in rank even above the king's own sons, is a slave. Instances of this kind might be afforded almost indefinitely.

Slaves are procured chiefly by conquest, sometimes in warfare as justifiable and even more so than the wars waged among civilized nations; at other times predatory, and undertaken solely for their capture. Not a few incur slavery as a penalty for crime. Some are sold to defray either their own debts, or it may be the debts of others for which they have become liable; and frequently children are kidnaped and sold away into distant parts.

Although but a few years since every heathen town in this region abounded with slave markets, there is now, doubtless through the influence of Christian civilization, nothing of the kind seen; and although it would be unsafe to say that slaves are not sometimes sold, yet if so, it is done secretly. The first and only marts we met for "this description of property," were at Ilorin, a Mohammedan kingdom. There was there, besides several small numbers exposed in different places throughout the town, a large market, the Gambari, almost exclusively devoted to their sale, and in which there were certainly not less than from five to six hundred. Christian America and Mohammedan Ilorin do with complacency what the heathens of Yoruba and Egba feel it a disgrace to practise.

At Ilorin we sojourned with Nasamo, the king's sheriff, in whose company only we were permitted to walk about the city. On arriving at the Gambari market in one of our excursions, he pointed to the slaves and jocularly asked whether I wished to purchase. I embraced the opportunity to show him the wrong of making slaves of our fellows, and the great injury which it inflicted not only upon those who suffer, but also on those who practise it. Nasamo fills a high position in the state, and is the master of a large number of slaves; nevertheless he is himself a slave, and doubtless thought of his youthful home and dear parents from whom he was stolen. He admitted all I said, and observed that he wished there was no such thing, but while it existed it was better that they be exposed in the markets than that they should be sold privately, "for then bad men would seize the defenseless and our children, and we would not know where to find them."

The Mohammedans do not sell their co-religionists into slavery: they sometimes hold them as slaves, but only when they were bought as heathens and converted after coming into their posses- sion; but these are never sold. Here is a vast difference from that class of Christians, so called, who buy and sell the members of their own church, the partakers of the same communion with themselves. How much better are such than the heathens, or even these benighted Mussulmans?

Although, as I have before shown, slavery in Africa is not like slavery in America, or even as it is in Cuba, yet it is still a fact which must not be disregarded, that, more or less, it is slavery— such, it is true, as the teachings and example of good men might quietly but certainly in time overthrow, but which might also by an obverse course assume most of the abhorrent phases of the American institution. My own opposition to slavery does not arise simply from the suffering and ill-treatment which the bond- man endures, for in that case I would have to acquit perhaps the majority of American masters. I oppose it because a human being is by it reduced to the condition of a thing, a mere chattel, to be bought or sold at the option of his fellow man, whose only right to do so is the accidental circumstance of superior power— a power which the good should use to protect rather than oppress the weak. I oppose it because I feel the common instinct that man has an inalienable right to "life, liberty and the pursuit of hap- piness." Hence I do not regard a slave-owner, even when he makes his slave as comfortable and happy as a slave can be—in all other respects, it may be, as well off as himself—I do not, I say, regard such a person as therefore less guilty; indeed if there is one class of them whom I detest more heartily than another, it is that class whose course is to render the slave, if possible, contented with his condition.

From this view, therefore, I place my opposition to African slavery on the same ground as to American slavery, and God helping me, shall labor as earnestly for the overthrow of one as for the other.*

---

* The following distinctions or grades of servitude prevail: one absolutely free through all generations is termed, *"Omo olu Wabi."* The issue of the child of slave parents, marrying an *"Omo olu wabi,"* is deemed *"eru idili,"* or a slave connected with the family. An absolute slave is called *"eru."* One in pawn, placed in that condition by another, is termed *"wafa":* one voluntarily placing himself in pawn is *"Faru so fa."* A favorite slave, *"eru,"* at the death of his master is seldom if ever considered any longer an *eru,* but becomes *"eru idili,"* and generally marries in the family, in which case his children, if by free mothers, become absolutely free.

EDWARD W. BLYDEN

Twentieth-century black nationalist and Pan-African ideas have their historical roots in the work of a brilliant West-Indian-born ideologue of the nineteenth century—Edward Wilmot Blyden (1832-1912). Summing up Blyden's achievements, Professor Hollis R. Lynch, author of a landmark study of Blyden, has written:

His teachings, incessantly propounded, that Negroes had a history and a culture of which they could be proud, and that with the help of New World Negroes a progressive civilization could be built in Africa, gave members of his race a new pride and hope, and inspired succeeding generations of African nationalists and New World Negro leaders.*

Some of the basic elements of Blyden's thought may be seen in the passages given below from his lecture at Lower Buchanan, Liberia, in 1908. Blyden was then seventy-five and had devoted his whole life to the strengthening of Liberian society and to preparing the intellectual and spiritual groundwork for a black renaissance in Africa and the diaspora. Tirelessly, in the face of repeated failures and discouragement, Edward Blyden had composed dozens of books, pamphlets, articles, and lectures, and had served in various high educational, government, and diplomatic posts of the Liberian republic. Often controversial and prob-

---

* Hollis R. Lynch, *Edward Wilmot Blyden: Pan-Negro Patriot,* (London 1967). This excellent book is the primary source for the present note. (Ed.)

lematic, his ideas were nevertheless thought out with rigor, imagination, and courage.

Born in St. Thomas, Virgin Islands, in 1832, Blyden had come to the United States as a promising boy of seventeen, under the sponsorship of a white American pastor, to apply for admission to the Rutgers Theological College. He was refused admission there because he was a Negro, and was later rejected by two other theological colleges. This bitter experience, together with the increasingly frightening atmosphere created by the Fugitive Slave Law, determined the race-proud young man to go to Liberia, which had just become an autonomous black republic. Blyden arrived in Liberia in 1851 and applied himself with tremendous seriousness and vigor to the tasks of self-development. In rapid succession he became a lay preacher, a tutor and then the principal of a high school, an ordained Presbyterian minister, and a Liberian commissioner to Britain and the United States. In 1862 he made the first of many trips to the United States to solicit emigration and support for Liberia.

One of Blyden's central themes was the particularist conception of the races as each having its own special character and its individual contribution to make to the world. However, in the atmosphere of nineteenth-century racial philosophies—like that of Count Arthur de Gobineau—which posited an innate biological basis for racial "talents" and "instincts," Blyden's particularism became an obsession with "pure" blackness, and went over into outspoken contempt for those of mixed blood. Blyden campaigned militantly against the mulatto as an enemy of the Negro both in Liberia and in the diaspora. While rationalizing his acceptance of certain distinguished leaders of mixed blood like Frederick Douglass and Bishop H. M. Turner, Blyden demanded that only "pure Negroes" be permitted to emigrate to Africa. His active hostility to the mulatto elements in the ruling ranks of Liberia resulted in his near-lynching by a Liberian mob in 1871. He had to flee to Sierra Leone after being rescued by a friend. This pattern of divisive hostility toward lighter-skinned Negroes was to be echoed a half-century later by Marcus Garvey, whose ideology, in other respects too, showed the influence of Blyden's ideas.

While Blyden was deeply involved in Christian theology, the thrust of his Negro nationalism, in the context of the Christian course in Africa, produced often contradictory twists in his ideology. He accepted the then-current Christian belief that it was the Divine plan to permit enslavement of Africans so that they could be civilized abroad and then return to civilize the pagan Africans. At the same time he castigated Christianity for being insufficiently appreciative of the soundness and merits of many indigenous African customs such as polygamy. He praised Mohammedanism—to which he gave much sympathetic study— for carrying out a civilizing mission without race prejudice and with less strain on the African social fabric. Blyden's most important book, *Christianity, Islam and the Negro Race* (1887), reflecting his deepening respect for the Muslim influence on Negro Africa, was well received in the American press, and especially in the Negro press, but greatly displeased European reviewers. However, even opponents were tremendously impressed by Blyden's erudition and cogency.

Blyden's early contacts with Jews in St. Thomas, as well as his serious study of the Hebrew language and Jewish history, brought him to see a parallel between the historical situations of the Negro and the Jew. He was intensely aware of "that marvelous movement called Zionism" from the time of the publication of Theodor Herzl's *Judenstaat* in 1896. Blyden's pamphlet *The Jewish Question* (1898) championed the right of the Jews to return to Palestine "to take their place in the land of their fathers as a great—a leading—secular power." He also urged Jews to settle in Africa and make their contribution to the solution of African problems as a "kindred" people. This seemed reasonable to Blyden because the Jews "in their early history, and in their impressionable condition, were more closely related to Africa, and to the Negro race, than to any other country or people."

In his 1908 lecture Blyden counseled European powers to desist from interfering with the wholesome fabric of African life, and he counseled Liberians to refrain from imposing American patterns on local conditions, but these caveats were not intended to pressure Europeans or Americans to withdraw from their activities in Africa. Blyden's conception was that for a certain period the Europeans and Americans, if they followed enlightened policies, could actually not only develop Africa materially, but play a role in furthering that distinctly "African personality" which would eventually animate and govern an independent

Africa. (In practical terms, Blyden was focused mainly on uniting English-speaking West Africa.)

After returning to Liberia from Sierra Leone in 1874, Blyden went on to hold such important posts as the presidency of Liberia College and the ministry of the interior. He was also ambassador to the Court of St. James's during three different periods. He was a great social success abroad and did much through his intellectual achievements to destroy notions of inherent Negro inferiority. His work toward a united West Africa was carried forward after his death in 1912 by his staunch disciple Casely Hayford, and in the next generation by Nnamdi Azikiwe and Kwame Nkrumah, both of whom became familiar with Blyden's writings while studying in the United States.

Progress is Difference*

This year we celebrate the eighty-sixth anniversary of the founding of the city of Monrovia by the Negro settlers from America. The colony is nearly ninety years old. The Republic has just celebrated its Diamond Jubilee. Still Liberia is called by foreigners an experiment. It is indeed an experiment, an unprecedented experiment. Nothing of the kind has ever happened before in the world's history. A group of returned exiles—refugees from the house of bondage—settled along a few hundred miles of the coast of their Fatherland, attempting to rule millions of people, their own kith and kin on a foreign system in which they themselves have been imperfectly trained, while knowing very little of the facts of the history of the people they assume to rule, either social, economic or religious, and taking for granted that the religious and social theories they have brought

---

* From a lecture originally entitled, "The Three Needs of Liberia", delivered January 26, 1908 at Lower Buchanan, Grand Bassa County, Liberia. Published in London: 1908.

from across the sea must be adapted to all the needs of their unexpatriated brethren.

Liberia is a little bit of South Carolina, of Georgia, of Virginia —that is to say—of the ostracized, suppressed, depressed elements of those States—tacked on to West Africa—a most incongruous combination, with no reasonable prospect of success; and further complicated by addition from other sources. We take a little bit from England, a little bit from France, a little bit from Germany, and try to compromise with all. We have no definite plan, no dominating race conception, with really nothing to help us from behind—the scene whence we came—and nothing to guide us from before—the goal to which are tending or should tend. We resemble those plants which we call "Life everlasting"—I do not know the botanical name—whose leaves severed from the stem, appear to survive apart from the whole plant, with no connection with root or branch. They can be pinned up against a wall or anywhere and yet appear to be green. But we know that this condition is not permanent. Liberia is like that plant; and it is a wonder to many that it has appeared to live so long. We are severed from the parent stock—the aborigines—who are the root, branch, and flower of Africa and of any Negro State in Africa.

Away from them we are cut off from the evolutionary process by which men and nations normally grow. And as evolution is the law of life, we can have neither real permanent life nor vigorous or continuous growth. Without the aborigines in our domestic, social, religious, and political life, there is nothing before this State but death. If you doubt this I will give you an illustration, which is before you every day. Take away the aborigines from our *industrial* life, where should we be? Where would be our farms? Where would be the tillers of our soil, our instruments of movement, of travel, of commercial enterprise? Who would work our canoes, our boats, carry our hammocks, load our ships and land our cargoes from abroad? No people can take root in any country where they cannot do these things for themselves. You see at once where we should be without the help and co-operation of the natives in the directions I have indicated. This is exactly where we are in our social, political, and religious life—*paralyzed*. A few among us see it, but the generality do not. After you had triumphantly carried last year the amendments to the Constitution, one of your most thoughtful and practical statesmen wrote to me: "We could not have succeeded without the aborigines." This was true. So in all the great changes and reforms to which the few leading men now look forward, there is no hope without the aborigines. We can take our proper place in Africa and in the world only by obeying the laws of the Fatherland. Our progress will come by connection with the parent stock. The question, therefore, which we should try to study and answer is, What are the underlying principles of African life—not American life—but *African* life? Every nation and every tribe has a right to demand freedom of life and abundance of life, because it has a contribution to make peculiar to itself towards the ultimate welfare of the world. But no nation can have this freedom of life, and make this contribution, which no other nation can make, without connection with its past, of which it must carefully preserve the traditions, if it is to understand the present and have an intelligent and inspiring hope of the future.

But we have no past across the sea of which we can be proud or to which we can look for inspiration. America, to which our fathers were carried by violence, where we lived and still live by sufferance as unwelcome strangers, is not the rock whence we were hewn. Our residence there was and is transitional, like that of the Hebrews in Egypt, or Babylon, looking to an exodus. That exodus may never come for all; but the feeling and aspiration on the part of the exile must ever be towards the Fatherland, as the Jew, wherever he is, looks to Palestine, and in the depths of his soul continually exclaims, "If I forget thee O Jerusalem, let my right hand forget her cunning." For Liberians the residence in America was an intermediate past—a past of which the elements were chains, whips, the auction block. There is nothing in that past to which we can look back with pride and satisfaction. We were victims, and we are still victims of that past—a past blurred, blotted, bloodstained. We cannot forget it. It is not given to us to follow the optimistic admonition of the poet: "Let the dead Past bury its dead."

No: for us the past has left its dead to be daily confronted by us. There are moments when, feeling the contaminating atmosphere and oppressive drawbacks of this corpse, we exclaim from the depths of our souls, "Who shall deliver us from the body of this death?" The "White Man's Burden" is with us. We are obsessed by the literature and prejudices of the age. We are continually reminded of past days. Every time we read our Declaration of Independence, many of whose phrases are out of date and should be eliminated, depressing and misleading reminiscences are brought before us, and following their inept suggestions we fancy that we are here to heal up an old sore, instead of developing a new bud in the garden of the nations. We find here in the kingdom of nature a different flora and fauna from what we left in America. We cannot introduce American natural conditions here, neither can we introduce its religious, social or economic conditions.

We were born under natural conditions, with the book of Nature open wide before us and written in characters so legible that he who runs may read. But Europe and America baffle us and shut out from us the pages we ought to read and study. By their literature, their books, their newspapers and the teachings of their philanthropists they are trying to introduce into Africa systems entirely incompatible with the racial and climatic conditions and necessities. Owing to the social, industrial and economic order of Europe and America, dislocations have been introduced which are the source of constant unrest in the countries whence they came; and the guardians of public order are at their wits end with the problems of labor, pauperism, lunacy and profligacy. The essential elements of European civilization today are pauperism, crime, lunacy, growing out of their social and economic order as naturally as showers from the clouds of summer.

* * *

Africa, away from foreign interference, has no such problems. Thieves do not arise, for there is no land or water so sacred that any woman or child can occupy it or any place near it and starve. Every man has enough or the means of getting enough for food, clothing and shelter. There are no spinsters, or professional outcasts, every woman being sheltered and protected, enjoying the privilege and sacred right of motherhood. No ecclesiastical law or foreign prejudice interferes with this right.

Africa, therefore, has a right to demand of Europe, in reply to its indiscriminate appeals for the demolition among us of immemorial customs, an answer to the following question: "If we abolished customs known and tried and helpful to us, and adopted yours, what shall we do with our submerged tenth, our thieves, and prostitutes?" But, alas, this is a question which Europe and America are trying in vain to answer for themselves. Then Africa must say to our would-be benefactors on these subjects:

> Great and good friends, *you* grapple with *your* domestic and social problems and leave us to grapple with *ours*. In political, military, material and financial problems we need and solicit your guidance and help, but as to the subtle problems which involve the physical, physiological and spiritual or psychological well-being of the people, we deprecate your benevolent but dislocating interference. As to your marriage laws, we beseech you to believe that for Africa you are mistaken—fatally mistaken—and inasmuch as you admit that there is no Divine command in the matter (See debate in Parliament, on Marriage with a deceased wife's sister, 1907) we entreat you, whether as religious or political legislators, to withdraw your heavy hand and recognize that the laws of Nature, which are the laws of God, are wiser and stronger than all your theories.

*   *   *

The object of the great social movement in England is to abolish private ownership and nationalize the land, so that by this collective ownership all the means of production and livelihood shall be under the control of the people. Here in Africa where the system of collective ownership is an immemorial custom, we are trying to introduce private ownership. I say we are trying to introduce it, because we have not succeeded and cannot succeed. The stars in their courses are fighting against us. Private owners pass away, as a rule without heirs, owing to the abnormal domestic conditions, and the lands escheat to the Government. In Monrovia alone the number of lots which have reverted to the Government, which means back to the people, according to African law, is astounding, as anyone may see who will examine the subject. Nature cannot be thrust out with a pitchfork; and we have been fighting to do this for three generations. The unequal contest has left us prostrate; yet we cannot or will not see.

Owing to our false training we have been legislating as Americans in America for Americans. We have been disposing of the lands of the country and are still disposing of them on the foreign system we have been taught. But everywhere amongst us this system has failed. We have been perpetrating the absurdity of measuring out and partitioning land to the natives, who are the lords of the soil. In many places they laugh at us because they know that in the order of Nature these lines of demarcation must disappear. By the system we are trying to introduce we always in the long run create wildnernesses instead of farms and cities. Let us then study African conditions and legislate according to the Constitution made and provided by the Divine lawgiver. Read "The manuscripts of God" and copy from them. Our laws will then stand permanent and unrepealable. All others will repeal themselves, whoever makes them.

* * *

In Liberia we have failed in Agriculture, as a permanent and successful feature in our industrial system, and shall always fail because we are trying to work the land on the gang system, which we learned in America. That is not the African system. It is not the natural system. It has been introduced into Europe and America and has led to the inequalities which are producing the unrest in those countries. In England farming is complicated by three distinct interests. First, there is the owner of the land; then there is the tenant or hirer of the land; then the laborer on the land. In Africa there is only one interest and that is the people's interest. Farming is communistic, allied to and guided by a patriarchal head. The land is owned by everybody. The men, women and children all work, engage in labor as a duty they owe to themselves and to each other, and all reap equal rewards. That is, unto each according to his several ability. Under the African system there can be no absolutely rich man and no absolutely poor man.

Now in coming from America with foreign ideas in our head, we have tried to reverse all this, and create the distinctions which exist in Europe and America, but we have nowhere succeeded. We have been striving to produce the independently rich man, with its opposite, the abjectly poor, but we have everywhere egregiously failed. There is not a man reputedly rich fifty years ago, who has left a single trace of his position. Not a single farmer who, thirty years ago, was at the height of prosperity, exists today. The fault is not in the climate but in those who persist in breaking its laws. White men tell us of the necessity and the importance of there being class distinctions—rich men and poor men—princes and beggars—in every community, but this was not Christ's idea, and it is not the African idea. The African idea is the idea of the first Christian church. "One for all and all for one."

* * *

The first Pilgrim fathers, before they left America, organized a Baptist Church, in Richmond, Virginia, went on board the "Elizabeth," as a Church, landed at Monrovia, thus organized and founded the Providence Baptist Church in Monrovia. There were a few individuals of other denominations among the first immigrants but they were not organized. The Baptist Church then was the first institution of the kind in Liberia—and the only institution of any kind which has maintained unbroken continuity for eighty-six years. This church then has a right and a claim which it ought at once to assert, to form itself into an organization to develop the true African Religion begotten by the teachings and nourished by the pure and sincere milk of the words of Christ.

* * *

Our white friends in America do not now take the same interest in the emigration of the Negroes to Africa that they did forty or fifty years ago. Then the politicians wished to get rid of the surplus Negro population as a burden and a menace, and the philanthropists wanted to found a nation on the American model of repatriated Africans in Africa; while the Christians wanted to establish a center in West Africa for the evangelization of the continent. But time has changed all that. The politicians now want the blacks to remain in America to plant cotton; the philanthropists do not see why they should not be happy in the South, especially in the Black Belt, where if they do not now they will soon outnumber the whites; while the Christians are not enthusiastic over the results of their two generations of expenditure of life and treasure upon what experience and science are now telling them is a hopeless task. They now feel that the work of evangelization had better be left to the Africans themselves. The white Presbyterian and white Baptist have retired from the scene.

Americans generally are also beginning to recognize that the manifest destiny in their country is the blending in material, political and religious work of the conglomerate forces existing in the land. So far as Liberia is concerned, the aim of its leaders is to make the Republic an essentially African State. That is what is implied in the recent amendment of the Constitution substituting the word *Negro* for *colored*. Liberia is, then, first and foremost a Negro State. That is its basis and that must be its superstructure. All efforts to de-Negroize it will prove abortive. To have a little bit of South Carolina, of Georgia, of Virginia as component elements of the State is not progress. We do not want the same thing in Africa we left in America. Progress is difference. The object of the Christianity we profess is that "the thoughts of many hearts may be revealed;" it is not to suppress individuality but to develop and emphasize it.

MARCUS GARVEY

In 1917, at a time of rising West Indian immigration, thirty-year-old Marcus Garvey came to the United States from his native Jamaica, and within a few years built the largest mass movement of blacks ever seen in America. He gave hundreds of thousands of people an inspiring vision of a worldwide African empire uniting the blacks of the diaspora with a homeland liberated from colonialism. The Universal Negro Improvement Association, together with the *Negro World,* a weekly newspaper edited by Garvey, were the central instruments for disseminating that vision, but there was a galaxy of other enterprises: a Black Star Steamship Company, the Negro Factory Corporation, the African Orthodox Church, the Universal African Legion, the Universal Black Cross Nurses, and still others. The officers and ranks of these entities were furnished with grand titles and uniforms, displayed in parades and rituals. All this had a powerful appeal for people of little education, who daily experienced a sense of powerlessness and oppression.

In practical affairs Garvey's reach far exceeded his grasp, and his business enterprises became entangled in fantastic mismanagement which led to his imprisonment for fraudulent use of the mails. He spent almost three years in jail until the commutation of his sentence by President Coolidge in 1927 and his deportation as an undesirable alien. He returned to Jamaica and later went to London, where he died in 1940. He was never able to rebuild his movement to its previous strength. Today small remnants of neo-Garveyite persuasion still exist in black ghettos of the United States and the Caribbean islands.

On the rising tide of interest in Africa, the name of Garvey has gained some dignity among the educated Negroes—the very class who had originally spurned his movement and against whom Garvey had waged war. W. E. B. Du Bois and Garvey had engaged in vicious polemics against each other, the latter persistently exploiting the resentments of dark-skinned Negroes against the caste discriminations practiced by some lighter-hued Negroes, whom Garvey identified with the National Association for the Advancement of Colored People and Negro intellectuals generally. Garvey accused all these people not only of being his personal enemies but of "a scheme to destroy the Negro Race." While pleading for worldwide unity of Negroes (under his leadership), he mounted divisive attacks on "the so-called intellectual Negroes" who maintained what he considered an utter absurdity, the notion "that the black man would ultimately work out his existence alongside of the white man in countries founded and established by the latter." Committed to a propaganda for a "pure black race," he found the Ku Klux Klan vision of a "pure white race" congenial, and publicly cooperated with them. In his article "Africa for the Africans," reproduced here, he excoriates Negro intellectuals, but praises southern United States senators for their interest in colonizing Africa with American Negroes.

Garvey himself never set foot in Africa, nor did any Garveyite settlement establish itself anywhere in Africa. For a few years the dream of a "Negro empire" lived in the minds of many black Americans and then quickly faded. But the emergence of the new African states in mid-century casts an aura of prophecy, for some, around the name of Garvey. In independent Jamaica today Garvey is officially designated a national hero, and his portrait appears on currency and postage stamps, though the government is far from accepting his total ideology.

*Africa for the Africans**

For five years the Universal Negro Improvement Association
has been advocating the cause of Africa for the Africans—that
is, that the Negro peoples of the world should concentrate upon
the object of building up for themselves a great nation in Africa.

When we started our propaganda toward this end several of
the so-called intellectual Negroes who have been bamboozling the
race for over half a century said that we were crazy, that the
Negro peoples of the western world were not interested in Africa
and could not live in Africa. One editor and leader went so far
as to say at his so-called Pan-African Congress that American
Negroes could not live in Africa, because the climate was too
hot. All kinds of arguments have been adduced by these Negro
intellectuals against the colonization of Africa by the black race.
Some said that the black man would ultimately work out his
existence alongside of the white man in countries founded and
established by the latter. Therefore, it was not necessary for
Negroes to seek an independent nationality of their own. The old
time stories of "African fever," "African bad climate," "African
mosquitos," "African savages," have been repeated by these
"brainless intellectuals" of ours as a scare against our people in
America and the West Indies taking a kindly interest in the new
program of building a racial empire of our own in our Motherland. Now that years have rolled by and the Universal Negro
Improvement Association has made the circuit of the world with
its propaganda, we find eminent statesmen and leaders of the
white race coming out boldly advocating the cause of colonizing
Africa with the Negroes of the western world. A year ago Senator
MacCullum of the Mississippi Legislature introduced a resolution
in the House for the purpose of petitioning the Congress of the
United States of America and the President to use their good
influence in securing from the Allies sufficient territory in Africa
in liquidation of the war debt, which territory should be used for
the establishing of an independent nation for American Negroes.
About the same time Senator France of Maryland gave expres-

---

* From *The Philosophy and Opinions of Marcus Garvey,* compiled by
Amy Jacques Garvey (New York, 1925). Reprinted with the permission
of Mrs. Garvey.

sion to a similar desire in the Senate of the United States. During
a speech on the "Soldiers' Bonus," he said:

We owe a big debt to Africa and one which we have too long ignored.
I need not enlarge upon our peculiar interest in the obligation to the
people of Africa. Thousands of Americans have for years been contributing to the missionary work which has been carried out by the
noble men and women who have been sent out in that field by the
churches of America.

Germany to the Front

This reveals a real change on the part of prominent statesmen
in their attitude on the African question. Then comes another
suggestion from Germany, for which Dr. Heinrich Schnee, a
former Governor of German East Africa, is author. This German
statesman suggests in an interview given out in Berlin, and published in New York, that America takes over the mandatories of
Great Britain and France in Africa for the colonization of American Negroes. Speaking on the matter, he says

As regards the attempt to colonize Africa with the surplus American
colored population, this would in a long way settle the vexed problem,
and under the plan such as Senator France has outlined, might enable
France and Great Britain to discharge their duties to the United States,
and simultaneously ease the burden of German reparations which is
paralyzing economic life.

With expressions as above quoted from prominent world statesmen, and from the demands made by such men as Senators
France and McCullum, it is clear that the question of African
nationality is not a far-fetched one, but is as reasonable and
feasible as was the idea of an American nationality.

A "Program" at Last

I trust that the Negro peoples of the world are now convinced
that the work of the Universal Negro Improvement Association is
not a visonary one, but very practical, and that it is not so far-
fetched, but can be realized in a short while if the entire race will
only co-operate and work toward the desired end. Now that the
work of our organization has started to bear fruit we find that
some of these "doubting Thomases" of three and four years ago
are endeavoring to mix themselves up with the popular idea of

rehabilitating Africa in the interest of the Negro. They are now advancing spurious "programs" and in a short while will endeavor to force themselves upon the public as advocates and leaders of the African idea.

It is felt that those who have followed the career of the Universal Negro Improvement Association will not allow themselves to be deceived by these Negro opportunists who have always sought to live off the ideas of other people.

The Dream of a Negro Empire

It is only a question of a few more years when Africa will be completely colonized by Negroes, as Europe is by the white race. What we want is an independent African nationality, and if America is to help the Negro peoples of the world establish such a nationality, then we welcome the assistance.

It is hoped that when the time comes for American and West Indian Negroes to settle in Africa, they will realize their responsibility and their duty. It will not be to go to Africa for the purpose of exercising an over-lordship over the natives, but it shall be the purpose of the Universal Negro Improvement Association to have established in Africa that brotherly co-operation which will make the interests of the African native and the American and West Indian Negro one and the same, that is to say, we shall enter into a common partnership to build up Africa in the interests of our race.

Oneness of Interests

Everybody knows that there is absolutely no difference between the native African and the American and West Indian Negroes, in that we are descendants from one common family stock. It is only a matter of accident that we have been divided and kept apart for over three hundred years, but it is felt that when the time has come for us to get back together, we shall do so in the spirit of brotherly love, and any Negro who expects that he will be assisted here, there or anywhere by the Universal Negro Improvement Association to exercise a haughty superiority over the fellows of his own race, makes a tremendous mistake. Such men had better remain where they are and not attempt to become in any way interested in the higher development of Africa.

The Negro has had enough of the vaunted practice of race superiority as inflicted upon him by others, therefore he is not prepared to tolerate a similar assumption on the part of his own people. In America and the West Indies, we have Negroes who believe themselves so much above their fellows as to cause them to think that any readjustment in the affairs of the race should be placed in their hands for them to exercise a kind of an autocratic and despotic control as others have done to us for centuries. Again I say, it would be advisable for such Negroes to take their hands and minds off the now popular idea of colonizing Africa in the interest of the Negro race, because their being identified with this new program will not in any way help us because of the existing feeling among Negroes everywhere not to tolerate the influence of race or class superiority upon them, as is the desire of the self-appointed and self-created race leadership that we have been having for the last fifty years.

The Basis of an African Aristocracy

The masses of Negroes in America, the West Indies, South and Central America are in sympathetic accord with the aspirations of the native Africans. We desire to help them build up Africa as a Negro Empire, where every black man, whether he was born in Africa or in the Western world, will have the opportunity to develop on his own lines under the protection of the most favorable democratic institutions.

It will be useless, as before stated, for bombastic Negroes to leave America and the West Indies to go to Africa, thinking that they will have privileged positions to inflict upon the race that bastard aristocracy that they have tried to maintain in this Western world at the expense of the masses. Africa shall develop an aristocracy of its own, but it shall be based upon service and loyalty to race. Let all Negroes work toward that end. I feel that it is only a question of a few more years before our program will be accepted not only by the few statesmen of America who are now interested in it, but by the strong statesmen of the world, as the only solution to the great race problem. There is no other way to avoid the threatening war of the races that is bound to engulf all mankind, which has been prophesied by the world's greatest thinkers; there is no better method than by apportioning every race to its own habitat.

The time has really come for the Asiatics to govern themselves in Asia, as the Europeans are in Europe and the Western world, so also is it wise for the Africans to govern themselves at home, and thereby bring peace and satisfaction to the entire human family.

LANGSTON HUGHES

From the time of his first published poem, *The Negro Speaks of Rivers* (1921), the work of Langston Hughes showed a romantic awareness of Africa as the ancient Negro homeland. He was then twenty. Two years later he was a member of the crew of the S.S. *Malone,* which visited over thirty West African ports. From those shores he began to send back prose pieces that appeared in the *Crisis,* edited by W. E. B. Du Bois, and that were later included with revisions in Hughes's autobiography, *The Big Sea* (1940). In that book he exclaims: "When I saw the dust-green hills in the sunlight, something took hold of me. My Africa, Motherland of the Negro peoples! And me a Negro! Africa! The real thing."

His West African sketches include sensitively realistic passages touching on the exploitation of Africans, along with youthfully lyric effusions. In the sketch given here his yearning identification with Africa is marred by the circumstance of his being a light-skinned Negro who can be teased by a Liberian friend for not being a black man, and in this way dissuaded from going to see native religious rites in one of the villages. "So I gave up going to Ju-Ju," he says somewhat sadly.

It is interesting to compare this incident with what happened a number of years later in New York after he had established himself as part of the Negro Renaissance. Hughes was receiving support from an elderly white lady of wealth, who, as Hughes tells it, felt that Negroes were "America's link with the primitive, and that they had something precious to give to the Western World." He finally broke with her, declining further largess, and he explains it thus: "... I did not feel the rhythms of the primitive surging through me, and so I could not live and write as though I did. I was only an American Negro—who had loved the surface of Africa and the rhythms of Africa—but I was not Africa. I was Chicago and Kansas City and Broadway and Harlem."

This point of view could hardly qualify him as a supporter of the Senghor school of Negritude. Hughes's own conception of blackness is embodied in his creation of the folk character of Jessie B. Semple, the earthy and unillusioned protagonist of the long series of sketches published in book form under such titles as *Simple Speaks His Mind* (1950), *Simple Takes a Wife* (1955), *Simple Stakes a Claim* (1957). When Simple, in a rare mention of his African heritage, speaks of his great-great grandfather (and he is speaking during the 1943 riots) he says, "He must of been simple—else why did he let them capture him in Africa and sell him for a slave to breed great-grandpa in slavery to breed my grandpa in slavery to breed my pa to breed me to look at that window and say, 'It aint mine! Bam—mmm-mm-m!' and kick it out!" But Simple's further connection with Africa was this: his stories were serialized in African papers, over the years of their fame both here and abroad, and Simple's creator also had become known to African readers for his poems and other writings.

With his now eminent position as one of the world's most published Negro authors, Hughes was able, as the tide of African independence rolled up, to take an active part in encouraging and promoting African writers. In 1960 he published a pioneering collection of the new African literature, *An African Treasury*. In 1962 he went to Uganda and Nigeria to take part in literary conferences. The next year he published his anthology *Poems from Black Africa*. These acts of literary fellowship with the new African writers were the happiest fruition of Hughes's feelings for Africa.

Looking in on West Africa

Sometimes life is a ripe fruit too delicious for the taste of man: the full moon hung low over Burutu and it was night on the Nigerian delta.

We walked through the quiet streets of the native town, Tom Pey, one of the Kru men from our boat, and I. There were no pavements, no arclights. Only the wide grassy streets, the thatched huts and the near low-hung moon. Dark figures with naked shoulders, a single cloth about their bodies, and bare feet, passed us often, their footsteps making no sounds on the grassy road, their voices soft like the light of the moon. Through the open doors of some of the houses fires gleamed. Women moved about preparing food. In the clearing, great mango trees cast purple shadows across the path. There was no wind. Only the moon.

"How still it is," I said to Pey.

"Yes," Pey replied, "but by and by they make Ju-Ju."

"Tonight? Where?" I cried excited. "I want to go."

Pey shook his head, but pointed toward the edge of the town, where the walls of the forest began. "Christian man no bother with Ju-Ju," Pey said politely. "Omali dance no good for Christian man."

"But I want to see it," I insisted.

"No," Pey cried. "White man never go see Ju-Ju. Him hurt you! Him too awful! White man never go!"

"But I'm not a white man," I objected. "I'll—"

"You no black man, neither," said Pey impatiently. So I gave up going to the Ju-Ju.

We were invited into the house of Nagary, the trader. It was a little larger than the other houses of the village. There were two or three small rooms. We sat down on the floor in the first room, the moonlight streaming through the doorway. A large green parrot slept on a wooden ring hung from the ceiling.

Nagary was an old Mohammedan in voluminous long robes. He must have been a large strong man in his youth. There was a lingering nobleness in his dark old face and proud carriage.

Nagary called his wife. She came, a pretty brown woman, much younger than Nagary. Her body was wrapped in a dull red cloth of rich fiber. She spoke no English, but she smiled.

Nagary sent her for two candles and the only chair, which she offered to me. Nagary sent her for three heavy boxes, which she placed before him. He opened two of the boxes and showed us beaten brass from up the Niger, statuettes that skilled hands had made, fiber-cloth woven by women in far-off villages, the skin of jungle animals, and the soft, white feathers of birds found in the dangerous forests of "the bush."

Nagary opened the third box with a rusty key. It contained a fortune in ivory. Great heavy bracelets for women when they marry; solid ivory tusks, smooth and milk-white; little figures and tiny panels intricately carved; and one great white tusk, circled with monkeys and coiled snakes. Nagary did not ask me to buy any of these things. He seemed satisfied with my surprise and wonder. He told me of his trips up the river to Wari and down to Lagos. He gave me a great spray of feathers. When I left, he said, with outstretched hands: "God be with you."

When we came out of Nagary's house, the moon had risen in the sky. It was not so large now, but it was much brighter. I had never seen a moon so bright.

W. E. B. DU BOIS

William Edward Burghardt Du Bois was born in Great Barrington, Massachusetts, in 1868. He died in Ghana in 1963, having settled and become a citizen there, and was eulogized by Kwame Nkrumah as "a great son of Africa" who had pioneered the Pan-African movement in the Western world. Du Bois had devoted his long lifetime and prolific talents to the cause of completing the Negro emancipation. He had achieved an unquestionable historic stature, but had failed to win the kind of mass support wielded by such men as Booker T. Washington and Marcus Garvey. As a man of intellect, of imperious personality and ambition, of rich scholarly and literary gifts, he did succeed in establishing an enduring ideological influence among educated and activist Negroes.

In vying for leadership with Washington, Du Bois advocated an aggressive struggle for uncompromised civic equality and a stronger emphasis on intellectual and cultural development side by side with the vocational and economic goals stressed by Washington. To sustain and nourish the "talented tenth" among the blacks, and to move toward justice all who would listen among the whites, Du Bois wrote eighteen books ranging from works of historical or sociological scholarship to volumes of essays, novels, and autobiography. He was one of the founders, in 1909, of the NAACP, editing their influential magazine the *Crisis* for twenty-three years. He also wrote numerous articles for national weeklies and monthlies like *Collier's, Nation, Outlook, Forum, Atlantic.*

A mulatto of French Huguenot, Dutch, and Negro ancestry, Du Bois was, from boyhood on, possessed of tremendous black pride and an ingrained distrust of whites even among his friends or allies. It was not only this race pride, however, which moved him to study and write about Africa, to initiate Pan-African conferences, and in his last years to emigrate to Ghana. His ever-closer identification with Africa evolved out of the demands of pro-Negro propaganda, the need for images of racial self-respect. It was necessary to reclaim a heritage of historic wholeness and depth. But beyond all this there was the promise of political leverage in the agitation of antiimperialist issues and in the formation of alliances overseas.

In 1919, as the Versailles Peace Conference was meeting, Du Bois organized in Paris the first Pan-African Congress with fifty-seven delegates, including sixteen Americans, twenty West Indians and twelve Africans. This gathering and three subsequent pan-African conferences which Du Bois organized in the twenties were of little consequence in their own time. The resolutions of a few self-appointed spokesmen could hardly begin to cope with the tremendous problems of developing movements toward self-government in the whole of colonial Africa. Du Bois, in pioneering the Pan-African idea, saw it as the "centralization of race effort and the recognition of a racial fount." This approach did not make much of an impression on the mass of Afro-Americans. But the colorful, emotional appeals of Marcus Garvey—which Du Bois scorned—did whip up a great, if shortlived, enthusiasm.

In 1945, recognizing a new and much more propitious set of circumstances in the world, Du Bois, now seventy-seven but as dynamic as ever, called together yet another Pan-African Conference in London. It was a brilliant success. Representatives from sixty nations and colonies, among them Nkrumah, reflected the confident expectations of colored peoples everywhere that they would soon win their struggles for self-rule.

But on the home grounds of the Afro-American leadership scene, Du Bois became more isolated than ever. He became more and more convinced that the only true friends of the Negro were the communist world and the colored world. It became part of Du Bois's peculiar racial ideology that when Japan, for example, annexed northern China, this was not imperialism but rather antiimperialism. The possibilities of races in Africa or Asia developing their own exploitations and imperialisms did not enter seriously into his reckonings.

The ambiguities of Du Bois's mystique about Africa are vividly revealed in his account, given below, of his visit to Liberia in 1924 as official representative of President Coolidge to the inaugural ceremonies of the Liberian president C. D. B. King.

Obviously, Du Bois takes pride and pleasure in his ancestral link with Africa. Yet he is careful to emphasize that "the physical bond is least and the badge of color relatively unimportant save as a badge; the real essence of this kinship is the social heritage of slavery; the discrimination and insult; and this heritage binds together not simply the children of Africa, but extends through yellow Asia and into the South Seas. It is this unity that draws me to Africa."

Maintaining that shared suffering is the essence of his relationship to Africa, and that discrimination and insult are to be resisted and abolished by the unity of the oppressed, he sees fit, nevertheless, to draw a romantic veil of idyllic scenes and elegiac prose over the harsh realities of Liberia in 1924, which included exploitation of the indigenous Liberians by the Americo-Liberians (the high-caste descendants of the American free Negroes who founded the Liberian republic.)

This anomaly is commented on by F. L. Broderick in his excellent book on Du Bois:

But when Liberia was guilty of practices that would have outraged his Negro sensibilities if performed by white nations, Du Bois was tolerant and understanding. When an American-born Liberian was burned to death in a building as he was being arrested, Du Bois excused the action as being merely the result of bad judgment. Several years later he acknowledged the existence of slavery in Liberia and urged its abolition, but for the time being he tolerated "pawning"—a form of compulsory labor little removed from slavery—as a way of raising the ignorant to an educated status; and, anyway, he added, the British had only just released two hundred thousand slaves in Sierra Leone. When he continued to defend Liberia even after George S. Schuyler published *Slaves Today,* a vigorous attack on the Liberian rulers, Schuyler commented that Du Bois's "belligerent and commendable Negrophilism" warped his vision.[1]

---

[1] Francis L. Broderick, *W.E.B. Du Bois: Negro Leader in Time of Crisis* (Stanford, 1959).

Du Bois's lyrical rendering of his Liberian visit (published, it should be noted, fully sixteen years after the event, when he had already attached himself fervently not only to antiimperialist but to many specifically communist positions and causes), deserves to be read for its revelations of the thought and character of this complex man. It also points to some of the basic dilemmas faced by the black diaspora when it seeks identification with particular African regimes.

An Official Visit to Liberia

What is Africa to me? Once I should have answered the question simply: I should have said "fatherland" or perhaps better "motherland" because I was born in the century when the walls of race were clear and straight; when the world consisted of mutually exclusive races; and even though the edges might be blurred, there was no question of exact definition and understanding of the meaning of the word. One of the first pamphlets that I wrote in 1897 was on "The Conservation of Races" wherein I set down as the first article of a proposed racial creed: "We believe that the Negro people as a race have a contribution to make to civilization and humanity which no other race can make."

Since then the concept of race has so changed and presented so much of contradiction that as I face Africa I ask myself: what is it between us that constitutes a tie which I can feel better than I can explain? Africa is, of course, my fatherland. Yet neither my father nor my father's father ever saw Africa or knew its meaning or cared overmuch for it. My mother's folk were closer and yet their direct connection, in culture and race, became tenuous; still, my tie to Africa is strong. On this vast continent were born and lived a large portion of my direct ancestors going back a thousand years or more. The mark of their heritage is upon me in color and hair. These are obvious things, but of little meaning in themselves; only important as they stand for real and more subtle differences from other men. Whether they do or not I do not know nor does science know today.

But one thing is sure and that is the fact that since the fifteenth century these ancestors of mine and their other descendants have had a common history; have suffered a common disaster and have one long memory. The actual ties of heritage between the individuals of this group vary with the ancestors that they have in common and many others: Europeans and Semites, perhaps Mongolians, certainly American Indians. But the physical bond is least and the badge of color relatively unimportant save as a badge: the real essence of this kinship is its social heritage of slavery, the discrimination and insult; and this heritage binds together not simply the children of Africa, but extends through yellow Asia and into the South Seas. It is this unity that draws me to Africa.

When shall I forget the night I first set foot on African soil? I am the sixth generation in descent from forefathers who left this land. The moon was at the full and the waters of the Atlantic lay like a lake. All the long slow afternoon as the sun robed herself in her western scarlet with veils of misty cloud, I had seen Africa afar. Cape Mount—that mighty headland with its twin curves, northern sentinel of the realm of Liberia—gathered itself out of the cloud at half past three and then darkened and grew clear. On beyond flowed the dark low undulating land quaint with palm and breaking sea. The world grew black. Africa faded away, the stars stood forth curiously twisted—Orion in the zenith —the Little Bear asleep and the Southern Cross rising behind the horizon. Then afar, ahead, a lone light shown, straight at the ship's fore. Twinkling lights appeared below, around, and rising shadows. "Monrovia," said the Captain.

Suddenly we swerved to our left. The long arms of the bay enveloped us and then to the right rose the twinkling hill of Monrovia, with its crowning star. Lights flashed on the shore— here, there. Then we sensed a darker shading in the shadows; it lay very still. "It's a boat," one said. "It's two boats!" Then the shadow drifted in pieces and as the anchor roared into the deep, five boats outlined themselves on the waters—great ten-oared barges with men swung into line and glided toward us.

It was nine at night—above the shadows, there the town, here the sweeping boats. One forged ahead with the flag-stripes and a lone star flaming behind the ensign of the customs floating wide; and bending to the long oars, the white caps of ten black sailors. Up the stairway clambered a soldier in khaki, aide-de-camp of the President of the Republic, a customhouse official, the clerk of the American legation—and after them sixty-five lithe, lean black stevedores with whom the steamer would work down to Portuguese Angola and back. A few moments of formalities, greetings and good-bys and I was in the great long boat with the President's aide—a brown major in brown khaki. On the other side, the young clerk, and at the back, the black barelegged pilot. Before us on the high thwarts were the rowers: men, boys, black, thin, trained in muscle and sinew, little larger than the oars in thickness, they bent their strength to them and swung upon them.

One in the center gave curious little cackling cries to keep up the rhythm, and for the spurts and the stroke, a call a bit thicker and sturdier; he gave a low guttural command now and then; the boat, alive, quivering, danced beneath the moon, swept a great curve to the bar to breast its narrow teeth of foam— "t'chick-a-tickity, t'chick-a-tickity," sang the boys, and we glided and raced, now between boats, now near the landing—now cast aloft at the dock. And lo! I was in Africa.

Christmas Eve, and Africa is singing in Monrovia. They are Krus and Fanti—men, women and children, and all the night they march and sing. The music was once the music of mission revival hymns. But it is that music now transformed and the silly words hidden in an unknown tongue—liquid and sonorous. It is tricked out and expounded with cadence and turn. And this is that same rhythm I heard first in Tennessee forty years ago: the air is raised and carried by men's strong voices, while floating above in obligato come the high mellow voices of women—it is the ancient African art of part singing, so curiously and insistently different.

So they come, gay appareled, lit by transparency. They enter the gate and flow over the high steps and sing and sing and sing. They saunter round the house, pick flowers, drink water and sing and sing and sing. The warm dark heat of the night steams up to meet the moon. And the night is song.

On Christmas Day, 1923, we walk down to the narrow, crooked wharves of Monrovia, by houses old and gray and step-like streets of stone. Before is the wide St. Paul River, double-mouthed, and beyond, the sea, white, curling on the sand. Before us is the isle—the tiny isle, hut-covered and guarded by a cotton tree, where the pioneers lived in 1821. We board the boat, then circle round—then up the river. Great bowing trees, festoons of flowers, golden blossoms, star-faced palms and thatched huts; tall spreading trees lifting themselves like vast umbrellas, low shrubbery with gray and laced and knotted roots—the broad, black, murmuring river. Here a tree holds wide fingers out and stretches them over the water in vast incantation; bananas throw their wide green fingers to the sun. Iron villages, scarred clearings with gray, sheet-iron homes staring, grim and bare, at the ancient tropical flood of green.

The river sweeps wide and the shrubs bow low. Behind, Monrovia rises in clear, calm beauty. Gone are the wharves, the low and clustered houses of the port, the tight-throated business village, and upsweep the villas and the low wall, brown and cream and white, with great mango and cotton trees, with lighthouse and spire, with porch and pillar and the color of shrubbery and blossom.

We climbed the upright shore to a senator's home and received his wide and kindly hospitality—curious blend of feudal lord and modern farmer—sandwiches, cake, and champagne. Again we glided up the drowsy river—five, ten, twenty miles and came to our hostess, a mansion of five generations with a compound of endless native servants and cows under the palm thatches. The daughters of the family wore, on the beautiful black skin of their necks, the exquisite pale gold chains of the Liberian artisan and the slim, black little granddaughter of the house had a wide pink ribbon on the thick curls of her dark hair, that lay like sudden sunlight on the shadows. Double porches, one above the other, welcomed us to ease. A native man, gay with Christmas and a dash of gin, sang and danced in the road. Children ran and played in the blazing sun. We sat at a long broad table and ate duck, chicken, beef, rice, plantain, collards, cake, tea, water and Madeira wine. Then we went and looked at the heavens, the uptwisted sky—Orion and Cassiopeia at zenith, the Little Bear beneath the horizon, now unfamiliar sights in the Milky Way—all awry, a-living—sun for snow at Christmas, and happiness and cheer.

The shores were lined with old sugar plantations, the buildings rotting and falling. I looked upon the desolation with a certain pain. What had happened, I asked? The owners and planters had deserted these homes and come down to Monrovia, but why? After all, Monrovia had not much to offer in the way of income and occupation. Was this African laziness and inefficiency? No, it was a specimen of the way in which the waves of modern industry broke over the shores of far-off Africa. Here during our Civil War, men hastened to raise sugar and supply New York. They built their own boats and filled the river and sailed the sea. But afterwards, Louisiana came back into the Union, colored Rillieux invented the vacuum pan; the sugar plantations began to spread in Cuba and the Sugar Trust Monopoly of refining machinery, together with the new beet sugar industry, drove Liberia quickly from the market. What all this did not do, the freight rates finished. So sugar did not pay in Liberia and other crops rose and fell in the same way.

As I look back and recall the days, which I have called great —the occasions in which I have taken part and which have had for me and others the widest significance, I can remember none like the first of January, 1924. Once I took my bachelor's degree before a governor, a great college president, and a bishop of New England. But that was rather personal in its memory than in any way epochal. Once before the assembled races of the world I was called to speak in London in place of the suddenly sick Sir Harry Johnston. It was a great hour. But it was not greater than the day when I was presented to the President of the Negro Republic of Liberia.

Liberia had been resting under the shock of world war into which the Allies forced her. She had asked and been promised a loan by the United States to bolster and replace her stricken trade. She had conformed to every preliminary requirement and waited when waiting was almost fatal. It was not simply money, it was world prestige and protection at a time when the little republic was sorely beset by creditors and greedy imperial powers. At the last moment, an insurgent Senate peremptorily and finally refused the request and strong recommendation of President Wilson and his advisers, and the loan was refused. The Department of State made no statement to the world, and Liberia stood naked, not only well-nigh bankrupt, but peculiarly defenseless amid scowling and unbelieving powers.

It was then that the United States made a gesture of courtesy, a little thing, and merely a gesture, but one so unusual that it was epochal. President Coolidge, at the suggestion of William H. Lewis, a leading colored lawyer of Boston, named me, an American Negro traveler, Envoy Extraordinary and Minister Plenipotentiary to Liberia—the highest rank ever given by any country to a diplomatic agent in black Africa. And it named this Envoy the special representative of the President of the United States to the President of Liberia, on the occasion of his inauguration; charging the Envoy with a personal word of encouragement and moral support. It was a significant action. It had in it nothing personal. Another appointee would have been equally significant. But Liberia recognized the meaning. She showered upon the Envoy every mark of appreciation and thanks. The Commander of the Liberian Frontier Force was made his special aide, and a sergeant, his orderly. At ten a.m. New Year's morning, 1924, a company of the Frontier Force in red fez and khaki, presented arms before the American Legation and escorted Solomon Porter Hood, the American Minister Resident, and myself as Envoy Extraordinary and my aide to the Presidential mansion—a beautiful white verandahed house, waving with palms and fronting a grass street.

Ceremonials are old and to some antiquated and yet this was done with such simplicity, grace and seriousness that none could escape its spell. The Secretary of State met us at the door, as the band played the impressive Liberian National hymn, and soldiers saluted:

> All hail! Liberia, hail!
> In union strong, success is sure.
> We cannot fail.
> With God above,
> Our rights to prove,
> We will the world assail.

We mounted a broad stairway and into a great room that stretched across the house. Here in semi-circle were ranged the foreign consuls and the cabinet—the former in white, gilt with orders and swords; the latter in solemn black. Present were

England, France, Germany, Spain, Belgium, Holland, and Panama, to be presented to me in order of seniority by the small brown Secretary of State with his perfect poise and ease. The President entered—frock-coated with the star and ribbon of a Spanish order on his breast. The American Minister introduced me, and I said:

The President of the United States has done me the great honor of designating me as his personal representative on the occasion of your inauguration. In so doing, he has had, I am sure, two things in mind. First, he wished publicly and unmistakably to express before the world the interest and solicitude which the hundred million inhabitants of the United States of America have for Liberia. Liberia is a child of the United States, and a sister Republic. Its progress and success is the progress and success of democracy everywhere and for all men; and the United States would view with sorrow and alarm any misfortune which might happen to this Republic and any obstacle that was placed in her path.

But special and peculiar bonds draw these two lands together. In America live eleven million persons of African descent; they are citizens, legally invested with every right that inheres in American citizenship. And I am sure that in this special mark of the President's favor, he has had in mind the wishes and hopes of Negro Americans. He knows how proud they are of the hundred years of independence which you have maintained by force of arms and by brawn and brain upon the edge of this mighty continent; he knows that in the great battle against color caste in America, the ability of Negroes to rule in Africa has been and ever will be a great and encouraging reenforcement. He knows that the unswerving loyalty of Negro Americans to their country is fitly accompanied by a pride in their race and lineage, a belief in the potency and promise of Negro blood which makes them eager listeners to every whisper of success from Liberia, and eager helpers in every movement for your aid and comfort. In a special sense, the moral burden of Liberia and the advancement and integrity of Liberia is the sincere prayer of America.

And now a word about the African himself—about this primitive black man: I began to notice a truth as I entered southern France. I formulated it in Portugal. I knew it as a great truth one Sunday in Liberia. And the Great Truth was this: efficiency and happiness do not go together in modern culture. Going south from London, as the world darkens it gets happier. Portugal is deliciously dark. Many leading citizens would have difficulty keeping off a Georgia "Jim Crow" car. But, oh, how lovely a land and how happy a people! And so leisurely. Little use of trying to shop seriously in Lisbon before eleven. It isn't done. Nor at noon; the world is lunching or lolling in the sun. Even after four p.m. one takes chances, for the world is in the Rocio. And the banks are so careless and the hotels so leisurely. How delightfully angry Englishmen get at the "damned, lazy" Portuguese!

But if this of Portugal, what of Africa? Here darkness descends and rests on lovely skins until brown seems luscious and natural. There is sunlight in great gold globules and soft, heavy scented heat that wraps you like a garment. And laziness; divine, eternal, languor is right and good and true. I remember the morning; it was Sunday, and the night before we heard the leopards crying down there. Today beneath the streaming sun we went down into the gold green forest. It was silence—silence the more mysterious because life abundant and palpitating pulsed all about us and held us drowsy captives to the day. Ahead the gaunt missionary strode, alert, afire, with his gun. He apologized for the gun, but he did not need to, for I saw the print of a leopard's hind foot. A monkey sentinel screamed, and I heard the whir of the horde as they ran.

Then we came to the village, how can I describe it? Neither London, nor Paris, nor New York has anything of its delicate, precious beauty. It was a town of the Veys and done in cream and pale purple—still, clean, restrained, tiny, complete. It was no selfish place, but the central abode of fire and hospitality, clean-swept for wayfarers and best seats were bare. They quite expected visitors, morning, noon, and night, and they gave our hands a quick, soft grasp and talked easily. Their manners were better than those of Park Lane or Park Avenue. Oh, much better and more natural. They showed breeding. The chief's son—tall and slight and speaking good English—had served under the late Colonel Young. He made a little speech of welcome. Long is the history of the Veys and comes down from the Eastern Roman Empire, the great struggle of Islam and the black empires of the Sudan.

We went on to other villages—dun-colored, not so beautiful, but neat and hospitable. In one sat a visiting chief of perhaps fifty years in a derby hat and a robe, and beside him stood a shy young wife done in ebony and soft brown, whose liquid eyes would not meet ours. The chief was taciturn until we spoke of schools. Then he woke suddenly—he had children to "give" to a school.

I see the last village fading away; they are plastering the wall of a home, leisurely and carefully. They smiled a good-by—not effusively, with no eagerness, with a simple friendship, as we glided under the cocoa trees and into the silent forest, the gold and silent forest.

And there and elsewhere in two long months I began to learn: primitive men are not following us afar, frantically waving and seeking our goals; primitive men are not behind us in some swift foot-race. Primitive men have already arrived. They are abreast, and in places ahead of us; in others behind. But all their curving advance line is contemporary, not prehistoric. They have used other paths and these paths have led them by scenes sometimes fairer, sometimes uglier than ours, but always toward the Pools of Happiness. Or, to put it otherwise, these folk have the leisure of true aristocracy—leisure for thought and courtesy, leisure for sleep and laughter. They have time for their children—such well-trained, beautiful children with perfect, unhidden bodies. Have you ever met a crowd of children in the east of London or New York, or even on the Avenue at Forty-second or One Hundred and Forty-second Street, and fled to avoid their impudence and utter ignorance of courtesy? Come to Africa, and see well-bred and courteous children, playing happily and never sniffling and whining.

RICHARD WRIGHT

The sadness of Richard Wright's embattled life of genius and alienation was summed up by James Baldwin, whose writing career owed much to Wright, in this way: "First America, then Europe, then Africa failed him." And in commenting on one of Wright's late short stories, Baldwin says, ". . . his imagination was beginning to grapple with that darkest of all dark strangers for him, the African."[1] In 1953, seven years before his death, Wright had gone to Africa to grapple in person with the meaning of Africa to him.

A good friend of Wright's, and a close associate of Kwame Nkrumah, the West Indian Pan-Africanist George Padmore had often urged Wright to visit Africa and write a book about it. Both Padmore and Wright had, for many years, been seriously involved in the communist movement. Padmore had been the leading African specialist for the Communist International. Wright had been a member of the American Communist Party for many years. Both had finally broken with the Communist Party when they discovered that they, and the cause of the Negro, were being used by the party for its own purposes. Wright was living in exile in Paris when he was at last prevailed upon by Mrs. Padmore and Mrs. Wright to go to the Gold Coast (now Ghana). In 1953 Nkrumah was already the unofficial prime minister of the Gold Coast, and leading the forces that would, within four years achieve complete independence from British rule. Wright received a warm

---

[1] James Baldwin, *Nobody Knows My Name* (New York, 1961), p. 189.

welcome from Nkrumah, and for three months, with the aid of official facilities and a crash reading program in West African history and anthropology, he made a hard-working tour of the Colony and Ashanti areas of the Gold Coast.

The resulting book, *Black Power* (1954), laid bare an intense experience, relentlessly inquiring and agonizingly ambivalent. While Wright hated what the West had done to Africa, he counted himself completely Western. He had an extreme rationalist antipathy to religion, be it African or any other kind, combined with a raging impatience to "modernize" all whom he considered backward. He could, on one occasion, tell an African chief, "I'm black, Nana, but I'm Western; and you must never forget that we of the West brought you to this pass. We invaded your country and shattered your culture in the name of conquest and progress." Yet, on leaving the Gold Coast, in an open letter to Nkrumah, he could passionately urge, "African life must be militarized . . . atomize the fetish-ridden past, abolish the mystical and nonsensical family relations that freeze the African in his static degradation . . . render impossible the continued existence of those parasitic chiefs who have too long bled and misled a naive people . . . project the African immediately into the twentieth century." We can only recall here what James Baldwin wrote about Wright's misapprehension of himself as a political thinker. "I never believed," wrote Baldwin, "that he had any real sense of how a society is put together."[2]

But Wright also shows the artist's sensitivity to human beings in all their concreteness. He probes his own sense of identity: "How much of me was *African*?" He makes the, to him, astonishing discovery that the dance style of celebrating African women—the "weaving, circular motion . . . snakelike, veering dances"—were the same he had seen before in America, "in storefront churches, in Holy Roller Tabernacles, in God's Temples, in unpainted wooden prayer-meeting houses on the plantations of the Deep South." But he confesses that he was never one for dances himself, and these dances meant as little to him in Africa as they did when he had seen them back home, and he painfully concludes that "racial qualities were but myths of prejudiced minds." He ac-

---

[2] *Ibid.*, p. 184.

knowledges, however, that he is at a loss to account for the evidence he observed of African dance style "survivals".

His frank talks with an illiterate cook or an educated village chief show Wright's sympathy and tact—qualities which were able to temper, if not quite to displace, the imperious urge to "project the African immediately into the twentieth century."

In his three major books—the novellas of *Uncle Tom's Children* (1938), the novel *Native Son* (1940), and the autobiography *Black Boy* (1945)—Richard Wright had created powerful imaginative projections of the psychic and social violence that shaped, and emanated from, a modern industrialized America. Yet, in confronting an indigenous violence in old African customs, his reflex was to fall back on "Westernism" as the cure. The dilemma of Wright as an artist was also his as an Afro-American. The ideology of materialist progress and social engineering (whether communist or capitalist) had alienated him from a more universal human perspective in which the conflicts and traumas of traditional African societies and of Western industrial societies are recognizably kin.

On Tour in the Gold Coast

Africa! Being of African descent, would I be able to feel and know something about Africa on the basis of a common "racial" heritage? Africa was a vast continent full of "my people" . . . Or had three hundred years imposed a psychological distance between me and the "racial stock" from which I had sprung? Perhaps some Englishman, Scotsman, Frenchman, Swede, or Dutchman had chained my great-great-great-great-grandfather in the hold of a slave ship, and perhaps that remote grandfather had been sold on an auction block in New Orleans, Richmond, or Atlanta. . . . My emotions seemed to be touching a dark and dank wall. . . . *But, am I African?* Had some of my ancestors sold their relatives to white men? What would my feelings be when I looked into the black face of an African, feeling that maybe his great-great-great-grandfather had sold my great-great-great-grandfather into slavery? Was there something in Africa that my feelings could latch onto to make all of this dark past clear and meaningful? Would the Africans regard me as a lost brother who had returned?

"Do you think that the Gold Coast will be self-governing soon?" I asked. I genuinely wanted to know about the political situation in the Gold Coast, yet another and far more important question was trying to shape itself in me. According to popular notions of "race," there ought to be something of "me" down there in Africa. Some vestige, some heritage, some vague but definite ancestral reality that would serve as a key to unlock the hearts and feelings of the African whom I'd meet. . . . But I could not feel anything African about myself, and I wondered, "What does being *African* mean . . . ?"

* * *

Was Africa "primitive"? But what did being "primitive" mean? I'd read books on "primitive" people, but, while reading them, their contents had always seemed somehow remote. Now a strange reality, in some way akin to me, was pressing close, and I was dismayed to discover that I didn't know how to react to it.

* * *

The fortuity of birth had cast me in the "racial" role of being of African descent, and that fact now resounded in my mind with associations of hatred, violence, and death. Phrases from my childhood rang in my memory: one-half Negro, one-quarter Negro, one-eighth Negro, one-sixteenth Negro, one thirty-second Negro. . . . In thirty-eight out of the forty-eight states of the American Federal Union, marriage between a white person and a person of African descent was a criminal offense. To be of "black" blood meant being consigned to a lower plane in the social scheme of American life, and if one violated that scheme, one risked danger, even death sometimes. And all of this was predicated upon the presence of *African* blood in one's veins. How much of me was *African*? Many of my defensive-minded Negro friends had often told me with passion:

We have a *special* gift for music, dancing, rhythm and movement. . . . We have a genius of our own. We were civilized in Africa when white men were still living in caves in Europe. . . .

To me talk of that sort had always seemed beside the point; I had always taken for granted the humanity of Africans as well as that of other people. And being either uninterested or unable to accept such arguments, I'd always remained silent in such conversations.

* * *

"I want to see your party and how it works," I said to the Prime Minister.

He nodded but did not answer.

"Free—dooom! Free—doooom!"

The roar came from all sides. Gratitude showed in the eyes of those black faces for the man who had taken their hand and told them that they had no need to fear the British, that they could laugh, sing, work, hope, and fight again.

I was astonished to see women, stripped to their waist, their elongated breasts flopping wildly, do a sort of weaving, circular motion with their bodies, a kind of queer shuffling dance which expressed their joy in a quiet, physical manner. It was as if they were talking with the movements of their legs, arms, necks, and torsos; as if words were no longer adequate as a means of communication; as if sounds could no longer approximate their feelings; as if only the total movement of their entire bodies could indicate in some measure their acquiescence, their surrender, their approval.

And then I remembered: I'd seen these same snakelike, veering dances before. . . . Where? Oh, God, yes; in America in storefront churches, in Holy Roller Tabernacles, in God's Temples, in unpainted wooden prayer-meeting houses on the plantations of the Deep South. . . . And here I was seeing it all again against a background of a surging nationalistic political movement. How could that be?

When I'd come to Africa, I didn't know what I'd find, what I'd see; the only prepossession I'd had was that I'd doubted that I'd be able to walk into the African's cultural house and feel at home and know my way around. Yet, what I was now looking at in this powerfully improvised dance of these women, I'd seen before in America! How was that possible? And, what was more, this African dance today was as astonishing and dumbfounding to me as it had been when I'd seen it in America.

Never in my life had I been able to dance more than a few elementary steps, and the carrying of even the simplest tune had always been beyond me. So, what had bewildered me about Negro dance expression in the United States now bewildered me in the same way in Africa.

I'd long contended that the American Negro, because of what he had undergone in the United States, had been basically altered, that his consciousness had been filled with a new content, that "racial" qualities were but myths of prejudiced minds. Then, if that were true, how could I account for what I now saw? And what I now saw was an exact duplicate of what I'd seen for so many long years in the United States.

I did not find an answer to that question that afternoon as I stared out of the window of the Prime Minister's car. But the question was lodged firmly in my mind, enthroned there so strongly that it would never leave until I had, at least to my satisfaction, solved the riddle of why black people were able to retain, despite vast distances, centuries of time, and the imposition of alien cultures, such basic and fundamental patterns of behavior and response.

We rode on through the cheering throngs. Whenever the car slowed, the black faces, laughing and excited, with heads thrown back, with white teeth showing, would press close to the windows of the car and give vent to:

"Free—doooom!"

But my emotions were preoccupied with another problem. How much am I a part of this? How much was I part of it when I saw it?

* * *

Last night I hadn't had time to question myself closely regarding that snakelike, shuffling dance, the strange veering and weaving of the body. . . . That there was some kind of link between the native African and the American Negro was undoubtedly true. But what did it mean? A certain group of American anthropologists had long clamored for a recognition of what they had quaintly chosen to call "African survivals," a phrase of which they had coined to account for exactly what I had observed. And now, as I reflected upon last night's experience, even more items of similarity came to me: that laughter that bent the knee and turned the head (as if in embarrassment!); that queer shuffling of the feet when one was satisfied or in agreement; that inexplicable, almost sullen silence that came from disagreement or opposition. . . . All of this was strange but familiar.

I understood why so many Negroes were eager to disclaim any relationship with Africa; they were being prompted by the same motives that made the Irish or the Jew or the Italian immigrant more militantly American than the native-born American. The American Negro's passionate identification with America stemmed from two considerations: first, it was a natural part of his assimilation of Americanism; second, so long had Africa been described as something shameful, barbaric, a land in which one went about naked, a land in which his ancestors had sold their kith and kin as slaves—so long had he heard all this that he wanted to disassociate himself in his mind from all such realities. . . .

The bafflement evoked in me by this new reality did not spring from any desire to disclaim kinship with Africa, or from any shame of being of African descent. My problem was how to account for this "survival" of Africa in America when I stoutly denied the mystic influence of "race," when I was as certain as I was of being alive that it was only, by and large, in the concrete social frame of reference in which men lived that one could account for men being what they were. I sighed; this was truly a big problem. . . .

*　　*　　*

Typical of a broader outlook and a more intelligent order of chiefs is one called the Efiduasihene, Nana Kwame Dua Awere II. Efiduasi is a little village (population indeterminate) of swish huts and is the center of trade and agriculture for an area which has a radius of ten miles. Sitting in his stuffy little office surrounded by his illiterate elders, the chief complained bitterly that his people were leaving the land in droves to go to the cities where life was more interesting. He frankly admitted that life in the villages was hard, that there were no modern amenities to lighten the burden, no conveniences for transportation, communication, etc. Yet, he pointed out, the government was crying out for the villages to grow more food.

The chief is president of the local council which has a membership of twenty-one, all of whom are members of the Convention People's Party. He has achieved a rare sort of psychological detachment about his position and spoke about it without lamenting.

It's hard for people to understand that what has happened to us in the past was done by the chiefs. The rise of our way of life was inspired by the chiefs. All crafts were under their leadership; the goldsmiths, the silversmiths, the blacksmiths—all trades were at the behest of the chief, and the people were loyal to him.

He paused and pointed openly to the half-clad men who sat around him, smiling and not understanding a word of what was being said.

Now, take these men. . . . All of them are older than I am. Yet I'm their chief. They serve me willingly. I don't ask them to; their serving me is the meaning of their lives. They want me to dress up in these bright garments. It's their sense of what's good; they yearn for something to serve, to fight for, to maintain. . . . You see? Their loyalty to the Stool is deep and genuine. They cannot grasp politics. Yet, history is making severe demands upon us and we are not prepared. How will this illiteracy fit into the machine age?

Yet, I don't see the end of the chief. He's closer to the people than anyone else. I'm convinced that it will take a long time for the social habits of the people to die out. The clan spirit is strong. We must find a way to bridge that gap. . . .

As the chief propounded the problem, there were in full view his huge state drums which he used to call his people together. And he knew that telephones and wireless and newspapers were taking the place of those drums. But could the new means of communication equal in emotional value the things that the drums said, drums which could, at a moment's notice, throw a people into anger, joy, sorrow, or the stance to fight and die? That was the problem. The base upon which the new order had to build was so slight. . . . How could these people be taken from these ancestral moorings and be made to live contented lives in a rational industrial order?

"You are an American," the chief said to me. "You fellows are, in a sense, our brothers. You've made the leap. What do you think of our chances?"

He was an intelligent man, an ex-schoolteacher, and I didn't want to misguide him. He had me stumped. The problems involved were stupendous. Above all, I had to disabuse him of the illusion that American Negroes had attained a kind of paradise, had solved all of their problems.

"Nana," I said, "you don't have a race problem as severe as ours. Your problem is much simpler and yet much harder, and much more important. . . . The American Negro has done no reflective thinking about the value of the world into which he fought so hard to enter.

He just panted to get into that world and be an American, that's all. The average American Negro is perhaps the least qualified person on earth to guide you in matters of this sort.

"I'm black, Nana, but I'm Western, and you must never forget that we of the West brought you to this pass. We invaded your country and shattered your culture in the name of conquest and progress. And we didn't quite know what we were doing when we did it. If the West dared have its way with you now, they'd harness your people again to solve their problems. . . . It's not of me, Nana, that you must ask advice. You men of Africa must be able to tell the West something about how to live. Get it out of your head that we are all happy and have no problems. That's propaganda. . . .

"If you go into the industrial world, Nana, go in with your eyes open. Machines are wonderful things; love them for what they can do for you; but remember that they cannot tell you how to live or what aims you should hold in life. If you have no sense of direction before you embrace the world of machines, machines will not give you one. . . ."

I was convinced that the meaning of the industrial world was beyond that chief. He could grasp it with his mind, but he could not feel or as yet know the emotional meaning of the lives of wage workers in Chicago or Detroit. The question facing him was a bigger one than merely becoming modern. Must he leave behind him his humanity, such as it was, as he moved into that industrial world, as he built his Volta Projects? Or could he take it with him? Must his culture, though condemned by the West—a culture evolved under unique conditions and over long centuries—be cast unthinkingly aside as he embraced plumbing, printing, and politics?

And what would the Akan religion be if grafted, in its present state, onto the techniques of atomic energy? The West had taken hold of the world of modern techniques with its old humanity intact, and now, in Paris where I lived, men were huddled together in indecision, numbed with despair, facing a myriad of possibilities, none of which they wanted, all of which sickened them. . . .

The pathos that rose from my talking to Africans about their problems was that their minds were uninformed—thanks to the contribution of a British education—about the bodies of knowledge relevant to their situation, bodies of knowledge which other peoples had erected at a great cost of suffering, toil, and sacrifice. Hence, I felt that almost any decision that the Africans would make, perhaps for some time to come, would be a hit-or-miss proposition, that they would have to tread ground already laboriously trampled by others. But there was no turning back; historic events had committed the Africans to change. . . . For good or ill, the die cast. The game was up. What had been done, could not now be undone. Africa was moving. . . .

JAMES BALDWIN

By 1956 there had already been quite a number of conferences —going back to 1900 and even earlier—at which African and diaspora Negroes had come together. But the Conference of Negro-African Writers and Artists held in Paris in 1956 was different. The previous conferences—notably those convoked by Du Bois—had had directly political objectives: loosening and removing European rule over Africans, completing the emancipation of American Negroes, freeing the island societies of the Caribbean. The 1956 conference had a basically cultural emphasis, although it, too, was unavoidably political. The black intellectual world was now ready to make a new beginning in assessing the spiritual and philosophical issues on which an international Negro fraternalism might be developed.

Any discussion of a homeland-diaspora relationship will naturally involve questions of assimilation and the loss of identity, and of what exactly this identity is which the people seek to preserve. James Baldwin argues, in the course of reporting on the 1956 colloquium, that the American Negro has a cultural and psychological identity quite different from that of the African Negro: "We had been dealing with, had been made and mangled by, another machinery altogether." Léopold Senghor, of Senegal, who so eloquently posits an African essence quite opposite to the European one, is himself, in his thought and art, inescapably of the French republic of letters. And when Senghor attempts to characterize Richard Wright's autobiography *Black Boy* as an essentially African work, Baldwin demurs. Senghor is, in effect, robbing Wright of his real identity as a black American, says Baldwin.

Baldwin makes an analogous point about the Martiniquan poet-politician Aimé Césaire (who was, with Senghor, a pioneer of the Negritude ideology). Césaire, says Baldwin, in spite of having made such a brilliant case against Europe, seemed not to recognize that he himself "had penetrated into the heart of the great wilderness which was Europe and stolen the sacred fire."

Baldwin feels more at home with the point of view of the Barbadian writer George Lamming than he does with those of his French-speaking colleagues. As Baldwin interprets it, Lamming's idea is that "part of the great wealth of the Negro experience lay precisely in its double-edgedness. He was suggesting that all Negroes were held in a state of supreme tension between the difficult, dangerous relationship in which they stood to the white world and the relationship, not a whit less painful or dangerous, in which they stood to each other."

If, therefore, life in the black diaspora over the generations has produced cultural identities quite distinct from those in the black homeland, where might the common ground between them be, except possibly in political alliances? And a highly politicized artist like Richard Wright illustrates some of the difficulties that would be involved in seeking such political common ground. For example, Baldwin is disturbed by Richard Wright's quickness to declare the West the heir to the future, his crude attacks on the "irrational past" of African tradition, and his readiness to give what might be called *carte noire* to future black dictators to deal with the "primitivism" of their own people. (On this, see also the selection from Richard Wright, pp. 87-96.)

In an essay Baldwin had written in 1950,* dealing with his personal contacts with Africans living in Paris, he found a great and disturbing difference between himself and them:

The African before him has endured privation, injustice, medieval cruelty; but the African has not yet endured the utter alienation of himself from his people and his past. His mother did not sing, "Sometimes I Feel Like a Motherless Child," and he has not all his life long,

---

* Reprinted in *Notes of a Native Son* (Boston, 1955) under the title "Encounter on the Seine: Black Meets Brown."

ached for acceptance in a culture which pronounced straight hair and white skin the only acceptable beauty. They face each other, the Negro and the African, over a gulf of three hundred years—an alienation too vast to be conquered in an evening's goodwill. . . .

In his report on the 1956 conference, Baldwin was still documenting this difference, but in a context of increasing effective communication in the black intellectual world.

The historic colloquy in Paris was the forerunner of the establishment of the Société Africaine de Culture and the affiliated American Society of African Culture, which also held several Negro conferences. Dialogues on the cultural plane between Africa and the diaspora have since continued in such events as the Negro Arts Festival in Dakar in 1966, and the Black and African Culture Festival scheduled to be held in Lagos in 1975.

Black Colloquium in Paris

Behind the table at the front of the hall sat eight colored men. These included the American novelist Richard Wright; Alioune Diop, the editor of *Présence Africaine* and one of the principal organizers of the conference; poets Léopold Senghor, from Senegal, and Aimé Césaire, from Martinique, and the poet and novelist Jacques Alexis, from Haiti. From Haiti, also, came the president of the conference, Dr. Price-Mars, a very old and very handsome man.

It was well past ten o'clock when the conference actually opened. Alioune Diop, who is tall, very dark and self-contained, and who rather resembles, in his extreme sobriety, an old-time Baptist minister, made the opening address. He referred to the present gathering as a kind of second Bandung. As at Bandung, the people gathered together here held in common the fact of their subjugation to Europe, or, at the very least, to the European vision of the world. Out of the fact that European well-being had been, for centuries, so crucially dependent on this subjugation had come that *racisme* from which all black men suffered. Then he spoke of the changes which had taken place during the last decade regarding the fate and the aspirations of non-European peoples, especially the blacks. "The blacks," he said, "whom history has treated in a rather cavalier fashion. I would even say that history has treated black men in a resolutely spiteful fashion were it not for the fact that this history with a large *H* is nothing more, after all, than the Western interpretation of the life of the world." He spoke of the variety of cultures the conference represented, saying that they were genuine cultures and that the ignorance of the West regarding them was largely a matter of convenience.

Yet, in speaking of the relation between politics and culture, he pointed out that the loss of vitality from which all Negro cultures were suffering was due to the fact that their political destinies were not in their hands. A people deprived of political sovereignty finds it very nearly impossible to recreate, for itself, the image of its past, this perpetual recreation being an absolute necessity for, if not, indeed, the definition of a living culture. And one of the questions, then, said Diop, which would often be raised during this conference was the question of assimilation. Assimilation was frequently but another name for the very special brand of relations between human beings which had been imposed by colonialism. These relations demanded that the individual, torn from the context to which he owed his identity, should replace his habits of feeling, thinking, and acting by another set of habits which belonged to the strangers who dominated him. He cited the example of certain natives of the Belgian Congo, who, *accablé des complexes,* wished for an assimilation so complete that they would no longer be distinguishable from white men. This, said Diop, indicated the blind horror which the spiritual heritage of Africa inspired in their breasts.

The question of assimilation could not, however, be posed this way. It was not a question, on the one hand, of simply being swallowed up, of disappearing in the maw of Western culture, nor was it, on the other hand, a question of rejecting assimilation in order to be isolated within African culture. Neither was it a question of deciding which African values were to be retained and which European values were to be adopted. Life was not that simple.

It was due to the crisis which their cultures were now under-going that black intellectuals had come together. They were here to define and accept their responsibilities, to assess the riches and the promise of their cultures, and to open, in effect, a dialogue with Europe. He ended with a brief and rather moving reference to the fifteen-year struggle of himself and his confreres to bring about this day.

*   *   *

When the morning session ended and I was spewed forth with the mob into the bright courtyard, Richard Wright introduced me to the American delegation. And it seemed quite unbelievable for a moment that the five men standing with Wright (and Wright and myself) were defined, and had been brought together in this courtyard by our relation to the African continent. The chief of the delegation, John Davis, was to be asked just *why* he con-sidered himself a Negro—he was to be told that he certainly did not look like one. He is a Negro, of course, from the remarkable legal point of view which obtains in the United States, but, more importantly, as he tried to make clear to his interlocutor, he was a Negro by choice and by depth of involvement—by experience, in fact. But the question of choice in such a context can scarcely be coherent for an African and the experience referred to, which produces a John Davis, remains a closed book for him. Mr. Davis might have been rather darker, as were the others—Mercer Cook, William Fontaine, Horace Bond, and James Ivy—and it would not have helped matters very much.

For what, at bottom, distinguished the Americans from the Negroes who surrounded us, men from Nigeria, Senegal, Bar-bados, Martinique—so many names for so many disciplines—was the banal and abruptly quite overwhelming fact that we had been born in a society, which, in a way quite inconceivable for Africans, and no longer real for Europeans, was open, and, in a sense which has nothing to do with justice or injustice, was free. It was a society, in short, in which nothing was fixed and we had therefore been born to a greater number of possibilities, wretched as these possibilities seemed at the instant of our birth. Moreover, the land of our forefathers' exile had been made, by that travail, our home. It may have been the popular impulse to keep us at the bottom of the perpetually shifting and bewildered populace; but we were, on the other hand, almost personally indispensable to each of them, simply because, without us, they could never have been certain, in such a confusion, where the bottom was; and nothing, in any case, could take away our title to the land which we, too, had purchased with our blood. This results in a psychology very different—at its best and at its worst—from the psychology which is produced by a sense of having been invaded and overrun, the sense of having no recourse whatever against oppression other than overthrowing the machinery of the oppressor. We had been dealing with, had been made and mangled by, another machinery altogether. It had never been in our interest to overthrow it. It had been necessary to make the machinery work for our benefit and the possibility of its doing so had been, so to speak, built in.

We could, therefore, in a way, be considered the connecting link between Africa and the West, the most real and certainly the most shocking of all African contributions to Western cultural life. The articulation of this reality, however, was another matter. But it was clear that our relation to the mysterious continent of Africa would not be clarified until we had found some means of saying, to ourselves and to the world, more about the mysterious American continent than had ever been said before.

* * *

Léopold Senghor is a very dark and impressive figure in a smooth, bespectacled kind of way, and he is very highly regarded as a poet. He was to speak on West African writers and artists.

He began by invoking what he called the "spirit of Bandung." In referring to Bandung, he was referring less, he said, to the liberation of black peoples than he was saluting the reality and the toughness of their culture, which, despite the vicissitudes of their history, had refused to perish. We were now witnessing, in fact, the beginning of its renaissance. This renaissance would owe less to politics than it would to black writers and artists. The "spirit of Bandung" had had the effect of "sending them to school to Africa."

One of the things, said Senghor—perhaps *the* thing—which distinguishes Africans from Europeans is the comparative urgency of their ability to feel. *"Sentir c'est apercevoir"*: it is perhaps a tribute to his personal force that this phrase then meant something which makes the literal English translation quite inadequate, seeming to leave too great a distance between the feeling and the perception. The feeling and the perception, for Africans, is one and the same thing. This is the difference between European and African reasoning: the reasoning of the African is not compartmentalized, and, to illustrate this, Senghor here used the image of the bloodstream in which all things mingle and flow to and through the heart. He told us that the difference between the function of the arts in Europe and their function in Africa lay in the fact that, in Africa, the function of the arts is more present and pervasive, is infinitely less special, "is done by all, for all." Thus, art for art's sake is not a concept which makes any sense in Africa. The division between art and life out of which such a concept comes does not exist there. Art itself is taken to be perishable, to be made again each time it disappears or is destroyed. What is clung to is the spirit which makes art possible. And the African idea of this spirit is very different from the European idea. European art attempts to imitate nature. African art is concerned with reaching beyond and beneath nature, to contact, and itself become a part of *la force vitale*. The artistic image is not intended to represent the thing itself, but, rather, the reality of the force the thing contains. Thus, the moon is fecundity, the elephant is force.

Much of this made great sense to me, even though Senghor was speaking of, and out of, a way of life which I could only very dimly and perhaps somewhat wistfully imagine. It was the esthetic which attracted me, the idea that the work of art expresses, contains, and is itself a part of that energy which is life. Yet, I was aware that Senghor's thought had come into my mind translated. What he had been speaking of was something more direct and less isolated than the line in which my imagination immediately began to move. The distortions used by African artists to create a work of art are not at all the same distortions which have become one of the principal aims of almost every artist in the West today. (They are not the same distortions even when they have been copied from Africa.) And this was due entirely to the different situations in which each had his being. Poems and stories, in the only situation I know anything about, were never told, except, rarely, to children, and, at the risk of mayhem, in bars. They were written to be read, alone, and by a handful of people at that—there was really beginning to some-

thing suspect in being read by more than a handful. These crea-
tions no more insisted on the actual presence of other human
beings than they demanded the collaboration of a dancer and a
drum. They could not be said to celebrate the society any more
than the homage which Western artists sometimes receive can be
said to have anything to do with society's celebration of a work
of art. The only thing in Western life which seemed even faintly
to approximate Senghor's intense sketch of the creative inter-
dependence, the active, actual, joyful intercourse obtaining among
African artists and what only a Westerner would call their public,
was the atmosphere sometimes created among jazz musicians and
their fans during, say, a jam session. But the ghastly isolation of
the jazz musicians, the neurotic intensity of his listeners, was
proof enough that what Senghor meant when he spoke of social
art had no reality whatever in Western life. He was speaking out
of his past, which had been lived where art was naturally and
spontaneously social, where artistic creation did not presuppose
divorce. (Yet he was not there. Here he was, in Paris, speaking
the adopted language in which he also wrote his poetry.)

*   *   *

The evening debate rang perpetual changes on two questions.
These questions—each of which splintered, each time it was
asked, into a thousand more—were, first: What *is* a culture?
This is a difficult question under the most serene circumstances—
under which circumstances, incidentally, it mostly fails to present
itself. (This implies, perhaps, one of the possible definitions of a
culture, at least at a certain stage of its development.) In the context of the conference, it was a question which was helplessly at
the mercy of another one. And the second question was this: Is
it possible to describe as a culture what may simply be, after all,
a history of oppression? That is, is this history with these present
facts, which involve so many millions of people who are divided
from each other by so many miles of the globe, which operates,
and has operated, under such very different conditions, to such
different effects, and which has produced so many different sub-
histories, problems, traditions, possibilities, aspirations, assump-
tions, languages, hybrids—is this history enough to have made
of the earth's black populations anything that can legitimately be
described as a culture? For what, beyond the fact that all black

men at one time or another left Africa, or have remained there, do they really have in common?

And yet, it became clear as the debate wore on, that there *was* something which all black men held in common, something which cut across opposing points of view, and placed in the same context their widely dissimilar experience. What they held in common was their precarious, their unutterably painful relation to the white world. What they held in common was the necessity to remake the world in their own image, to impose this image on the world, and no longer be controlled by the vision of the world, and of themselves, held by other people. What, in sum, black men held in common was their ache to come into the world as men. And this ache united people who might otherwise have been divided as to what a man should be.

Yet, whether or not this could properly be described as a *cultural* reality remained another question. Haiti's Jacques Alexis made the rather desperate observation that a cultural survey must have *something* to survey; but then seemed confounded, as, indeed, we all were by the dimensions of the particular cultural survey in progress. It was necessary, for example, before one could relate the culture of Haiti to that of Africa, to know what the Haitian culture was. Within Haiti there were a great many cultures. Frenchmen, Negroes, and Indians had bequeathed it quite dissimilar ways of life; Catholics, voodooists, and animists cut across class and color lines. Alexis described as "pockets" of culture those related and yet quite specific and dissimilar ways of life to be found within the borders of any country in the world and wished to know by what alchemy these opposing ways of life became a national culture.

And he wished to know, too, what relation national culture bore to national independence—was it possible, really, to speak of a national culture when speaking of nations which were not free?

Senghor remarked, apropos of this question, that one of the great difficulties posed by this problem of cultures within cultures, particularly within the borders of Africa herself, was the difficulty of establishing and maintaining contact with the people if one's language had been formed in Europe. And he went on, somewhat late, to make the point that the heritage of the American Negro was an African heritage. He used, as proof of this, a poem of Richard Wright's which was, he said, involved with African tensions and symbols, even though Wright himself had not been aware of this. He suggested that the study of African sources might prove extremely illuminating for American Negroes. For, he suggested, in the same way that white classics exist—classic here taken to mean an enduring revelation and statement of a specific, peculiar, cultural sensibility—black classics must also exist. This raised in my mind the question of whether or not white classics *did* exist, and, with this question, I began to see the implications of Senghor's claim.

For, if white classics existed, in distinction, that is, to merely French or English classics, these could only be the classics produced by Greece and Rome. If *Black Boy,* said Senghor, were to be analyzed, it would undoubtedly reveal the African heritage to which it owed its existence; in the same way, I supposed, that Dickens' *A Tale Of Two Cities,* would, upon analysis, reveal its debts to Aeschylus. It did not seem very important.

And yet, I realized, the question had simply never come up in relation to European literature. It was not, now, the European necessity to go rummaging in the past, and through all the countries of the world, bitterly staking out claims to its cultural possessions.

Yet *Black Boy* owed its existence to a great many other factors, by no means so tenuous or so problematical; in so handsomely presenting Wright with his African heritage, Senghor rather seemed to be taking away his identity. *Black Boy* is the study of the growing up of a Negro boy in the Deep South, and is one of the major American autobiographies. I had never thought of it, as Senghor clearly did, as one of the major *African* autobiographies, only one more document, in fact, like one more book in the Bible, speaking of the African's long persecution and exile.

Senghor chose to overlook several gaps in his argument, not the least of which was the fact that Wright had not been in a position, as Europeans had been, to remain in contact with his hypothetical African heritage. The Greco-Roman tradition had, after all, been *written down;* it was by this means that it had kept itself alive. Granted that there was something African in *Black Boy* as there was undoubtedly something African in all American Negroes, the great question of what this was, and how it had survived, remained wide open. Moreover, *Black Boy* had been written in the English language which Americans had inherited from England, that is, if you like, from Greece and Rome; its form, psychology, moral attitude, preoccupations, in short, its cultural validity, were all due to forces which had nothing to do with Africa. Or was it simply that we had been rendered unable to recognize Africa in it?—for, it seemed that, in Senghor's vast re-creation of the world, the footfall of the African would prove to have covered more territory than the footfall of the Roman.

Thursday's great event was Aimé Césaire's speech in the afternoon, dealing with the relation between colonization and culture. Césaire is a caramel-colored man from Martinique, probably around forty, with a great tendency to roundness and smoothness, physically speaking, and with the rather vaguely benign air of a schoolteacher. All this changes the moment he begins to speak. It becomes at once apparent that his curious, slow-moving blandness is related to the grace and patience of a jungle cat and that the intelligence behind those spectacles is of a very penetrating and demagogic order.

The cultural crisis through which we are passing today can be summed up thus, said Césaire: that culture which is strongest from the material and technological point of view threatens to crush all weaker cultures, particularly in a world in which, distance counting for nothing, the technologically weaker cultures have no means of protecting themselves. All cultures have, furthermore, an economic, social, and political base, and no culture can continue to live if its political destiny is not in its own hands. "Any political and social regime which destroys the self-determination of a people also destroys the creative power of that people."

* * *

This speech, which was very brilliantly delivered, and which had the further advantage of being, in the main, unanswerable (and the advantage, also, of being very little concerned, at bottom, with culture) wrung from the audience which heard it the most violent reaction of joy. Césaire had spoken for those who could not speak and those who could not speak thronged around the table to shake his hand, and kiss him. I myself felt stirred in a very strange and disagreeable way. For Césaire's case against Europe, which was watertight, was also a very easy case to make. The anatomizing of the great injustice which is the irreducible fact of colonialism was yet not enough to give the victims of that injustice a new sense of themselves. One may say, of course, that the very fact that Césaire had spoken so thrillingly, and in one of the great institutions of Western learning, invested them with this new sense, but I do not think this is so. He had certainly played very skillfully on their emotions and their hopes, but he had not raised the central, tremendous question, which was, simply: What *had* this colonial experience made of them and what were they now to do with it? For they were all, now, whether they liked it or not, related to Europe, stained by European visions and standards, and their relation to themselves, and to each other, and to their past had changed. Their relation to their poets had also changed, as had the relation of their poets to them. Césaire's speech left out of account one of the great effects of the colonial experience: its creation, precisely, of men like himself. His real relation to the people who thronged about him now had been changed, by this experience, into something very different from what it once had been. What made him so attractive now was the fact that he, without having ceased to be one of them, yet seemed to move with the European authority. He had penetrated into the heart of the great wilderness which was Europe and stolen the sacred fire. And this, which was the promise of their freedom, was also the assurance of his power.

* * *

George Lamming is tall, raw-boned, untidy, and intense, and one of his real distinctions is his refusal to be intimidated by the fact that he is a genuine writer. He proposed to raise certain questions pertaining to the quality of life to be lived by black people in that hypothetical tomorrow when they would no longer be ruled by whites. "The profession of letters is an untidy one," he began, looking as though he had dressed to prove it. He directed his speech to Aimé Césaire and Jacques Alexis in particular, and quoted Djuna Barnes: "Too great a sense of identity makes a man feel he can do no wrong. And too little does the same." He suggested that it was important to bear in mind that the word Negro meant black—and meant nothing more than that; and commented on the great variety of heritages, experiences, and points of view which the conference had brought together under the heading of this single noun. He wished to suggest that the nature of power was unrelated to pigmentation, that bad faith was a phenomenon which was independent of race. He found—from the point of view of an untidy man of letters—something crippling in the obsession from which Negroes suffered as regards the existence and the attitudes of the Other—this other being everyone who was not Negro. That black people faced great problems was surely not to be denied and yet the greatest problem facing us was what *we,* Negroes, would do among ourselves "when there was no longer any colonial horse to ride." He pointed out that this was the horse on which a great many Negroes, who were in what he called "the skin trade," hoped to ride to power, power which would be in no way distinguishable from the power they sought to overthrow.

Lamming was insisting on the respect which is due the private life. I respected him very much, not only because he raised this question, but because he knew what he was doing. He was concerned with the immensity and the variety of the experience called Negro; he was concerned that one should recognize this variety as wealth. He cited the case of Amos Tutuola's *The Palm-Wine Drinkard,* which he described as a fantasy, made up of legends, anecdotes, episodes, the product, in fact, of an oral story-telling tradition which disappeared from Western life generations ago. Yet "Tutuola really *does* speak English. It is *not* his second language." The English did not find the book strange. On the contrary, they were astonished by how truthfully it seemed to speak to them of their own experience. They felt that Tutuola was closer to the English than he could possibly be to his equivalent in Nigeria; and yet Tutuola's work could elicit this reaction only because, in a way which could never really be understood, but which Tutuola had accepted, he was closer to his equivalent in Nigeria than he would ever be to the English. It seemed to me that Lamming was suggesting to the conference a subtle and difficult idea, the idea that part of the great wealth of the Negro experience lay precisely in its double-edgedness. He was suggesting that all Negroes were held in a state of supreme tension between the difficult, dangerous relationship in which they stood to the white world and the relationship, not a whit less painful or dangerous, in which they stood to each other. He was suggesting that in the acceptance of this duality lay their strength, that in this, precisely, lay their means of defining and controlling the world in which they lived.

* * *

Richard Wright had been acting as liaison man between the American delegation and the Africans and this had placed him in rather a difficult position, since both factions tended to claim him as their spokesman. It had not, of course, occurred to the Americans that he could be anything less, whereas the Africans automatically claimed him because of his great prestige as a novelist and his reputation for calling a spade a spade—particularly if the spade were white. The consciousness of his peculiar and certainly rather grueling position weighed on him, I think, rather heavily.

He began by confessing that the paper he had written, while on his farm in Normandy, impressed him as being, after the events of the last few days, inadequate. Some of the things he had observed during the course of the conference had raised questions in him which his paper could not have foreseen. He had not, however, rewritten his paper, but would read it now, exactly as it had been written, interrupting himself whenever what he had written and what he had since been made to feel seemed to be at variance. He was exposing, in short, his conscience to the conference and asking help of them in his confusion.

There was, first of all, he said, a painful contradiction in being at once a Westerner and a black man. "I see both worlds from another, and third, point of view." This fact had nothing to do with his will, his desire, or his choice. It was simply that he had been born in the West and the West had formed him.

As a black Westerner, it was difficult to know what one's attitude should be toward three realities which were inextricably woven together in the Western fabric. These were religion, tradition, and imperialism, and in none of these realities had the lives of black men been taken into account: their advent dated back to 1455, when the church had determined to rule all infidels. And it just so happened, said Wright, ironically, that a vast proportion of these infidels were black. Nevertheless, this decision on the part of church had not been, despite the church's intentions, entirely oppressive, for one of the results of 1455 had, at length, been Calvin and Luther, who shook the authority of the church in insisting on the authority of the individual conscience. This might not, he said accurately, have been precisely their intention, but it had certainly been one of the effects. For, with the authority of the church shaken, men were left prey to many strange and new ideas, ideas which led, finally, to the discrediting of the racial dogma. Neither had this been foreseen, but what men imagine they are doing and what they are doing in fact are rarely the same thing. This was a perfectly valid observation which would, I felt, have been just as valid without the remarkable capsule history with which Wright imagined he supported it.

Wright then went on to speak of the effects of European colonialism in the African colonies. He confessed—bearing in mind always the great gap between human intentions and human effects —that he thought of it as having been, in many ways, liberating, since it smashed old traditions and destroyed old gods. One of the things that surprised him in the last few days had been the realization that most of the delegates to the conference did not feel as he did. He felt, nevertheless, that, though Europeans had not realized what they were doing in freeing Africans from the "rot" of their past, they had been accomplishing a good. And yet —he was not certain that he had the right to say that, having forgotten that Africans are not American Negroes and were not, therefore, as he somewhat mysteriously considered American Negroes to be, free from their "irrational" past.

In sum, Wright said, he felt that Europe had brought the Enlightenment to Africa and that "what was good for Europe was good for all mankind." I felt that this was, perhaps, a tactless way of phrasing a debatable idea, but Wright went on to express a notion which I found even stranger. And this was that the West, having created an African and Asian elite, should now "give them their heads" and "refuse to be shocked" at the "methods they will feel compelled to use" in unifying their countries. We had not, ourselves, used very pretty methods. Presumably, this left us in no position to throw stones at Nehru, Nasser, Sukarno, etc., should they decide, as they almost surely would, to use dictatorial methods in order to hasten the "social evolution." In any case, Wright said, these men, the leaders of their countries, once the new social order was established, would voluntarily surrender the "personal power." He did not say what would happen then, but I supposed it would be the second coming.

HORACE MANN BOND

Horace Mann Bond (1904-1972) had a long and distinguished career in the education of Afro-Americans and Africans. He was president of both Fort Valley State College in Georgia and Lincoln University in Pennsylvania. He also served as dean of the college at Dillard University and dean of the school of education at Atlanta University. In his article on the historic role that Lincoln University has played in the education of Africans in this country, Dr. Bond proudly singles out Nnamdi Azikiwe and Kwame Nkrumah because of their rise to power in Nigeria and Ghana, but he also indicates how many other African alumni of Lincoln have gone on to hold important positions of service to their governments and peoples in Africa.

From its founding in 1853 until 1945, the control of Lincoln University was in the hands of the Presbyterian Church. The founder, a minister, John Miller Dickey, was under the influence of the French Enlightenment which believed in the equal capacity of all races. Dickey was active in the movement to send freedmen to Liberia. One of the earliest students of the Ashmun Institute (renamed Lincoln University in 1866) was a young Liberian, American-born Armistead Miller. Starting with the early Liberian students, Lincoln's work with African students is now over a century old.

One interesting episode was the break between the university and Liberia caused by the quasi-conversion of the Liberian leader

113

and scholar Edward W. Blyden to Mohammedanism. This led to the absence of Liberian students from the university for about fifty years.

As Dr. Bond points out, the student residences, perhaps more than the classrooms, were the place where Africans and Afro-Americans shared ideas, experiences and aspirations: ". . . The student body itself constituted Lincoln University's most important faculty." Outside jobs during school holidays were also of great importance in giving African students intimate contact with the Negro masses and the American workaday world. As we learn from Kwame Nkrumah's autobiography, those experiences helped to shape their leadership potential and political ideas.

Forming African Youth at Lincoln University

In October, 1949, on the occasion of my first visit to West Africa, I discovered that there was magic in the name of Lincoln University. I was in the Airport Hotel, at Accra, in transit to Nigeria, walled in by that isolation that is the lot of the foreigner in a strange city and by the suspicion that surrounded the outlander at a time of great political tension. The British officials were eminently correct and hospitable. They smiled forgivingly when I naively said I hoped to see Nkrumah; he was in the "doghouse," almost in hiding, and it was obviously my ignorance of propriety that impelled me to seek the company of this "fanatical rabble rouser" as he was regarded—then.

I did finally corner a porter on my hotel floor and almost in desperation told my story. I told him I must see Nkrumah; further discovering that he was an Ibo from Nigeria, I babbled that Nkrumah and Azikiwe had attended the Lincoln University where I was then President.

I had said the magic words that opened up the treasure-house of confidence and friendship. "You know Zik? You know Nkrumah? You come from Lincoln University?"—and the world was mine, or at least that not inconsiderable part of it bounded by the African workers at the Airport Hotel, and by the widening circles of their friends and acquaintances in Accra. Within a half-hour I was visited by one of Nkrumah's assistants to arrange a meeting. Even by 1949, Nnamdi Azikiwe and Kwame Nkrumah had lit a flame in the hearts of Africans everywhere; and Lincoln University had become the name of an educational institution better known among the great masses of Africans than any other educational institution in the world. The record is astonishing.

This is an institution, small, even microscopic in size, by the measurement of "universities" anywhere in the world, whose enrollment before the post–World War II era never exceeded three hundred and fifty. The record of its 4,000 American-born alumni has been extraordinary; the attainments of 161 African born alumni (through 1954) can only be described as unbelievable. Even the great British universities count it as exceptionally noteworthy when they can point to two prime ministers in office at the same time among the Commonwealth nations; Lincoln University can point to two men who are prime ministers, but who have done even more; they are the fathers of their own countries and of other nascent new States into whose citizens Azikiwe and Nkrumah have breathed the breath of lively nationalism.

Besides the two great names that have principally helped make Lincoln University synonymous with African nationalism, one can count four other cabinet ministers of lesser rank in Nigeria and Ghana; a member of the Sierra Leone legislative Assembly; public health officials of distinction in Sierra Leone and Nigeria; lecturers at the University Colleges in Sierra Leone, Liberia, Ghana, and Nigeria; and directors of important civil service bureaus throughout West Africa. Even in South Africa, there still live venerable patriarchs who proudly recall their graduation from Lincoln University more than fifty years ago. More recently, students have come from Southwest Africa, the Cameroons, Kenya and Somaliland.

Throughout Africa, the name of Lincoln University symbolizes "Free-dom!"; it is the lodestone for ambitious youth everywhere on the continent. During my active presidency at the institution from 1945 to 1957, each year more than a thousand African youth wrote seeking admission; and they represented all Africa—from North to South, from every State and Colony, from every major tribe, almost from every department or province.

The influence of Lincoln University in Africa is a part of the original design of the institution. In 1853, some months preceding the grant of the original charter, its founder, John Miller Dickey, set forth in a sermon the principal objective he hoped the institution would attain through its graduates—that they would raise Africans in America, and in Africa, "to an elevated position, social and civil, among the people of the earth". When the first building was dedicated on December 31, 1856, and christened "Ashmun Hall" in honor of Jehudi Ashmun, first Governor of Liberia for the American Colonization Society, the principal address included this prophecy:

> Feet that tread these halls shall stand on soil once wet with the crime of the slave trade. . . . Educated laymen will be sent forth to Africa from the Ashmun Institute. . . . The Ashman institute stands like a nursing mother, and she longs to rescue some noble Africans from their bark of slime and to train them for the statesmanship of a great growing Republic.

There is scarcely another example in educational history of so close an approximation between the originally designed objective and the successful attainment of that goal. That Lincoln University has been precisely the instrument its founder hoped it would be surpassed imagination. But the improbable has happened; this essay proposes to explore some of the reasons why.

*   *   *

Three periods in Lincoln University's attraction for African students may be described. The first was the Liberian phase, extending from Armistead Miller's enrollment to the graduation in 1895 of Charles B. Dunbar. In this period, thirty-two African students enrolled at Lincoln University. All but two were from Liberia. One, whose future career is unknown, was from the Gabun; another, George William Bell, was the son of a rebel against the great Menelik of Ethiopia. Bell later attained eminence in the State of Arkansas as physician and State senator.

Of the early Liberian graduates, Dunbar was the only one to achieve great distinction. He served as Attorney General of Liberia, and as its representative to many international conferences, including the Versailles Peace Conference. Several Liberian graduates remained in the United States. For those who returned, high mortality was characteristic; several died, apparently of tuberculosis contracted in the United States. Most were from the Liberian tribes, not of American-Liberian stock. Despite their superior education, the survivors were unable to overcome the poverty and isolation then characteristic of the country. As ministers and teachers, they found no outlet in political preferment. Among their descendants are to be found many persons now prominent in Liberian life.

* * *

The second phase in Lincoln's African history began in 1896, with the enrollment of two Xosa youths. They had been members of a "Zulu Choir" brought to America in the hope of raising money for a South African school, through singing engagements in Canada and at the World's Columbian Exposition at Chicago. The choir was disbanded in 1896, and the members entered various schools in the United States; Thomas Katiya and Edward Magaya came to Lincoln University.

Five years later, in the declining days of the Boer War, a far-sighted pastor, the Reverend P. J. Mzimba, personally conducted seven young men, including his son, Livingstone Mzimba, to Lincoln University. Umfundisi Mzimba considered that with the ending of the Boer revolt, the condition of the Africans would be greatly improved. He had, twenty years before, organized a separatist African church, splitting from the Scottish Church on the issue of an African pastorate. He saw that an educated ministry would be required for the new day; and so he brought his young men to Lincoln University.

Only three Liberians enrolled from 1896 to 1899. There were no more until 1949. The original African source dried up in 1896 because of the severance of ties between Presbyterians of the United States and their missionary field in Liberia. In turn this divorce had resulted from the *furore* created when the Liberian scholar, Edward W. Blyden, much esteemed in American Presbyterian circles and recipient of two honorary degrees from Lincoln University, demitted the Christian faith in 1894. He shocked Christendom by publicly announcing his conversion to Mohammedanism, a religion he thought devoid of the racial prejudices by which he believed Christianity was ensnared.

(This writer took pleasure in 1949 in welcoming to Lincoln University, as its first Liberian student since 1899, Edward W. Blyden III, the grandson of the elder statesman).

South Africans compensated for the Liberian loss. Twenty-two were enrolled between 1896 and 1924. This stream ceased flowing because of growing "color bar" restrictions that finally stopped all but extraordinary exit from the country.

By contrast with more famous African graduates of Lincoln University, careers of South African alumni reflect the tragedy of human repression. Men of the utmost cultivation and highest character, they have lived noble lives, principally as unsung shepherds of impoverished flocks on South African "native reserves".

Their children and their children's children give hope for the future. P. J. Mzimba's grandson—who is Lincoln-educated Livingstone Mzimba's son—was the first African to complete a medical course at Witwatersrand before *Apartheid*. There are others to testify that a good and noble idea has an immortality no restriction can forever contain.

Lincoln University's third African period began when Nnamdi Azikiwe of Nigeria came to Lincoln University in 1929. There followed disciples in 1935 from Ghana, Sierra Leone, and Uganda; among them Kwame Nkrumah. In 1939 eleven enrolled, including Mbonu Ojike and K. O. Mbadiwe, of Nigeria. The flow was momentarily halted by World War II; but afterward, a flood began. In 1946, nine came from Nigeria, two from Ghana, and five from Sierra Leone; in 1949, three from Liberia, seventeen from Nigeria, and one from Ghana.

In 1952, three came from Kenya among the first students from that country in the United States. In 1954, one came from the French Cameroons, the first at Lincoln University, and one from Southwest Africa, the first African to escape from that immense prison to any higher educational institution out of Africa.

*   *   *

The magic distilled by Lincoln University for these African students was therefore a potion made up of elements contributed by the institution but also derived from its setting. Enrollment in it gave access to a tremendously vital world—that of the American Negro—where he who would lead an oppressed people, might learn all of the difficulties of his trade but also the skills by which those difficulties might be mastered. These were principles of leadership and techniques for exercising leadership for colonial peoples, not available for the student at any University in the

British Commonwealth of Nations, nor in Western Europe, nor in any Soviet Republic, nor in Asia, nor elsewhere in the world.

These principles and appropriate experiences were exemplified both off and on the Lincoln University campus in diverse settings, and through varied instruments, all interwoven into the fabric of a complete educational design for the objectives sought. They include: faith in the capacity of the humblest to acquire the noblest stature in learning and life; freedom to think, write, and speak; hourly converse with fellow youth similarly situated economically, similarly bent on personal and racial improvement; daily intellectual stimulation by mature minds whose ideal was academic perfectionism; daily association and identification with the toils and tribulations of the very poor; observation of, and participation in, the instruments and techniques of power available to those who have not but wish to have.

A leader must greatly believe: in himself, in other people, and in a cause. He must have that aura best defined, even in an irreligious world, by the words of Paul to the Hebrews: "Now faith is the substance of things hoped for, the evidence of things not seen." This faith Azikiwe and Nkrumah brought with them to Lincoln University. Both set forth in their first letters of application what they hoped to do in Africa. It is the glory of Lincoln University that it helped nourish in Azikiwe, Nkrumah, and scores of other Africans men who fulfilled the founding prophecy. Though these men brought a bright faith with them to the University, without the University's long-standing reputation for devotion to the African cause, Azikiwe might not have come, and Nkrumah came because Azikiwe directed him to do so. It is the greater glory that these men left the University with their faith intact and with new arts and skills wherewith to build the substance of things hoped for, the evidence of things not seen.

RALPH ELLISON

Ralph Ellison has held aloof from any moves to link Africa and its diaspora culturally, and this may have been one reason why the French magazine *Preuves* sought to draw him out on this and cognate topics in an interview in 1958, just two years after the famous conference of Negro-African Writers and Artists in Paris (on which see James Baldwin's report, p. 97.) The interview produces a forthright dissent from what Ellison considers vague and ill-founded concepts of "Negro culture."

Ellison's writing has always aimed at the most concrete and deeply pondered accounts of the black experience in America, most notably in his powerful and influential novel *Invisible Man* (1952). Throughout the *Preuves* interview Ellison stays close to specifics and to his firsthand knowledge, which, as he repeatedly emphasizes, is that of a Negro American. As a former jazz musician and a lifelong student of Negro music, he does not hesitate to speak of "the Afro-American rhythmical sense" and of special qualities in "the sound of the Negro voice." Indeed, in his essay "Blues People"[1] (a review of a book by Leroi Jones), Ellison holds that it was the Negroes' "cultural tendencies inherited from Africa," blended with borrowings from European music, which finally produced "the most authoritative rendering of America in music" and, further, that "it was the African's origin in cultures in which

---

[1] Reprinted in *Shadow and Act* (New York, 1964).

art was highly functional which gave him an edge in shaping the music and dance of this nation."

As a writer, he affirms his "using in my own work the music and the idiom of American Negro speech." He has always wanted to reflect the "reality of life as seen by my own people." But he rejects what he calls "the racist terms 'white culture' or 'black culture'." While he is quite ready to speak of an "American Negro culture" in terms of folklore, spirituals, blues, jazz, cuisine, dance forms, and styles of worship, he is flatly skeptical of any unities underlying the multiplicities of black African cultures, and he doubts that much else unites "peoples of partially African origin" besides "an identity of passions"—the bond of common suffering.

Seven years after the *Preuves* interview (and after more than two dozen black African nations had won their independence), Ralph Ellison, at a Conference of the American Negro,[2] restated his skepticism about an African orientation in the following exchange with two other participants, Thomas F. Pettigrew and Martin Kilson, both of the Harvard University faculty:

> Ellison: Mr. Pettigrew, is there any possibility that, in answering your questions about Africa, people were put on the defensive? That is, everybody seems to feel that he has to have a "homeland." In this country, no one is free not to have a homeland. Over and over again, this idea gets into the literature. One has to have some place to feel proud of. Well, I am proud of Abbeville, South Carolina, and Oklahoma City. That is enough for me.
>
> Kilson: I am not sure that is enough for many people.
>
> Ellison: In my experience, by raising the possibility of Africa as a "homeland," we give Africa an importance on the symbolic level that it does not have in the actual thinking of people. Does that make any sense?

---

2 Held by the American Academy of Arts and Sciences, May 14–15, 1965, and recorded in the academy's journal *Daedalus*, vol. 95, no. 1, (winter, 1966).

"Negro Culture": Some Questions and Some Answers

What do you understand today by "Negro culture"?

What I understand by the term "Negro culture" is so vague as to be meaningless. Indeed, I find the term "Negro" vague even in its racial connotations, for in Africa there are several non-white racial strains and one suspects that the term came into usage as a means of obliterating cultural differences between the various African peoples. In this way the ruthless disruption of highly developed cultures raised no troubling moral questions. The term, used mainly by whites, represented a "trained incapacity" to make or feel moral distinctions where black men were concerned.

As for the term "culture," used in this connection, I know of no valid demonstration that culture is transmitted through the genes.

In Africa the blacks identify themselves by their tribal names; thus it is significant that it is only in the United States that the term "Negro" has acquired specific cultural content. Spelled with a capital "N" by most publications (one of the important early victories of my own people in their fight for self-definition), the term describes a people whose origin began with the introduction of African slaves to the American colonies in 1619, and which today represents the fusing with the original African strains of many racial blood lines—among them English, Irish, Scotch, French, Spanish and American Indian. Although the American Civil War brought an end to the importation of African peoples into the United States, this mixture of bloods has by no means ceased—not even in the South where the whites are obsessed with racial purity—so that today the anthropologists tell us that very few American Negroes are of pure African blood. It occurs to me that in the light of this, even if culture were transmitted through the blood stream, we would encounter quite a problem in explaining just how the genes bearing "Negro" culture could so overpower those bearing French or English culture, which in all other ways are assumed to be superior.

But to continue, the American Negro people is North American in origin and has evolved under specifically American conditions: climatic, nutritional, historical, political and social. It takes its character from the experience of American slavery and the struggle for, and the achievement of, emancipation; from the dynamics of American race and caste discrimination, and from living in a highly industrialized and highly mobile society possessing a relatively high standard of living and an explicitly stated equalitarian concept of freedom. Its spiritual outlook is basically Protestant, its system of kinship is Western, its time and historical sense are American (United States), and its secular values are those professed, ideally at least, by all of the people of the United States.

Culturally this people represents one of the many subcultures which make up that great amalgam of European and native American cultures which is the culture of the United States. This "American Negro culture" is expressed in a body of folklore, in the musical forms of the spirituals, the blues and jazz; an idiomatic version of American speech (especially in the Southern United States); a cuisine; a body of dance forms and even a dramaturgy which is generally unrecognized as such because still tied to the more folkish Negro churches. Some Negro preachers are great showmen.

It must, however, be pointed out that due to the close links which Negro Americans have with the rest of the nation these cultural expressions are constantly influencing the larger body of American culture and are in turn influenced by them. Nor should the existence of a specifically "Negro" idiom in any way be confused with the vague, racist terms "white culture" or "black culture"; rather, it is a matter of diversity within unity. One could indeed go further and say that, in this sense, there is no other "Negro" culture. Haitians, for instance, are an "American" people and predominantly dark but their culture is an expression of Haitian conditions: it reflects the influence of French culture and the fusion of Catholic and native Haitian religious outlooks. Thus, since most so-called "Negro cultures" outside Africa are necessarily amalgams, it would seem more profitable to stress the term "culture" and leave the term "Negro" out of the discussion. It is not culture which binds the peoples who are of partially African origin now scattered throughout the world, but an identity of passions. We share a hatred for the alienation forced upon us by Europeans during the process of colonization and empire and we are bound by our common suffering more than by our pigmentation. But even this identification is shared by most non-white peoples, and while it has political value of great potency, its cultural value is almost nil.

In your opinion was there before the arrival of Europeans a single Negro culture that all Negroes shared, or was it the case, as among the whites, that there had been many different cultures, such as Judeo-Christianity, Brahmanism, etc. . . . ?

Before the arrival of Europeans there were many African cultures.

What is the role of modern industrial evolution on the spiritual crisis of the Negro people of our times? Does industrial progress (capitalist or socialist) endanger the future of a genuine Negro culture?

The role of modern industrial evolution in the spiritual crisis of those whom you refer to as "Negro" peoples seems to me to be as ambiguous as its role in the lives of peoples of any racial identity: it depends upon how much human suffering must go into the achievement of industrialization, upon who operates the industries, upon how the products and profits are shared and upon the wisdom used in imposing technology upon the institutions and traditions of each particular society. Ironically, black men with the status of slaves contributed much of the brute labor which helped get the industrial revolution under way; in this process they were exploited, their natural resources were ravaged and their institutions and their cultures were devastated, and in most instances they were denied anything like participation in the European cultures which flowered as a result of the transformation of civilization under the growth of technology. But now it is precisely technology which promises them release from the brutalizing effects of over three hundred years of racism and European domination. Men cannot unmake history; thus it is not a question of reincarnating those cultural traditions which were destroyed, but a matter of using industrialization, modern medicine, modern science generally, to work in the interest of these peoples rather than against them. Nor is the disruption of continuity with the past necessarily a total negative phenomenon; sometimes it makes possible a modulation of a people's way of life which allows for a more creative use of its energies. The United States is ample proof of this, and though we suffer much from the rupture of tradition, great good has come to the world through those achievements which were made possible. One thing seems clear, certain possibilities of culture are achievable only through the presence of industrial techniques.

It is not industrial progress per se which damages peoples or cultures, it is the exploitation of peoples in order to keep the machines fed with raw materials. It seems to me that the whole world is moving toward some new cultural synthesis, and partially through the discipline imposed by technology. There is, I believe, a threat when industrialism is linked to a political doctrine which has as its goal the subjugation of the world.

Is the birth of various religions in the present Negro societies progressive or regressive as far as culture is concerned?

I am unacquainted with the religious movements in the societies to which you refer. If the Mau Mau is one of these, then I must say that for all my disgust for those who provoked the natives to such obscene extremes, I feel it to be regressive indeed.

Several Negro poets from Africa explain that they write in French or English because the ancient languages are not adequate to express their feeling any longer. What do you think about this?

When it comes to the poet the vagueness of the term "Negro" becomes truly appalling, for if there is a "Negro" language I am unacquainted with it. Are these people Bantu, Sudanese, Nigerian, Watusi or what? As for the poets in question, it seems to me that in a general way they are faced by the problem confronted by the Irish, who for all their efforts to keep their language vital have had nevertheless their greatest poets expressing themselves in English, as in the case of Shaw, Yeats, Joyce and O'Casey. Perhaps the poet's true language is that in which he dreams. At any rate, it is true that for some time now poets throughout the world have drawn freely from all the world's tongues in order to create their vocabularies. One uses whatever one needs, to best express one's vision of the human predicament.

Another way of approaching the matter is to view the poem as a medium of communication—to whom do these poets wish to speak? Each poet creates his own language from that which he finds around him. Thus if these poets find the language of Shakespeare or Racine inadequate to reach their own peoples, then the other choice is to re-create their original language to the point where they may express their complex emotions. This is the manner in which the poet makes his contribution to literature, and the greatest literary creation of any culture is its language. Further, language is most alive when it is capable of dealing with the realities in which it operates. In the myth, God gave man the task of naming the objects of the world; thus one of the functions of the poet is to insist upon a correspondence between words and ever-changing reality, between ideals and actualities. The domain of the unstated, the undefined is his to conquer.

In my own case, having inherited the language of Shakespeare and Melville, Mark Twain and Lincoln and no other, I try to do my part in keeping the American language alive and rich by using in my work the music and idiom of American Negro speech, and by insisting that the words of that language correspond with the reality of American life as seen by my own people. Perhaps if I were a member of a bilingual society I would approach my task differently, but my work is addressed primarily to those who have my immediate group experience, for I am not protesting, nor pleading, my humanity; I am trying to communicate, to articulate and define a group experience.

What do you think of the present level of Negro sculpture? What future do you see for it?

I know little of current work in sculpture by Africans, but that which I have seen appears to possess little of that high artistic excellence characteristic of ancient African art. American Negro sculpture is, of course, simply American sculpture done by Negroes. Some is good, some bad. I don't see any possibility of work by these artists being created in a vacuum outside of those influences, national and international, individual and abstract, which influence any other American artist. When African sculpture is one influence it comes to them through the Cubists just as it did to most contemporary artists. That phenomenon which Malraux calls the "Imaginary Museum" draws no color line.

As for the future of African sculpture, it depends upon the future role which art will play in African societies which are now struggling into being. I doubt, however, that sculpture will ever play the same role that the so-called primitive art played, because the tribal societies which called this art into being have either been shattered or are being rapidly transformed. And if the influences of the primitive sculptures are to be seen in European art wherever one turns, so have the influences of modern Western art found their way into Africa. This process is more likely to increase rather than lessen. To the extent that art is an expression of transcendent values, the role of sculpture in these societies will depend upon the values of those societies.

What do you think of the future of "Negro music"?

I know only American Negro music, in this sense of the term. This music consists of jazz and the spirituals, but as with all things cultural in the United States these forms have been and are still being subjected to a constant process of assimilation. Thus, although it was the specific experience of Negroes which gave rise to these forms, they expressed and gave significance to feelings and sounds so characteristically American that both spirituals and jazz have been absorbed into the musical language of the culture as a whole. On the other hand, American Negro music was never created in a vacuum; it was the shaping of musical elements found in the culture—European, American Indian, the Afro-American rhythmical sense, the sound of the Negro voice— to the needs of a particular group. Today jazz is a national art form, but for me personally the source of the purest stream of this music is the Negro community, wherein the commercial motive in popular music is weaker, and where jazz remains vital because it is still linked with the Saturday night or the Sunday morning breakfast dance, which are still among the living social forms functioning within the Negro community.

Nor does this in any way contradict the fact that some of the leaders in the modern jazz movement are Negroes; we still move from the folk community to a highly conscious acquaintance with the twelve-tone composers and their methods in less time than it takes to complete a course in counterpoint, and these modern methods are quickly absorbed into the body of classical jazz. A man like Duke Ellington remains a vital and imaginative composer precisely because he has never severed his tie with the Negro dance and because his approach to the world's musical speech is eclectic.

Nevertheless there is the danger that the rapid absorption of Negro American musical forms by the commercial interests and their rapid vulgarizations by dissemination through the mass media will corrupt the Negro's own taste, just as in Mexico the demand for modern designs in silver jewelry for export is leading to a dying away of native design. Thus I say that so much of the future depends upon the self-acceptance of the Negro composer and his integrity toward his musical tradition. Nor do I exclude the so-called serious composer; all are faced with the humanist American necessity of finding the balance between progress and continuity; between tradition and experimentation. For the jazz artist there is some insurance in continuing to play for dance audiences, for here the criticism is unspoiled by status-directed theories; Negroes simply won't accept shoddy dance music thus the artist has a vital criticism danced out in the ritual of the dance.

Since the spirituals are religious music it would seem that their future is assured by the revitalization of the Negro American churches as is demonstrated in the leadership which these churches are giving in the struggle for civil rights. The old songs play quite a part in this and they in turn throb with new emotion flowing from the black American's revaluation of his experience. Negroes are no longer ashamed of their slave past but see in it sources of strength, and it is now generally recognized that the spirituals bespoke their birth as a people and asserted and defined their humanity. The desegregation struggle is only the socio-political manifestation of this process. Commercial rock-and-roll music is a brutalization of one stream of contemporary Negro church music, but I do not believe that even this obscene looting of a cultural expression can permanently damage the vital source—not for racial reasons but because for some time to come Negroes will live close to their traditional cultural patterns. Nor do I believe that as we win our struggle for full participation in American life we will abandon our group expression. Too much living and aspiration have gone into it, so that drained of its elements of defensiveness and alienation it will become ever more precious to us, for we will see it ever clearer as a transcendent value. What we have counterpoised against the necessary rage for progress in American life (and which we share with other Americans) will have been proved to be at least as valuable as all our triumphs of technology. In spilling out his heart's blood in his contest with the machine, John Henry was asserting a national value as well as a Negro value.

What do you think of the attempt of Brazilian and American Negroes to adopt "white values" in place of "Negro values"? Is this only an illusion on their part, or will it be a source of creative development?

I am unqualified to speak of Brazil, but in the United States, the values of my own people are neither "white" nor "black," they are American. Nor can I see how they could be anything else, since we are a people who are involved in the texture of the American experience. And indeed, today the most dramatic fight for American ideals is being sparked by black Americans. Significantly, we are the only black peoples who are not fighting for separation from the "whites," but for a fuller participation in the society which we share with "whites." And it is of further significance that we pursue our goals precisely in terms of American Constitutionalism. If there is anything in this which points to "black values" it must lie in the circumstance that we really believe that all men are created equal and that they should be given a chance to achieve their highest potentialities, regardless of race, creed, color or past condition of servitude.

The terms in which the question is couched serve to obscure the cultural fact that the dynamism of American life is as much a part of the Negro American's personality as it is of the white American's. We differ from certain white Americans in that we have no reason to assume that race has a positive value, and in that we reject race thinking wherever we find it. And even this attitude is shared by millions of whites. Nor are we interested in being anything other than *Negro* Americans. One's racial identity is, after all, accidental, but the United States is an international country and its conscious character makes it possible for us to abandon the mistakes of the past. The point of our struggle is to be both Negro and American and to bring about that condition in American society in which this would be possible. In brief, there is an American Negro idiom, a style and a way of life, but none of this is inseparable from the conditions of American society, nor from its general modes or culture—mass distribution, race and intra-national conflicts, the radio, television, its system of education, its politics. If general American values influence us, we in turn influence them—speech, concept of liberty, justice, economic distribution, international outlook, our current attitude toward colonialism, our national image of ourselves as a nation. And this despite the fact that nothing which black Americans have won as a people has been won without struggle. For *no* group within the United States achieves anything without asserting its claims against the counterclaims of other groups. Thus as Americans we have accepted this conscious and ceaseless struggle as a condition of our freedom, and we are aware that each of our victories increases the area of freedom for all Americans, regardless of color. When we finally achieve the right of full participation in American life, what we make of it will depend upon our sense of cultural values, and our creative use of freedom, not upon our racial identification. I see no reason why the heritage of world culture—which represents a continuum—should be confused with the notion of race. Japan erected a highly efficient modern technology upon a religious culture which viewed the Emperor as a god. The Germany which produced Beethoven and Hegel and Mann turned its science and technology to the monstrous task of genocide; one hopes that when what are known as the "Negro" societies are in full possession of the world's knowledge and in control of their destinies, they will bring to an end all those savageries which for centuries have been committed in the name of race. From what we are witnessing in certain parts of the world today, however, there is no guarantee that simply being non-white offers any guarantee of this. The demands of state policy are apt to be more influential than morality. I would like to see a qualified Negro as President of the United States. But I suspect that even if this were today possible, the necessities of the office would shape his actions far more than his racial identity.

Would that we could but put the correct questions in these matters; perhaps then great worlds of human energy could be saved—especially by those of us who would be free.

MALCOLM X

As a child, Malcolm X (born Malcolm Little in 1925) may already have been under the influence of extreme separatist and "Back-to-Africa" ideas, for his father was a loyal follower of Marcus Garvey. As an adult, his conversion while in jail to the fast-growing cult of the Nation of Islam (Black Muslims) was an upsurge and continuation of the black nationalist ideas that were his patrimony.

Malcolm rose spectacularly in the Muslim movement to a position very near the power pinnacle occupied by Elijah Muhammad. Then Malcolm's growing awareness of his own gifts of leadership, and his widening vision of how these gifts might better serve his own ambitions and those of his people, burst the bonds of Muhammad's control. On March 8, 1964 Malcolm left the Nation of Islam and announced his formation of a new movement. He began to hedge his previous positions on the need for a separate black nation or a mass return to Africa. He wanted to reach out to a broader non-Muslim constituency, and for this purpose he formed the secular Organization of Afro-American Unity, the name echoing that of the Organization of African Unity which the newly independent states of Black Africa had formed just the year before to promote cooperation among themselves and with the northern African states.

On April 13, 1964, Malcolm X left the United States on an ambitious and shrewdly conceived visit to Egypt, Lebanon, Saudi

Arabia, Nigeria, Ghana, Morocco, and Algeria. His pilgrimage to Mecca served as the occasion for another revision of his previous thinking. Upon his return, he announced, "I no longer subscribe to sweeping indictments of one race."

He returned briefly to the United States on May 21 and on July 9 was off again to Africa and the Middle East. He was intent on "internationalizing" the Afro-American struggle and at the same time scoring a publicity coup for his new organization. He secured acceptance for himself as an observer at the second conference of the OAU which met in Cairo July 17–21 attended by almost all heads of the thirty-four member states. With this status, he won permission to submit an eight-page memorandum to the delegates urging their support for the Negro cause in the United States and also in the United Nations. It became clear in the months that followed Malcolm's African campaign, on which he had spent almost half a year abroad, that his reputation in Africa and Afro-America had been spectacularly advanced. By the same token, his competitors and opponents must have taken sharp notice and alarm. He was back in the United States on November 24. In the early morning of February 14, his home in Queens was fire-bombed, but he and his family escaped injury. On February 21, 1965, he was assassinated by three gunmen, two of whom were later identified as Black Muslims.

The excerpts reprinted here are taken from a letter he sent from Accra, Ghana, and from two speeches he made after his African visits. Malcolm X had made himself a superb orator, a master of audiences. In one powerfully orchestrated passage he plays on the theme, "You can't hate Africa and not hate yourself." He is stating the minimum basis for personal dignity, the compelling necessity of accepting one's origins. In another passage he very clearly redefines the "return to Africa" as a spiritual act and not the mass migration that his Garveyite father may have dreamed of. Moreover, this cultural or psychological migration is not tricked out with mystical overtones. It is a common sense matter of "our mutual effort toward a mutual objective [which] will bring mutual benefit to the African as well as to the Afro-American." He takes his stand here on a pragmatic platform where the Negro leaders whom he scornfully called "Uncle Roy" and "Uncle Whitney" and "Uncle A. Philip" might have been quite ready to join him.

After the African Visits

Accra, Ghana
May 11, 1964

I arrived in Accra yesterday from Lagos, Nigeria. The natural beauty and wealth of Nigeria and its people are indescribable. It is full of Americans and other whites who are well aware of its untapped natural resources. The same whites, who spit in the faces of blacks in America and sic their police dogs upon us to keep us from "integrating" them, are seen throughout Africa, bowing, grinning and smiling in an effort to "integrate" with the Africans —they want to "integrate" into Africa's wealth and beauty. This is ironical.

This continent has such great fertility and the soil is so profusely vegetated that with modern agricultural methods it could easily become the "breadbasket" of the world.

I spoke at Ibadan University in Nigeria, Friday night, and gave the *true* picture of our plight in America, and of the necessity of the independent African nations helping us bring our case before the United Nations. The reception of the students was tremendous. They made me an honorary member of the "Muslim Students Society of Nigeria," and renamed me "Omowale," which means "the child has come home" in the Yoruba language.

The people of Nigeria are strongly concerned with the problems of their African brothers in America, but the U. S. information agencies in Africa create the impression that progress is being made and the problem is being solved. Upon close study, one can easily see a gigantic design to keep Africans here and the African-Americans from getting together. An African official told me, "When one combines the number of peoples of *African descent* in South, Central and North America, they total well over 80 million. One can easily understand the attempts to keep the Africans from ever uniting with the African-Americans." Unity between the Africans of the West and the Africans of the fatherland will well change the course of history.

Being in Ghana now, the fountainhead of Pan-Africanism, the last days of my tour should be intensely interesting and enlightening.

Just as the American Jew is in harmony (politically, economically and culturally) with world Jewry, it is time for all African-Americans to become an integral part of the world's Pan-Africanists, and even though we might remain in America physically while fighting for the benefits the Constitution guarantees us, we must "return" to Africa philosophically and culturally and develop a working unity in the framework of Pan-Africanism.

*   *   *

When I was in Africa in May, I noticed a tendency on the part of the Afro-Americans to—what I call lollygag. Everybody else who was over there had something on the ball, something they were doing, something constructive. Let's take Ghana as an example. There would be many refugees in Ghana from South Africa. . . . Some were being trained in how to be soldiers but others were involved as a pressure group or lobby group to let the people of Ghana never forget what happened to the brother in South Africa. Also you had brothers there from Angola and Mozambique. All of the Africans who were exiles from their particular country and would be in a place like Ghana or Tanganyika, now Tanzania—they would be training. Their every move would be designed to offset what was happening to their people back home where they had left. . . . When they escaped from their respective countries that were still colonized they didn't try and run away from the family; as soon as they got where they were going, they began to organize into pressure groups to get support at the international level against the injustices they were experiencing back home.

But the American Negroes or the Afro-Americans, who were in these various countries, some working for this government, some working for that government, some in business—they were just socializing, they had turned their back on the cause over here, they were partying, you know. When I went through one country in particular, I heard a lot of their complaints and I didn't make any move. But when I got to another country, I found the Afro-Americans there were making the same complaints. So we sat down and talked and we organized a branch in this particular country of the Organization of Afro-American Unity. That one was the only one in existence at that time. Then during the summer when I went back to Africa, I was able in each country that I visited to get the Afro-American community together and organize them and make them aware of their responsibility to those of us who are still here in the lion's den.

They began to do this quite well, and when I got to Paris and London—there are many Afro-Americans in Paris, and many in London—in November, we organized a group in Paris and within a very short time they had grown into a well-organized unit. In conjunction with the African community, they invited me to Paris Tuesday to address a large gathering of Parisians and Afro-Americans and people from the Caribbean and also from Africa who were interested in our struggle in this country and the rate of progress that we have been making. But the French government and the British government and this government here, the United States, know that I have been almost fanatically stressing the importance of the Afro-Americans uniting with the Africans and working as a coalition, especially in areas which are of mutual benefit to all of us. And the governments in these different places were frightened.

*   *   *

I might point out here that colonialism or imperialism, as the slave system of the West is called, is not something that is just confined to England or France or the United States. The interests in this country are in cahoots with the interests in France and the interests in Britain. It's one huge complex or combine, and it creates what's known not as the American power structure or the French power structure, but an international power structure. This international power structure is used to suppress the masses of dark-skinned people all over the world and exploit them of their natural resources, so that the era in which you and I have been living during the past ten years most specifically has witnessed the upsurge on the part of the black man in Africa against the power structure.

He wants his freedom and now. Mind you, the power structure is international, and its domestic base in London, in Paris, in Washington, D.C., and so forth. The outside or external phase of the revolution which is manifest in the attitude and action of the Africans today is troublesome enough. The revolution on the outside of the house, or the outside of the structure, is troublesome enough. But now the powers that be are beginning to see that this struggle on the outside by the black man is affecting, infecting the black man who is on the inside of that structure—I hope you understand what I am trying to say. The newly awakened people all over the world pose a problem for what is known as Western interests, which is imperialism, colonialism, racism and all these other negative isms or vulturistic isms. Just as the external forces pose a grave threat, they can now see that the internal forces pose an even greater threat. But the internal forces pose an even greater threat only when they have properly analyzed the situation and know what the stakes really are.

Just advocating a coalition of African, Afro-Americans, Arabs, and Asians who live within the structure automatically has upset France, which is supposed to be one of the most liberal countries on earth, and it made them expose their hand. England is the same way. And I don't have to tell you about this country that we are living in now. When you count the number of dark-skinned people in the Western hemisphere you can see that there are probably over 100 million. When you consider Brazil has two-thirds what we call colored, or non-white, and Venezuela, Honduras and other Central American countries, Cuba and Jamaica, and the United States and even Canada—when you total all these people up, you have probably over 100 million. And this 100 million on the inside of the power structure today is what is causing a great deal of concern for the power structure itself. . . .

We thought that the first thing to do was to unite our people, not only internally, but with our brothers and sisters abroad. It was for that purpose that I spent five months in the Middle East and Africa during the summer. The trip was very enlightening, inspiring, and fruitful. I didn't go into any African country, or any country in the Middle East for that matter, and run into any closed door, closed mind, or closed heart. I found a warm reception and an amazingly deep interest and sympathy for the black man in this country in regards to our struggle for human rights.

*   *   *

Now what effect does the struggle over Africa have on us? Why should the black man in America concern himself since he's been away from the African continent for three or four hundred years? Why should we concern ourselves? What impact does what happens to them have upon us? Number one, you have to realize that up until 1959 Africa was dominated by the colonial powers. Having complete control over Africa, the colonial powers of Europe projected the image of Africa negatively. They always project Africa in a negative light: jungle savages, cannibals, nothing civilized. Why then naturally it was so negative that it was negative to you and me, and you and I began to hate it. We didn't want anybody telling us anything about Africa, much less calling us Africans. In hating Africa and in hating the Africans, we ended up hating ourselves without even realizing it because you can't hate the roots of a tree, and not hate the tree. You can't hate your origin and not end up hating yourself. You can't hate Africa and not hate yourself.

You show me one of these people over here who has been thoroughly brainwashed and has a negative attitude toward Africa, and I'll show you one who has a negative attitude toward himself. You can't have a positive attitude toward yourself and a negative attitude toward Africa at the same time. To the same degree that your understanding of and attitude toward Africa become positive, you'll find that your understanding of and your attitude toward yourself will also become positive. And this is what the white man knows. So they very skillfully make you and me hate our African identity, our African characteristics.

You know yourself that we have been a people who hated our African characteristics. We hated our heads, we hated the shape of our nose, we wanted one of those long dog-like noses, you know, we hated the color of our skin, hated the blood of Africa that was in our veins. and in hating our features and our skin and our blood, why, we had to end up hating ourselves. And we hated ourselves. Our color became to us a chain—we felt that it was holding us back; our color became to us like a prison which we felt was keeping us confined, not letting us go this way or that way. We felt that all of these restrictions were based solely upon our color, and the psychological reaction to that would have to be that as long as we felt imprisoned or chained or trapped by black skin, black features and black blood, that skin and those features and that blood holding us back automatically had to become hateful to us. And it became hateful to us.

It made us feel inferior; it made us feel inadequate; made us feel helpless. And when we fell victims to this feeling of inadequacy or inferiority or helplessness, we turned to somebody else to show us the way. We didn't have confidence in another black man to show us the way, or black people to show us the way. In those days we didn't. We didn't think a black man could do anything except play some horns—you know, make some sound and make you happy with some songs and in that way. But in serious things, where our food, clothing, shelter and education were concerned, we turned to the man. We never thought in terms of bringing these things into existence for ourselves, we never thought in terms of doing things for ourselves. Because we felt helpless. What made us feel helpless was our hatred for ourselves. And our hatred for ourselves stemmed from our hatred for things African.

* * *

(Malcolm was asked how he thought Afro-Americans would be received by the Africans if they should go back to Africa.)
After lengthy discussions with many Africans at all levels, I would say some would be welcome and some wouldn't be welcome. Those that have a contribution to make would be welcome, but those that have no contribution to make would not be welcome. I don't think any of us, if we look at it objectively, could find fault with that.

And I believe this, that if we migrated back to Africa culturally, philosophically and psychologically, while remaining here physically, the spiritual bond that would develop between us and Africa through this cultural, philosophical and psychological migration, so-called migration, would enhance our position here, because we would have our contacts with them acting as roots or foundations behind us. You never will have a foundation in America. You're out of your mind if you think that *this* government is ever going to back you and me up in the same way that it backed others up. They'll never do it. It's not in them.

As an example, take the Chinese. You asked me about Red China. The Chinese used to be disrespected. They used to use that expression in this country. "You don't have a Chinaman's chance." You remember that? You don't hear it lately. Because a Chinaman's got more chance than they have now. Why? Because

China is strong. Since China became strong and independent, she's respected, she's recognized. So that wherever a Chinese person goes, he is respected and he is recognized. He's not respected and recognized because of what he as an individual has done; he is respected and recognized because he has a country behind him, a continent behind him. He has some power behind him. They don't respect him, they respect what's behind him.

By the same token, when the African continent in its independence is able to create the unity that's necessary to increase its strength and its position on this earth, so that Africa too becomes respected as other huge continents are respected, then, wherever people of African origin, African heritage or African blood go, they will be respected—but only when and because they have something much larger that looks like them behind them. With that behind you, you will get some respect. Without it behind you, you can do almost anything under the sun in this society—pass any kind of law that Washington can think of—and you and I will still be trying to get them to enforce that law. We'll be like that Chinaman [about whom] they used to say, "He doesn't have a Chinaman's chance." Now you don't have a Negro's chance. But with Africa getting its independence, you and I will have more of a chance. I believe in that 100 per cent.

And this is what I mean by a migration or going back to Africa —going back in the sense that we reach out to them and they reach out to us. Our mutual understanding and our mutual effort towards a mutual objective will bring mutual benefit to the African as well as to the Afro-American. But you will never get it just relying on Uncle Sam alone. You are looking to the wrong direction.

LESLIE ALEXANDER LACY

One of the most massive concentrations of Afro-American ex-patriates in recent years was to be found in Ghana during the Nkrumah regime. Coming for various reasons, but with a common despair about the prospect of blacks in the United States, these expatriates formed a very busy and lively community in Ghana, mostly in the capital city of Accra. As Leslie Alexander Lacy points out in his autobiographical volume *The Rise and Fall of a Proper Negro* (1970), they provided Nkrumah's state with an arsenal of the most diverse talents and services.

Mr. Lacy's personal road to Ghana had its early source in his bewildered youth, when he found that in his native Louisiana, even his wealthy and powerful father, a physician, could be humiliated by gun-toting white racists; that his elegant private schooling did not suffice to make his quite dark complexion acceptable to the pretty colored girls he wanted; and that his beloved parents came, unexpectedly and shockingly for him, to a parting of the ways. Never wanting for material things, Lacy's anguished search for a meaningful life led him to the world of white radicals, then to that of black nationalists. (By that time he had garnered a master's degree in political science, a Jewish mistress who was sternly disapproved of by his black friends, and a psychiatric release from the draft.) Finally, it was the example of W. E. B. Du Bois, when he formally announced his member-ship in the Communist Party and moved to Ghana, which brought

Lacy to his own decision to go there too, for had not Du Bois said, "A socialist Africa is the future"?

On his way Lacy visited Senegal, Guinea, Sierra Leone, Liberia, and the Ivory Coast, but in none of these—probably for want of the desired political ambience—did he find that ecstatic feeling that was his when he set foot in Ghana: "My first days in Ghana were wild and beautiful. . . . I walked the streets of Accra, kissed and put my arms around strangers, calling them brother and sister. . . ."

Very early in his stay, however, Lacy had to make his peace with some disturbing facts. The baleful white presence which he and his fellow expatriates had fled was to be seen in Ghana. And not merely Europeans, but white South Africans. It was not only that H. M. Basner, a white communist from South Africa, was writing a daily column in the government-controlled *Ghanaiian Times,* and acting as a speech writer and consultant to Nkrumah, but that other white South Africans were working as doctors and teachers around the country, and even operating the richest gold-mines in Ghana.

As one of Lacy's Ghanaian students remarked to him once, "This is what you could not have learned in America." The things which he relates in the pages reprinted here, help us to comprehend the perilous ambiguities faced by enthusiastic pilgrims in quest of a racial identity who become involved in something more than a humanistic person-to-person relationship. When Lacy's "Politicals" commit themselves to the bottomless pit of intrigue in their adoptive homeland, they make themselves aliens, targets of demonstrators who shout, "Deport the expatriates", and are indeed deported, as was Wendell Jean Pierre, the stalwart black nationalist friend of Lacy; or else they abandon their friends and shout with the shouters.

Lacy makes poignant comment on this elsewhere in his book:

Ironically, and tragically, the perceptive and conscious New World Black is likely to find himself doing a little black Uncle Tomming in Africa in order not to be disliked, since that is why he came, and also because, in his confused inferiority he believes that criticism of Africans would support the racist notions Whites have about all black people. Any *serious exchange* is ultimately impossible, because it hurts too much to be honest.

After witnessing the Nkrumah debacle Mr. Lacy ended his two-year stay in Ghana and returned to the United States to take up a career of writing and teaching at Howard University.

Black Bodies in Exile

Black bodies in Ghana? A Ghanaian friend of mine called us that because he said we were weird. "Weird" may not have described us, but we were probably strange to some, disjointed to others. On the whole I think we were a rather fascinating group, joined together in an amorphous community to express from different points of experience and knowledge our dislike and outrage for American racialism. Out of that madness we had come to this West African state, pressed by the words of Countee Cullen—"What is Africa to me?"—hoping to find for an incurable American sickness a drug of identity, a feeling of kinship with Africa and its "strong bronzed men . . . women from whose loins I sprang."

Consciously and unconsciously our presence was not just a second to that motion which had indicted America. More significantly, we were a confirmation, of immense importance, of those black voices—some loud, like Marcus Garvey, some adventurous, like Paul Cuffee, clever, like Martin Robinson Delany, some speaking about the pyramids as our dear Langston did, crying "among the skyscrapers"—which (however romantic, forgotten, or denied) have always, since the first day, damned the New World and cried out for the Old. And in rejecting America, for whatever reason, we had carried forth this glorious history. No, we did not speak Hausa, Twi, Akan, or Ga; our language and values had come from the States, from reservations of America, which had never become *America* because we were of African descent; and that fact—and that alone—established our historical legitimacy. Without arrogance, our presence in the country forged the link between the New World and the Old and made Ghanaian political independence complete. That occurred to me when I saw Du Bois. One of us had made all this possible. Because he had started it. True, there had been slave revolts, other men, other causes, and other forces, past and present, traditional and modern, which produced the complex pattern of independence. But as *Ghana* was the autobiography of Kwame Nkrumah, *African Freedom* was the autobiography of W. E. B. Du Bois. And we were a part of him. Strange, isn't it? I had more history there than I had in America, and by extension, more involvement in the revolution than the average Ghanaian.

It was beautiful—a day-to-day history, a living history. If you entered the country, you probably would see a group of Afros drinking beer at the airport hotel. If you stayed in that hotel or another and watched a television program you liked, you'd have to thank Shirley Du Bois because she was the director. If you wanted a book or speech written or to talk to the editor of the country's leading magazine, the *African Review,* the man to see was Julian Mayfield. Need Julian's magazine in the French edition? See Richard Wright's daughter Julia—absolutely beautiful—but don't touch, because she's got an Algerian husband. Trouble with language? Don't worry, because there's an Afro to teach you at the Institute of Languages. Need an artist? Got three: Tom Feelings, Ted Pontiflet, Herman Bailey. And if you don't like artists, what about a sculptor? Just ask for Ray. Designer? Architect? Max Bond (M.A., Harvard School of Design), Jerry Bard (M.A., University of Paris). Advisor for a president? Go to Legon and ask for Preston King. Want to have fun, real fun—need a dancer, singer, poetry? See Maya Maka at the Institute of African Studies. Need someone to build what Max designs? See Frank Robertson and the other brothers at All Afro; they deal in heavy industry. Need a good doctor who is developing new techniques in tropical medicine? See Julian's lovely wife, Dr. Ana Livia Corderia. Want a creative children's book? See Jean Bond. Historian? Dr. Lewis. Have bad teeth? See Bobby Lee, and if you don't like him, his pretty wife, Dr. Sarah Lee, is right next door. Business? What kind?—legitimate, illegitimate, honest, underground, some other kind? Well, ask me, and I'll whisper it to you. Need a man of honor and integrity? Got a lot of them, but you can start with Jim Lacy, my namesake. Want a scholar? Well now, there's Dr. St. Clair Drake, and if he's too radical, see Dr. Martin Kilson. Want some soul? Ask for Jerry Harper. Want a really pretty girl (Southern too) with a lot of talent? Ask for Miss Lucretia Collins. If you want to go back to the States, go see Curtis Morrow; every hurt in our history is in his face. Want to see a happy Afro family? Go to Legon and ask to see the McCleans. Want charm, beauty, and intelligence? See Sylvia Boone; we all love her. Need a French master? See Wendell, he's a good friend of mine and a fine scholar. Want to start a revolution? See Vicky Garvin and Alice Windom. And for the women, how about a lover, a sixty-minute man replete with an authoritarian discussion about the history of China? Go to Tema and just ask for Max; he'll fix you up. Need a quick course in journalism? See the director at the Ghana School of Journalism; he is a brother too. Need a photographer who talks a lot? Well go to Job 600 and get Earl Grant. Want to laugh, have fun, and see black people who have gotten the white man off their backs? Go to the YWCA in Accra any day at noon; you'll find them, sitting at their same table with their Ghanaian friends, having a ball, and you'll probably find me there too.

These people, and many others I have not named, were our tribe in Ghana. Like most tribes, clans, ethnic groups, or whatever, we had leaders and followers, assorted interest-class differentiation and political attitudes. Although each of us had the final say over his individual fate, there tended to be three distinct sectors in the community; the Politicals, the Nonpoliticals, and the Opportunists.

For lack of a better description, the Politicals can be called professional protesters. Many of them had been influenced by the same revolutionary ideology, and most had had similar activist experiences, in France, America, or England. The Politicals had had, as I did before coming to Ghana, connections—ties or membership involvement—with the white left in the countries they had come from. But they had dissolved or modified these connections for a more pan-Africanist perspective. Most of the men were married to European women, and the black women, except two, were single or divorced and faced the usual problem of chauvinism in a male-dominated society. The majority of the political exiles were near or over thirty, well educated or highly talented in literary and artistic ways. All were religiously loyal to Nkrumah, zealously rationalizing his political moves, and generally, if not always ostensibly, following the ruling party's line.

From the point of view of the government and from the vantage point of their various jobs, this minority in the community had a considerable amount of power. What they said or didn't say carried weight. When the government or party (a procedural distinction, since in substance they were synonymous) wanted an official statement, they were the ones who were consulted. Moreover, since, as a West Indian writer said, "They walked in the corridors of power," they had direct access to the mass media and could be as critical of any political position as they wished—just as long as their stand was not at variance with the prevailing party ideology. Like only a very few others in the country, they had a direct line to the President, as well as intimate associations with some of his key advisors. The President used their skills, including their literary talents, for speech writing took their advice rather seriously. In every sense, they identified with and were a part of the Ghanaian ruling elite.

Such benefits of power usually carry correlative burdens; and so it was with this Afro elite. They were watchdogs in the community and generally responsible for the activity within it. Negroes believed to be working for the CIA or carrying out subversive activities against the state always sent waves of fear and anxiety through the group. Its position of trust and power was always vulnerable. From inside and outside the party, Nkrumah's enemies were always trying to discredit the Politicals, either to weaken their position as an expatriate force or to embarrass the government. They were also attacked from the inner circle, by Ghanaian and European friends of the President who resented or hated them for their ideology, privileges, or more often than not, simply because they were Afro-Americans. Beyond all this, their power rested upon the overall stability of the CPP [the Convention Peoples Party, Nkrumah's instrument for the single-party rule of the country]. Any day, hour, second, power can shift right or left, depending upon the exigencies of the moment, the strength of the opposition, or unrest in the army. A move to the right would have decreased their power, and a move to the left could have had the reverse effect. Either way, your position would change, and you would inevitably take on more friends or more enemies, probably both.

Being on guard against both external and internal forces coming at your heart produces a strange kind of head. You *must* suspect everyone, since you can never be sure. Everyone, Afro-Americans, even ones you rallied with in Harlem, are potential CIA agents or potential enemies. Every change in government or army and every presidential trip abroad is another headache to consider. In time, therefore, as an exile, you develop what I call a "refugee" mentality. The moves you make appear to reflect political acumen, but in reality they are based on acute anxiety, blind acceptance of an ideology you vaguely comprehend, a confused fusion of the political rhetoric you learned back home (which of course has nothing to do with the present political culture), and equally irrelevant, what you read in the daily newspaper. Naturally, you call all this nonsense "revolutionary," and are so smothered by this cloak that if real agents like the CIA . . . if CIA agents came to the country (as I'm sure they did), they could probably move around freely, because nothing in your political training would have prepared you to detect them.

I should say here that this group had a close alliance with the group of South African freedom fighters, which suffered from the same disposition. Small wonder that fascism still rides herd in their country. By default, Julian Mayfield was the unofficial leader of this neurotic contingent. He was very much aware of the psychology of his flock. But little could he do, since he spent most of his hours watching out for the knife against his own neck, trying to convince his immediate supervisor that a monthly magazine should come out each month, and doing his own writing. He worked on the average of fourteen hours a day just to keep ahead.

In the Politicals' behalf—one of their many virtues—they were honest, individuals of integrity, and in spite of their lack of revolutionary sophistication, devoted to their work. They could be trusted and did only what they believed. Also, they believed that Nkrumah was honest and committed and that some of the problems of political change—inevitable in these countries, given the world situation in which independence occurred—would be solved. If more of the Ghanaians had possessed their sense of history and honesty, at the very least there would have been much less corruption.

The Nonpoliticals would have faced the same problems, but fortunately they were not interested in "what was happening." I found that rather amazing, since what was happening would nevertheless affect their lives. Younger, they were the "hippies" of Ghana, and unlike the white hippies in America, had seen the worst in America, the side which had twisted and broken much of their spirit. Psychologically, Africa was good for them. It allowed them moments to think, relax, and feel a sense of development in a changing culture. Unlike the Politicals, with very few exceptions, they lived among the people and learned considerably more about the "real culture" than their radical brothers. Neither were they dogmatic believers. Conditioned by the hard steel of American racism, they were also hard, tough, and cynical, they had patience, a wait-see, or as the Ghanaians say "wait-small," philosophy which gave them a comfortable home among the urban masses. Most were artists and unpublished writers, a few students, and one, maybe two, did nothing. They were for Nkrumah, too, but expressed their support by loving the people they met. They taught the Ghanaian high school youngsters (who always flocked to them because they were "cool") black American music, especially jazz.

Tom Feelings, a talented artist from Brooklyn, led the Non-politicals, although neither he nor they wanted, needed, or would have approved had they thought of themselves in that way. But he stood out like a happy little boy, always joyful, always smiling, and drawing the happy children who smiled back. You could see the change in his work. His Brooklyn children looked angry, as our children feel as they grow up. Africa allowed Tom to live his youth all over, and this time he would be black, strong, and free. Tom did not know about their insides, their hurtings, their lack of nourishment—black bodies deformed by malaria, bodies which would not get old. Tom saw what he wanted and needed to see, and that was beautiful, because he created something, made them happy when they saw themselves, and that made him part of their lives.

And Ted Pontiflet, a fine artist too, became the model for many Ghanaian children. When he talked to them about music, I pretended to read, but listened too. The thought of coming to appreciate Charlie Parker, Miles Davis, John Coltrane, and Horace Silver in Africa blew my mind, because I was learning from men, brother men, beautiful men whom I probably would not have met back home. I had come from a mansion; Tom, Ted, Ray, Curtis from tenements, but they were giving and I was taking, because they, collectively and individually, were always closer to what we all were.

Naturally and understandably this group resented the power of the Politicals. Not out of envy, but because the existence of power creates pressures, conformity, obedience, and all our hippies wanted was a new sun, an undiscovered humanity, and as Ray said, "a little time to be me."

The Opportunists were many, always coming, always leaving, always stealing, never feeling—just going along with the tide. When business was right, Nkrumah was right, when business was bad, Nkrumah was bad. Men like these are always around. They are seen in American communities, and they look and smell the same out here.

Leslie Lacy was shaped by the Toms and the Julians. (And once or twice I sold some dollars on the Lebanese black market.) Whatever failings they had, I had. I was of both sectors. Sometimes, through me the community could express a wholeness. Both groups were honest, naive—each in its own way trying to find itself. When Smith of Southern Rhodesia declared "his country" (isn't that a laugh?) unilaterally independent from Britain, Nkrumah called for the mobilization of a people's army. The Political males stayed up all night convincing me that I should join up with them, even if it meant the loss of citizenship. Finally I felt that it was the logical extension of what I said I believed in, so I—and all the Politicals—signed up. Heading the list were the brothers from the world of music and art, the first volunteers in the country. The Politicals were surprised. I was not.

Most Ghanaians viewed us, the Afros, as a community, and as far as they were concerned, we were the same breed. The more politically conscious Ghanaians, including some students and intellectuals, were aware of our political differences and levels of involvement and related to us accordingly. But overall, given their own ethnic orientations, they tended to view us as a group, because like any other tribe in the country, we spoke the same language: a language which was critical of America, a language which defended Nkrumah, a tongue which constantly spoke of brotherhood, which never complained about inefficiency or the corruption we knew about. We wanted so much to ask for love that we sometimes lied in order not to hurt someone's feelings; and sometimes we did a little Uncle Tomming (seems strange, doesn't it?) to convince the Ghanaians that, in spite of everything, we were glad to be Home.

And sometimes we didn't want to be around any Ghanaians. Blacks passing through or newly arrived invariably accused us of segregating ourselves from the people. We just said, "Okay, man," or, "Whatever you say, sister," and kept on doing our thing.

*　　*　　*

Nearing the turn of my first year at the university, a year full of new discoveries, there developed a bitter and protracted struggle between the university and the government. The character of this particular confrontation was new, but the cause was the result of years of government-university controversy about the objectives of education in a developing society. For almost two weeks the university had been under constant attack from the government press. Not a new occurrence, but now it was coupled with irate threats to specific staff and students. The *masses* (CPP activists, screaming market women, trade unionists, and idle streetwalkers that they had picked up on their way) had stormed Ghana's highest institution of learning, breaking windows, carrying out acts of physical violence, making political speeches about socialism, and screaming and shouting, "Deport the expatriates; discipline the Ghanaians."

In the middle of this scary confusion, Wendell Jean Pierre paid me a sudden visit. He had a strange look about him, like a man looks when he brings you tragic news, news which has affected him, news which he does not understand but is forced to tell you nevertheless.

"Have you heard the news?" Wendell asked, smiling just a bit to cover his real look.

"I guess everybody has," I said indifferently. "From the looks of things, Nkrumah's people will take over the university."

Wendell walked around the room, and as he always did, looked at me in a questioning manner. "That's not what I mean, I'm talking about me."

"What about you?"—again indifferently. I fumbled through my notes on the thesis I had just started.

"I'm being deported."

"Yeah, and so is Nkrumah," I said jokingly.

"It's true, Leslie. The Ghana government is deporting me. I have twenty-four hours to leave the country." He then handed me the deportation order, which read:

Dear Dr. Pierre,

Your presence in the country is injurious to the health and welfare of the Ghanian revolution. You are no longer welcome in our People's Republic. You have 24 hours to leave the country.

By order of the President,
Osagyefo Dr. Kwame Nkrumah

"They have to be kidding. Look, Wendell, somebody's playing a joke on you." I handed him back the deportation order and continued looking through my index cards.

Wendell came up behind me, gripped my shoulders, and in a voice I had never heard from his lungs, said, "Les, this is not a joke. Police have surrounded my house, abused my family. It's dead serious."

I was shocked, confused, but because I knew Wendell, my belief still was not complete. "There must be some mistake," I said with authority. "Look, have you told Julian about this? What about Preston? Have you told him?" But Wendell did not hear my questions. His eyes were fixed on the wall in my little room in Mensah Sabbah Hall. His crying was disturbing, irritatingly disturbing. But what can you tell a man who is being put out of the country he has come to love? Who would do something like this to him?

"Les, my whole life will be ruined."

I put my arms around him and tried to assure him that the Afro-American community would do all that was in its power to make things right. After a few minutes he got himself together and went home to see after his family.

That was the beginning of an ugly experience. I could not for a moment believe that Wendell Jean Pierre, the Wendell that Eve had met in Paris, the Wendell of Legon, who I had heard over and over in his university classes trying desperately and painstakingly to get his students to understand the revolutionary thoughts of black men in the Third World—this Wendell, a man I knew, respected, and loved—could be working for the Central Intelligence Agency. There had been a gross error, a tragic mistake that a man—a man like Father—would make if he had lost his mind and developed in his insanity the unmitigated gall to accuse Malcolm X of being a CIA. The accusation would be absurd and heretical, and if you had a gun, you would probably kill the man. Certainly Wendell (or for that matter, any of us) was not Brother Malcolm, but I was unequivocally certain that Malcolm would have trusted him as I did. Fortunately, and shortly after Wendell left my room, I received a telephone call from Preston King informing me that the twenty-four hour deadline had been extended. Now we had time to work on a defense for Wendell, which we hoped would go through our channels directly to the president. The first thing was to rally support in the Afro-American community. Wendell had been an effective and serious voice at every level of life in our tribe. In French, he and Preston could discuss their letters to Fanon's wife, and with the "hippies" he was equally as responsive and involved. But the Afros, individually or collectively, did not come to his defense. We knocked on door after door, phoned until our ears were full of clicks and rings, and the response was always negative: "He's gone for the weekend." "Never did like that nigger." "Should'na got mixed up with that devil." "Told you so." "My name is Hess and I ain't in this mess." "I knew that nigger couldn't have believed all that shit he was saying." "Well, Pierre is all right, and I'd like to help, but. . . ." And so it was on and on.

I could understand, although I had to condemn it, the self-interested attitudes of the few, very few (brothers and sisters) who were afraid to get involved. Preston and I were both being watched, and the white cloud of guilt by association was beginning to form. But the overwhelming majority of our tribe members refused to form a defense committee because they were convinced of Wendell's guilt. Now, that was odd. Yesterday, the day before, all the days of their lives with Wendell, such a thought would have offended them, and if anyone of them accused him, the accuser would have found his neck on the block. With the exception of Julian Mayfield, who wrote a letter to the President in Wendell's defense, every other soul was on ice.

Because the Ghana government had accused him, he was guilty. Who were we to question the sovereign and progressive black government? We had never worked for the CIA, and did not, therefore, know its member agents. Maybe Wendell had infiltrated? But these doubts—questions however true, probing— did not enter my head. All I know was that the day before Wendell was cut down, he was my friend, our friend, a militant and understanding giant in the Afro-American hierarchy. Now the Ghana government had said that its judgment was clearer than ours and we had given him up.

Fear can cause people to do strange things; it is the timeless excuse for having acted irrationally. But our tribe was affected by a deeper illness, a sickness which went far beyond our inability to stand up for a principle, and in a very real sense, defined the twisted meaning of our black bodies in exile and the overall existential content of our human alienation. We had come from America because we hated it too much. Feeling ourselves sinking in a world of all-absorbing nations, worlds, parties, creeds and spirits, we, like others all over the damned earth, desperately needed something to hold on to. Nkrumah's kingdom was our promised land, a cubistic panacea for our lost souls. And in it, we lived honestly, did our jobs and whatever was our thing. It didn't matter if it was leaking, standing, falling, growing, or stopping; it was here, and we were in it.

Black, yes. But like most Americans, we were bent over by pragmatism, mixed up by poppycock. Because we saw the pragmatism and rejected the poppycock and ran into the kingdom's door, we thought we were free at last. And we were. But rather than do something un-American—like think—we simply got a robe from the kingdom keepers and covered over our self-hatred. We had power, prestige, and other things America could never give us; in addition, we had new norms, which we happily believed in. But we never used any of these things to create an effective ideology which our presence would have made useful to those of us still in America. We never understood power politics, least of all the Ghanaian kind. We could not be critical, as all creative revolutionaries must be, from a point of commitment. (We confused that with disloyalty.)

So when the government said, "Put Wendell out," we retreated, not so much in fear, but because we had not developed the tool to view Wendell in the changing complexities of an African political culture. We did not know about political culture. We did not know about political deals; right and left movements, you take this and I'll take that; political envies and jealousies, suspicions, disputes; international economy, American pressures—all the dirty work politicians all over the world do every day. For the first time in our lives, we had power, black power, real power— not screams from the road. Nkrumah needed us, as we needed him. For we were a radical extension of thirty million other people in a country he constantly attacked. If the widow of Dr. Du Bois, Shirley Graham Du Bois, had said no, deals would have been made, and Wendell might have remained. Like a chief in Ghana said later, "They sold you once and they'll sell you again."

Preston King, his devoted wife Hazel, Julian, and I put Wendell and his family on the plane. It was evening, the air filled with mosquitoes and suspicion. Waiting to hide from the sun.

The black bodies in exile. . . . We were the believers, the affirmers of Nkrumah's justice. And from that perspective, Wendell

Jean Pierre was a guilty nigger who had come to Africa to help the white man. We had not ascertained his guilt. We knew nothing about it. And if Nkrumah or any of his irretrievably corrupt ministers called for Julian Mayfield's blood the next morning, Shirley Graham Du Bois's the next day, and the beautiful person called Jim Lacy the day afterward—until we all had been asked for—we would have all left, blaming the white man as usual, never questioning, never knowing. Always believing.

WILLIAM SUTHERLAND

William Sutherland was brought up in a well-to-do family which made a point of living in an all-white neighborhood. "Like many other Negro families, my family thought that if I was in a better neighborhood, went to better schools and had that sort of background, I would stand a better chance in the world." But he found, as he grew up, that "being in that kind of community increases one's sense of being an alien."

The affluent white people, he observed, were unhappy, and had no real values that he could respect. The only whites who seemed to him to be "genuine" were the small minority, of a "Christian Socialist pacifist point of view," with whom he came to associate and work in various causes. He became an outstanding and resolute activist in civil rights and peace movements. As a conscientious objector in World War II, he spent three years in prison, one of which was endured in punishment quarters because he carried on a "strike" against racial segregation in the federal prisons.

In 1948 he campaigned with Bayard Rustin and A. Philip Randolph against segregation in the armed forces. In 1951, while he was in Europe on a propaganda mission seeking an end to the Korean war, he met some African leaders in Paris. Shortly thereafter he met some more Africans in England. To these meetings he attributes the crystallization of his interest in Africa as the way out of his deep sense of alienation. He no longer thought the

American way of life was worth the struggle, and "if there were other places—naturally, being an Afro-American and emotionally attached to Africa I thought of that continent—I would go to a place where there was more fluidity, where there was more chance to have the kind of society that *I* believed in." He stresses however, that it "wasn't merely a racial thing."

In 1966 the Afro-American journalist Ernest Dunbar, a senior editor of *Look* magazine, interviewed Sutherland in Tanzania. The interview, excerpted here, sums up Sutherland's experiences as consultant, organizer, and publicist for several African governments and conferences. In discussing strains and difficulties that occur between Afro-Americans and Africans, Sutherland points out that the differences occur in zones of leadership: "Let me put it this way: the emotional attachment of the man in the street here was still the same. If you were Afro-American and you came over and talked to somebody, there would be a real warmth of expression. But among the more politically aware people, there was a wary look that spelled caution." The most difficulty is likely to be experienced by the Afro-American who comes as an official representative of the government. Sutherland is, however, very frank to point out that as an unofficial volunteer, with the highest credentials as a social idealist, he also had difficulties, but did not take these as a personal affront. He simply tried to understand them in a historical perspective.

He affirms that for himself, as a free lance, the choice of an African "battleground"—in the struggle for human rights—was the better theater of operations, preferable, in his own case, to the civil rights struggle in America. At the same time, he insists that the two struggles are "inextricably linked."

The interesting thing about Sutherland's "Christian Socialist pacifist" orientation is that he is prepared to find the same vitiating traits in the new African societies that he found in the advanced technological societies: "I'm thinking of the desire for affluence, of the thirst for power. The real aim in some of these states is to be exactly the same as the great powers—only black instead of white." This is a curiously other-worldly perspective for one who participates actively in the grimy political process, if only as an adviser and technician. One is tempted to speculate that in this Afro-American's particular case, his act of going into exile on the African continent was the "equal and opposite" reaction to his family's going into virtual exile in an all-white community when he was growing up. But whatever the root impulses, this idealistic publicist was able to give of his skills and energies to African regimes which he could view without illusions.

*Bill Sutherland: Pacifist Expatriate**

How did you get to Africa?

Well, I went back to the States in May of 1951, and worked with an organization helping South African resistance people for about a year and a half. After that Bayard Rustin had had an offer to go to Nigeria and work with Nnamdi Azikiwe, and he couldn't make it at the time. I was invited in his place. I went to London in 1953 and met Azikiwe in the summer, so that I was present there at the first Nigerian Conference for Independence in August, 1953, and I worked with some of the Nigerian leaders. In spite of the fact that Nigeria had invited me, they were not successful in getting a visa for me from the British, who were still in control. I waited for months, then I finally gave it up and concentrated on Ghana, a country that was a little more politically advanced. Through the intercession of friends I got a visa for Ghana and I went there at the end of 1953.

At that time I didn't really know anything about the Ghanaian revolution. I just thought it would be better to be in Ghana than cooling my heels in London waiting for the Nigerian visa to come through.

I spent six months just being at the University in Ghana, trying to see if there was a place where I could fit in. There came an opening up-country where they were trying to start a school with a different type of educational system than the conventional British approach. They wanted to establish a high school which had

---

* From the interview by Ernest Dunbar.

an emphasis on practical activity: courses in agriculture, public health and public works and other things. So for two years I tried to make a go of this.

At Shito, as the place was called, I met Efua, the Ghanaian girl who was to become my wife. After about four or five months from the time I came to Ghana, we married. She had been educated both in Ghana and at Cambridge. She went to a teachers' training college in Cambridge and took a two-year course.

I was at the school from the beginning of 1951 until the beginning of 1957, and I met almost absolute resistance from the British who were still influential in the country's ministries even though the Gold Coast [Ghana] had "self-government" status. They didn't accept the idea of this school we were trying to start, that was very much like an Antioch College—but at the high school level—with a work-study program.

Then I got a job with the Ghana Finance Minister, Komla A. Gbedemah, as his personal secretary.

How long were you there in that job?

Four years. He was Minister of Finance throughout the time I was employed by him. In sixty I left that job.

I was asked to go to India to speak about another project I had been involved in which was called "Resistance against the French Explosion of Nuclear Devices in the Sahara." And I was in India for about six weeks during the end of sixty, and the beginning of sixty-one.

When I came back to Ghana in 1961 it was very difficult to find new employment. There was a certain undercurrent of sentiment against Gbedemah even during this period, and I don't know whether my difficulties had to do with him or not. You may recall that he fled the country a year later, after breaking with Nkrumah. For a while I couldn't find a niche that was satisfactory to me. Then I got an offer from Israel to go there and help as an adviser to them on the African program being put on by the Histadrut, Israel's equivalent of the AFL-CIO.

It was also at this time that the Non-Violent League, which I was connected with, got the idea of setting up another group known as the World Peace Brigade, to see what the possibilities were of "direct action," much along the lines of what we see so much of in the United States today, but on an international level. One of their first ideas was that we should work along with those people in Africa who were part of the freedom movement out there. Presidents Julius Nyerere of Tanganyika and Kenneth Kaunda of the now Zambia were people who were interested in this approach.

So I left Israel in 1962 and came to Addis Ababa, Ethiopia, to be an observer at a conference of the Pan-African Freedom Movement for East and Central Africa. It was at this conference that I met Kaunda again. I had been in touch with him and he had asked Britain's Reverend Michael Scott, Bayard Rustin and myself to help in a campaign for the freedom of what is now Zambia. Our efforts were coordinated from a base, here in Dar es Salaam, Tanganyika, which I ran. When that struggle was over I remained here in Dar es Salaam to become an employee under contract to the Tanganyika government.

At this point in my life I would like to get back into some nongovernmental role. At the moment I am an assistant secretary in the Ministry of Information and Tourism. In addition, ever since I've been in the government, I have been given special duties. I worked first in the office of the Tanzanian Second Vice-President with alien refugee groups who were trying to settle in this country, among them the Kikuyus of Kenya. I have also been sent to Geneva to help negotiate with the UN concerning aid to these refugees and at one point, later on, I was assigned to the Tanganyika delegation to the United Nations.

Have you reflected much on your Ghanaian experience and what you derive from it?

First, I discovered that this emotional idea of identification that I had was a little bit out of whack, historically. During the early period of the late W. E. B. Du Bois and Marcus Garvey, there was this idea of a *color-based* Pan-Africanism, a feeling of unity among people of African descent all over the world. I came along when it was changing from a color thing to a continental thing. In 1947 there was a conference in Manchester, England, which Nkrumah attended along with other African leaders, and at that point the *African* leaders took over the Pan-African movement. Prior to that time *West Indians*, such as the late George Padmore, had been dominant on the African nationalist scene. The West Indians were more than willing and happy to see the African leaders coming up and taking over, but it did change the whole Pan-African idea from a *universal* unity of colored people to a *continent*-wide unity. This was one factor which really changed my idea of what I could do in Africa, since *I* was not an *African* or from this continent.

Second, I hadn't been aware—though I soon became aware—of another fact: there had been a great deal of African alienation from Afro-American in West Africa because of the Liberian situation: the fact that over a long period of history "Americo-Liberians"—ex-American slaves resettled in Liberia—had behaved in the same way colonial rulers had elsewhere. Other Africans knew this and reacted negatively to it. Let me put it this way: the emotional attachment of the man on the street here was still the same. If you were Afro-American and you came over and talked to somebody, there would be a real warmth of expression. But among the more politically aware people, there was a wary look that spelled caution.

There was one other thing that I'm going to have to acknowledge: that in the previous period before I ever came to Ghana, there had been some Afro-Americans who had come to Ghana and who had pulled some fast deals. I'm afraid that those of us who came after these men had to suffer because of the actions which they took. However, I will say this, that as far as the Pan-African activity was concerned, I felt very much a part of it; because the late George Padmore, the West Indian who encouraged African nationalism, had been invited down to Ghana by Nkrumah. He was a very trusted person and I did a great deal of work with him at several Pan-American conferences. The opportunity to meet leaders from all over the continent and to work with them was great and I got a lot of insights in Ghana. And, of course, I did marry a Ghanaian and I was able, through my family relationships, to get a certain feel of the people and of the country.

You come in from outside the society and you marry a person who's Ghanaian. Family ties mean much in Africa and you would not have these ties, especially the tribal tie. How does this affect you?

Well, first of all there's a very natural fear of the outsider on the part of the family. They don't know who he is or why he has come. Because my wife [the writer Efua Theodora Sutherland, from whom he is now divorced], who was a Fanti, was very much a strong personality and because she was very much respected by her family, I think I had a degree of acceptance which might not have been usual. I think it's also true that had I been a member of the Fanti tribe I would have been accepted more easily. But if I had been, say, of the Ga tribe I would have had more problems than I did as a foreigner. I would say that as far as my wife's family is concerned, they really did everything possible to make me feel one of them.

What are the pros and cons of being an American in a government in Africa? Let's put it this way: you are an educated person, you have held a substantial job in a country which itself had young men possibly wanting the same kind of job. Would not such young men have feelings of jealousy and envy and try to get you ousted, perhaps using the fact that you were a foreign person?

I think that whatever my problems were about being an American, they would have been the same for any foreigner.

But Americans do occupy a certain role in the world and have a certain African policy, and I would expect that people react to you differently as an American than if you were of some other nationality.

When I worked for Gbedemah, it wasn't so much in evidence. As I mentioned before, the problem of people being cautious about Afro-Americans has also expressed itself here in Tanzania. Less, I think, when they got to know me, but there were also certain factors having to do with my own personality, because I wasn't content to just stay in the background. If there were certain things that I thought were wrong, I tended to speak up about them. This did cause a certain amount of trouble, but never enough that I was ever deported.

Have you any thoughts on the role an expatriate can play, politically, in a newly adopted country?

When you go into a country where America's foreign policy has definitely rubbed the leaders and the people the wrong way, naturally you would have a very rough, tough row to hoe, if you became active politically. But even in West Africa, I can see differences. I can see where a person might be able to take a much more active role in Nigeria than he would, say, in Ghana at this particular time. But I think, first of all, that one would have to remain in the country for a good length of time and have the people get to know you fairly well because, after all, there is this idea of "outsiders." Particularly there is this feeling in parts of Africa that America is going to use its Afro-Americans as a possible "fifth column" or something of that sort, and use them and their color to get "in."

Has that feeling gotten stronger over the years you've been here in Africa?

I don't think in general that it's as strong in East Africa as it is in West Africa. I don't mean to imply that if a man comes out to East Africa and he's, let's say, a U.S. Embassy employee or a U.S. Information Service employee, that he will have an easy time, because there's no question but that the suspicion is very definite.

What would be your observation on the ability of the Afro-American to get along with Africans? How would you rate the Afro-American vis-a-vis the white American coming here in an official capacity for the U.S. Government? Does it make a difference if you're white or black and is the difference positive or negative?

I'm convinced that it does make a difference and that the difference is negative. Let's relate this, to, say, American policy in the Congo, to which most Africans object. Let's say you are an American government employee and you are an Afro-American. It's your job to interpret the American point of view on your government's actions in the Congo. When you do that and you're black, it somehow becomes much worse than if you were a white American.

As a black man who is also a U.S. official, what is one going to say about the racial situation in the United States? Are you going to point toward the "positive" things at a time when there are riots or there are Selmas? If one is an Afro-American, it's a very tough thing to handle.

When I came here there was an accusation of an American plot here; that America was plotting against Tanzania. At that time they had American officials going around to the houses where Americans were living alerting them. One came to me and handed me a mimeographed paper saying that there was information that there were going to be anti-American riots and demonstrations and thaat I absolutely shouldn't go downtown. He said that he was the warden of the area and he had come to find out where my house was so I could be evacuated if need be. This was part of the Embassy plan for safeguarding American nationals.

As far as I was concerned, my first reaction to him was simply to tell him that I was sure he had many other people to handle and that he should sort of pass by my house. But I didn't say anything to *him* because he wasn't responsible. I did get to some of the Embassy people I knew and asked them what the hell was going on. They said, "Well, after all, we've had experience with these things in Asia and so we wanted to be sure you were all right." So I said to my American Embassy friends, "*If* you were really concerned about *me*, then what you should do is to set up your machinery in Mississippi and Georgia and Alabama. *That's* where I'm really in danger!"

You know, I have attended meetings and I have gone with no hesitation into the middle of Dar es Salaam at the height of disturbances— anti-American ones. The thing is, I'm in more relative danger *in the United States* than I would be here. Now can you imagine somebody who's Afro-American being assigned to some task like that Embassy man had?

But I know of a few Afro-American officials who have done very well at African posts.

Perhaps people with exceptional personalities could overcome this built-in liability, this conflict of interest, but generally I would say that it's very difficult during these times. I know that there are various Negro organizations that press to have more and more Negroes sent here. I would say that this is a mistake. I understand these organizations' point of view; they want to have more and more Negroes in the foreign service, but putting it in terms of *Africa*, I think they are making a mistake.

You are saying, really, that such an individual has almost got to lie, to put the most favorable face on things?

I would say that the possibility of divided loyalties would weigh heavily on any individual in this sort of situation. If he *doesn't* have divided loyalties, he's not going to be much use anyhow.

The year before last, on the Fourth of July celebration, an Afro-American group that was here decided to boycott the traditional Fourth of July party given at the U.S. Embassy because they felt there was nothing to celebrate. It was to celebrate "Independence" and *they* weren't independent. There was an Afro-American official here who had to develop a diplomatic "illness" because he was in a fix. He didn't know what to do. He didn't know whether to join the Embassy crowd or stay away with his friends. So he pleaded "sick" but he got called on the carpet by his superiors and he had to explain himself anyway. So I don't feel they should come, that is, as *official people*.

What about the Afro-American who is not a U.S. Government employee?

There still will be a problem, but it will be less of a problem for him as time goes on because he will be able to express himself. Then the way he is regarded by the Africans will depend on his own point of view, his own personality, much more.

We—the private people—are in a better position than the official Negroes, but we're not completely out of possible suspicion. One can always be attacked in a certain way. Even though I came with the World Peace Brigade, a private peace organization, I was constantly being confused with the Peace *Corps* and there were all kinds of rumors about the Peace Corps here, some very unfair rumors. From time to time I was linked to supposed "spying" by the Peace Corps. But I must point out that this kind of thing is a universal problem. If you are in the United States and take an active role in some civil rights organizations, in some communities you are immediately going to be thought of as a Communist. So it is not something that is unique here.

You said earlier that when you came you had "stars in your eyes" and now you don't. What do you mean?

I mean I no longer have the idea that Africa, as a newly developing and emerging continent, is going to be able to withstand completely the pressures of the way of life that I was opposed to in the United States. There are great forces that operate on this continent and the people within it are in some cases going to build the same kind of society that I opposed in America. But I am convinced of this: one chooses his own battleground. It's not a question of finding a "perfect" society. What you do is say, "It's one world." I'm sure you will agree that the fight for African freedom is inextricably linked up with the fight for human rights in America. So one chooses a place where one feels the situation is more fluid and where one has a better chance of operating. And I've come to this conclusion: as far as I'm concerned, I feel that here in Africa there are more opportunities for new experimentation, new values, a society which more represents what I am seeking than the society I lived in in the United States.

It's not a matter of absolutes at all. It is very much a matter of degree and how open the chances are.

You say that in some cases African societies will develop some of the things you opposed in America. Perhaps you can be more specific about which developments you found disturbing in African countries.

I'm not speaking so much of color or race. I'm thinking of the desire for affluence, of the thirst for power. The real aim in some of these states is to be exactly the same as the present great powers—only black instead of white.

What about the graft, the payoffs, one hears of even in so-called revolutionary states professing austerity?

When you take not just the African experience but that of the world, you find that the more this kind of corruption and this power hunger complex seems evident, the more developed you will find the society surrounding it. Since these countries say they are "developing" countries, one wonders what they are "developing" to! But I think that, as far as I can judge, in Tanzania there is less of this. Right down the line, I've found it better on this kind of thing than practically any part of the world. But that doesn't say that it does not exist here.

As a black American, what are the things you miss away from the black community in America?

I think you can find important lacks in intangibles like . . . like a certain kind of sense of humor. Of course, as an *American* and a big city boy, I miss being able to go out at one in the morning and get apple pie and a cold glass of milk. But I have discovered something important about myself and that is: I don't miss the kind of comforts and amenities that I find some of my other Afro-American friends missing. They're really not out of that society because they *reject* that society; they're out of it because they want to be a *full part of it* and they can't be. They miss it so therefore they have a kind of love-hate relationship with America that I don't feel I have. What I miss in America, let's say, are my friends in my community. But I don't have a love-hate relationship because my friends are a minority community within America. I miss them because we had an identity of struggle, but we still have it and they know that I still feel a part of them; I just wish that there were more of that type of person over here.

Do you feel any twinges of conscience about not being there at this time?

At different times I do. I never, for example, conceived that there would be a Montgomery bus boycott. When I left in 1952, I never thought it possible that what happened would happen in terms of the civil rights struggle. I certainly feel sometimes the great urge to be back there with the people I knew there who are working in that struggle. But nevertheless, I've also overcome that feeling because those very friends that I'm talking about—I see them when I go to the States or they come here, and I communicate with them by letter—indicate to me that this struggle is still one where the basic aim is to become part of *that* society. As long as that's true, I don't feel that that's my place in the world-wide struggle for human rights. As long as American civil rights groups want to be part of a society that I feel is basically rotten, then I don't—although I have an emotional urge to go there, it's not in any sense overpowering.

Yet as you have already noted many of these undesirable traits seem to go along with industrialization. May that not happen here?

The leadership in Tanzania is very aware of this and emphasizes in its village development programs, in its cooperative program, even in the industries they have developed, a different attitude toward human beings. It's not a question of whether they're wholly successful or not, but there is this *effort* and it's made at a very important place in the nation's power structure. There's an awareness among the leadership here of the pitfalls. They are not willing to just say "Industrialization at any price!" I think this is very significant and important. I can't say that it's going to be successful, but my God, the only thing you can do these days is throw your weight onto the side that you believe in, because if you don't, you're going to be taxed anyway to do something you don't believe in.

Has being in Africa, in an all-black country, changed your own racial attitudes?

Well, I don't know if this is going to be an answer to this question, but I'll come back again to this whole position of white people here. I haven't gone into this question before but I'd like to mention, in relation to it, the visit of CORE's Jim Farmer to Tanzania. When Farmer came here, although he wasn't representing the American Government at all, American officialdom met him at the airport. They arranged for him to see the ambassador and had dinner with him at other times; they had a special meeting to discuss civil rights with the American community, they had certain of the U.S. officials from Zanzibar come to meet him at a luncheon immediately *after* he had gone to Zanzibar to have a meeting with the Second Vice-President of Tanzania. This completely enraged me because I feel that by surrounding him that way the American Embassy really gave him the kiss of death. Their defense was that if they didn't pay proper attention to a prominent Afro-American citizen coming to Tanzania, they would catch it at home from people who, if they had ignored him or hadn't given him the proper VIP treatment, would have said they were prejudiced.

I made strong representations to them that it was time they got a little education in minority psychology. I told them to imagine themselves as a group of Northern Negroes who came, not into Mississippi, but at least into Tennessee, and that as Northern Negroes they had been aggressive in ways that the Tennessee community didn't like. Then a white liberal from the North comes and visits them. I would say that though the white liberal might not be in total sympathy with them, he still might be able to do them some good, but *never* if they fell all over him and tried to monopolize him. I told them it was definitely time that they began to project a little bit and to benefit from the experience of what it meant to be an unpopular minority. Because I think that in the white community here you see people who are so used to being the dominant group that, even with what one assumes are the best intentions, they just act in a totally stupid way.

I think the experience in Africa is very good for American white people. I think that at least *some* of them may emotionally go through some of the things that Afro-Americans go through in America such as wondering, "Why should this happen? I'm trying my best, but no matter what I do people still dislike me."

Now, this has nothing to do with the question of my racial attitude. I haven't found that my relations with white people have changed, except that I have gone through, now, some of the experiences which perhaps a white liberal would go through when he doesn't know whether to own up to his black brother or not. In one instance it happened when I tried to get some of the young white Americans here involved in part of the national cultural celebrations that I was helping to arrange. Tanzanians indicated to me that the presence of these young whites wasn't desirable. I had thought I could use their services at some of these celebrations, but it was indicated to me that they just weren't wanted. So then I had to go to these white people and say, "Well, I'm afraid you just can't be there." There was a certain reversal of roles.

It is also true that it is a definite disadvantage to me at times to associate with white Americans. Often I have to make up my mind, "Well, I will just operate as an individual and I will accept certain people as my friends, even though it may hurt me, if I think it's worthwhile." The roles are definitely reversed.

Would you come to Africa if you were doing it all over again?

Coming to Africa has been very exciting, very stimulating. There have been a lot of heartbreaks, but most of that was caused by my own blindness. And much more than the heartbreaks has been the feeling of definitely being a part of something which is ongoing, alive and moving. Who wants to stop being part of a new, moving, experimental society and go back to where people spend most of their time watching television or going to the movies? It raises a real question about a country like America—or the Soviet Union, for that matter—whether this drive for materialistic gain is going to mean happiness.

What advice would you give to an Afro-American who's coming out here to live?

I think I would say that any person who wants to come out to Africa owes it to Africa and to himself not to idealize but to be very, very hardheaded. He should examine the place he wants to go to very carefully and realize that people are going to be people, with a lot of the same failings. But, in addition, he must be ready to "identify" with the African. He can't come out here and not "leave home." And if he thinks he's going to come here and somehow get a better life quickly, he might as well forget about it because he cannot expect to get rich quick, or live at the same economic level as at home. If material things are all-important to him, he shouldn't come because he will be very unhappy and bitter.

Lastly, he has to put himself in perspective in order to realize that what may happen to him here, because of the *history* of the country, is not a personal affront. That's a very important thing. For example, if he were to go to West Africa even with the best intentions in the world, he would find certain kinds of suspicion and hostility. That suspicion and hostility must always be looked on as the result of actions that took place long before he came. So if he thinks, therefore, that the people don't trust *him* or are hostile toward *him*, he's going to be very unhappy. I suppose he should also have a sense of adventure; be willing to go along with a certain kind of experimentation in living. This is a frontier in a way and there's not going to be air conditioning in every place.

Did I ever tell you about one of my friends from the States who came down and went to stay at the Ambassador Hotel in Accra? I went to see him and he was tremendously agitated about the room and I said, "What's the matter?" And he said: "The air conditioning isn't working and I'm bringing up the engineer to find out what's wrong." So I told him, "Look man, the air conditioning is fine, it's the *air*!"

There *are* people who have been here for many years who identify with Africans by the way they wear their hair, by the way they dress, the things they put in their homes, who *do* identify with African aspirations. There are others who haven't been here who have an idealized picture of what life here is and what Africa's all about, and to them it would be quite a jolt.

Those who knew Richard Wright, who came seeking his own salvation in Africa, say he was putting too much of a burden on the country. One can't expect a country to solve a problem that is a personal one. If one is seeking a psychological home, then one may automatically project upon that country the home one seeks. But if it doesn't answer his need, that doesn't mean that the *country* is lacking.

ALBERT MURRAY

Albert Murray was born and brought up in Alabama. He is a major (retired) in the U.S. Air Force and has studied at Tuskegee Institute, University of Michigan, University of Chicago, University of Paris, Northwestern University, and New York University. He has taught literature at Tuskegee, published in various national publications, and served as a consultant for National Educational Television and the U.S. Information Service. He has published two books, *The Omni-Americans* (1970) and *South to a Very Old Place* (1971).

The title *The Omni-Americans* refers to his conception of American Negro culture as a specifically American amalgam very much part of the mainstream of American life. On the culture-historical plane, he draws on the scholarly findings of Constance Rourke, to maintain that the prototypical "image of the American is a composite that is part Yankee, part backwoodsman and Indian, and part Negro." A specific corollary of this premise follows in his assertion that "the blues idiom at its best is Omni-American," and that the blues express the complexities` not only of Negro life but of American life as a whole. Clearly, Murray is not inclined toward racialist clichés. It is not surprising, therefore, to find him ticking off Negritude as "an all but hopelessly confused theory or doctrine of international Negroism or is it black nationalist internationalism?"

It is from this point of view that Murray's consideration of the role of the Negro's pre-American past proceeds. He does not want at all to belittle the importance of the African heritage, but he insists on enforcing the rule of historical common sense. He concludes that what survives of the original culture of immigrant groups are patterns needed to adapt to the American environment, whether the immigrants were brought here in chains on slave ships or came in steerage from Europe and elsewhere. Thus, the Afro-American's development of "riff-style flexibility and an open disposition towards the vernacular" are far more worthy of study and praise than all the African beliefs and practices of which they were brutally stripped. The Africans of today, he adds, are moving toward the acquisition of world technologies and cultures as fast as their leaders can move them under the given circumstances. The backward look, therefore, is not the common ground on which Africans and Afro-Americans are likely to meet.

The Role of the Pre-American Past

Many Americans of African (and part-African) ancestry who are forever complaining, mostly in the vaguest of generalities, and almost always with more emotion than intellectual conviction, that their black captive forefathers were stripped of their native culture by white Americans often seem to have a conception of culture that is more abstract, romantic, and in truth, pretentious than functional. Neither African nor American culture seems ever to have been, as most polemicists perhaps unwittingly assume, a static system of racial conventions and ornaments. Culture of its very essence is a dynamic, ever accommodating, ever accumulating, ever assimilating environmental phenomenon, whose components, (technologies, rituals, and artifacts) are emphasized, de-emphasized, or discarded primarily in accordance with pragmatic environmental requirements, which of course are both physical and intellectual or spiritual.

There is, to be sure, such a thing as the destruction of specific cultural configurations by barbarians and vandals. But even so, time and again history reveals examples of barbarian conquerors becoming modified and sometimes even dominated by key elements of the culture of the very same people they have suppressed politically and economically. In other words, cultural continuity seems to be a matter of competition and endurance in which the fittest elements survive regardless of the social status of those who evolved them. Those rituals and technologies that tend to survive population transplantation seem to do so because they are essentially compatible to and fundamentally useful in changed circumstances. So, for example, the traditional African disposition to refine all movement into dance-like elegance survived in the United States at work rhythms (and playful syncopation) in spite of the fact that African rituals were prohibited and the ceremonial drums were taken away. On the other hand, the medicine man was forcibly replaced by the minister and the doctor—and he has met or is meeting the same fate in Africa!

As for those white American immigrants who faced no slave system and so presumably were not stripped of their "culture," in point of fact they were still stripped by the necessities of pioneer readjustment. Needless to say, they were not stripped altogether—but neither were the black chattel bondsmen. If the African in America was unable to remain an African to the extent that he may have chosen to do so, neither were very many Europeans able to remain Europeans even though they were able to construct exact duplicates of European architecture in Virginia and Maryland—and to the extent that they did remain Europeans, they often were out of practical touch with life around them. Nothing can be more obvious than the fact that for most practical everyday intents and purposes almost all non-English-speaking immigrants were stripped of their native tongue. Nor are French, German, Spanish, and Italian taught in American schools in the interest of ethnic identity and pride. They are taught primarily as tools for research. In any case, that the black man was the victim of brutal treatment goes without saying, but how much of his African culture he would have or could have kept intact had he come over as a free settler is a question that should be discussed against the fact that the pressure on "free white Americans" to conform is (as non-Protestants, for example, know very well) greater than is generally admitted. The question of African survival should also be discussed in full awareness of the fact that the dynamics of American culture are such that the average American citizen is a cultural pluralist.

*   *   *

Many black New Yorkers seem to be insisting on their loss of African culture not so much because they actually feel deprived of it but because they have somehow allowed themselves to be theorized into imitating and competing with white and somewhat white immigrants whose circumstances are not really analogous. There is, for instance, much theorizing by the Jewish friends, sweethearts, spouses, and colleagues of black New Yorkers about the importance of a Jewish ancestral homeland—but no one has as yet demonstrated that United States Jews are in any practical sense better off since the establishment of the vest pocket state of Israel, as marvelous as that little nation has turned out to be— nor has it been shown that the fall of Lumumba, Tschombe, or Nkrumah added to the problems of black Americans.

It is not Jewish culture as such that accounts for the noteworthy academic performance of Jewish pupils—which performance seems to impress black New Yorkers no end. Rather it is much more likely to be the traditional Jewish cultural orientation to the written word as the basis of formalized and routinized education. Indeed, so far as specific cultural details are concerned, a significant number of outstanding American Jewish intellectuals appear to represent Germany to a far greater extent than they represent the Middle East.

The definitive academic conditioning or intellectual "occupational psychosis" or mental orientation of the American Jewish intellectual, scientist, technician, and even journalist seems to have been derived largely from the tradition of the talmudic scholar, that inimitable master of research and midrash. In any case, it is the Talmudic scholar's traditional orientation to painstaking documentation which appears to be most functional. What sustains the fine Jewish student, that is to say, is neither Hebrew nor Yiddish, nor specific precepts from the synagogue, but rather his overall conditioning to (or attitude toward) written communication and linguistic discipline, plus a respect for prescribed procedures.

The Afro-American tradition, on the other hand, is largely oral rather than written. Even its music is likely to be transmitted largely through auditory means rather than by notation, even when both pupil and teacher are musically literate. The great Jewish conductors, concert masters, and virtuosi, by contrast, proceed very much as if they were Talmudic scholars with scores and instruments. Indeed Euro-Americans in general are Talmudic scholars in the sense that they tend to read and talk about such musical qualities as, say, dissonance, cacophony, atonality, and so on perhaps nearly as much as they listen to or perform music that contains these characteristics. Afro-American performers and listeners alike tend to proceed directly in terms of onomatopoeia.

In his very perceptive books, *Made in America* and *A Beer Can by the Highway*, John A. Kouwenhoven, whose observations on the nature of America belong beside those of Constance Rourke, states that contemporary American culture is the result of the conflict or interaction of two traditions in the United States over the years. He called one the learned or academic and the other the vernacular, or folk or native. This distinction is a particularly useful one in the present context. The learned or documentary orientation to experience is of its very nature esssentially conservative and even antiquarian. In traditions that are essentially learned, even revolutionary action is likely to be based almost as much on the documentation and analysis of past revolutions as upon the urgencies of a current predicament. Literacy, that is to say, is always indispensable to such a cultural orientation or life style.

Americans from Africa, however, are not derived from a life style that has been, or indeed has even needed to be as concerned with preserving and transmitting the past per se as Europeans have been. Not that the past was considered entirely forgettable. Far from it. But the African concept of time and continuity (or of permanence and change) seems to have been different, and certainly the concept of history, heritage, and documentation was different. (Afro-Americans, of course, came neither from Egypt nor from the famous Lost Cities.) It is hardly surprising if African conceptions of education were also different.

In all events, it is not only possible but highly probable that the "cultural dislocation trauma" suffered by Africans transported to frontier America was considerably less than European-oriented polemicists imagine, precisely because the African's native orientation to culture was less static or structured than they assume, precisely, that is to say, because the African may have been geared to improvisation rather than piety, for all the taboos he had lived in terms of. The fact that these taboos were not codified in writing may have contributed to a sense of freedom, once he was beyond the "pale."

But perhaps most important of all, it should never be forgotten that nothing is more important to man's survival as a human being than is his flexibility, his adaptability, his talent for accommodating himself to adverse circumstances. Perhaps it is a one-dimensional and essentially snobbish conception of culture which prevents some black-and-white-oriented polemicists from realizing that there is probably more to be said for the riff-style life style that Negroes have developed in response to the adverse circumstances of their lives in the United States than can be said for the culture they were so brutally stripped of. And, besides, look at what actually happened to the Africans who remained at home with their culture intact. Some "African bag" polemicists cop out at this point. But contemporary African leaders, spokesmen, and intellectuals do not. They are the first to explain that they were invaded and colonized by Europeans—and by European technology, upon which they are now more dependent than they ever were before. Nor do African officials hesitate to send as many students as possible to Europe and to segregationist America. Not to become white, but to enable the students to extend themselves in terms of the culture of the world at large.

Perhaps it is also pretentiousness that prevents some psychopolitical theorists from realizing that just as "Talmudic scholarship," applied to technology may account for the ability of Jewish and other literate peoples to survive and thrive in alien cultures all over the world, including South Africa, so may riff-style flexibility and an open disposition towards the vernacular underlie the incomparable endurance of black soulfulness or humanity.

There is, nevertheless, as much to be said for the vernacular tradition as for the learned tradition—and as Kouwenhoven's investigations suggest, even more to be said for the interaction of the two. At the advent of the phonograph, to take an example from recent cultural history, the typical United States Negro musician, not unlike his African ancestors, was clearly more interested in playing and enjoying music than in recording it for posterity. As a matter of fact, many Afro-Americans in general still tend to regard phonograph recordings more as current duplications (soon to be discarded as out of date) which enable them to reach more people simultaneously than as permanent documents. Euro-Americans, on the other hand, started record collections and archives, which eventually came to include the music of black Americans. Thus, it is the Euro-American whose tradition of scholarship and research has provided at least the rudiments of a source of musicological data that black historians and students in quest of musical heritage may someday make the most of.

Similarly, it is African creativity that has produced in African art one of the most marvelous achievements of the human imagination. But, as every art dealer knows, it is the Europeans who have been most interested in preserving it, and its fantastic value on the world art market is geared not to the valuation made by Africans but to the valuation of galleries and museums in Europe and America. African scholars, artists, and art dealers seem far more interested in what white European and American art dealers and museum directors think about African culture than what Harlem polemicists think.

When outraged Afro-Americans indict those whose bigotry is the cause of the omissions, distortions, the wholesale falsification and outright suppression of information about black people of the United States, the merits of their case are beyond question. Indeed, the deliberate debasement of the black image has been so viciously systematic and often times so exasperatingly casual that the scope of white malevolence is hard to exaggerate.

The absence of readily available documentary materials in Africa on the history and culture of the peoples of that continent, however, can hardly be blamed on the vandalism of slave traders and certainly not entirely upon the ruthless disregard by European colonials for African culture. Though some missionaries were Huns of a sort, the British Museum, the Musée de l'Homme, and the American Museum of Natural History contain impressive evidence that not all Europeans were set on obliterating African history or denying the significance of its culture. The fact of the matter is that white archaeologists and anthropologists have been instrumental in stimulating contemporary Africans to develop a European-type concern with the documentation and glorification of the past—and glorification of the present for posterity.

It is quite true that conventional European histories of the world have largely ignored African achievements. But what of histories of the world written by Africans down through the years? Were all of these destroyed by European barbarians, or did they never exist? The chances are that those African peoples for whom there is little or no "autobiographical" record conceived of time, reckoned time, and dealt with the passage of time in ways that, as suggested earlier, belonged to an orientation that was essentially different from that of most of the peoples of Europe. It is not impossible that some African cultures were as profoundly conditioned by the vanity of vanities as the preacher in *Ecclesiastes*—or as the traveler in Shelley's "Ozymandias."

That United States Negroes should enjoy the privilege of introducing additional African elements, including new fashion accents, ornaments, and trinkets, into the pluralistic culture of the United States not only goes without saying but, as the ads in *Ebony*, *Jet*, and the black weeklies suggest, give as big a boost to black business as to black vanity. Nevertheless, those who are so deeply and fervently concerned about the status of black culture and the prestige of black studies are likely to be motivated by forces and precedents that are not nearly so African as European or Euro-Talmudic, as it were. Thus, it is all too true that the "Americanization" process that captive Africans were forced to undergo stripped them of many of the native accoutrements that they held most dear and wished to retain. But it was also a process of Americanization that has now equipped and disposed them not only to reclaim and update the heritage of black Africa but also to utilize the multicolored heritage of all mankind of all the ages.

II

The
African Response
to the Diaspora

KWAME NKRUMAH

Kwame Nkrumah entitled his autobiography *Ghana*, thus emblazoning the fact that the new African state of that ancient name had been his lifelong dream, and had been achieved under his leadership. From humble beginnings in a mud-hut village in the Gold Coast, where he was born in 1909, Nkrumah had risen to a preeminent position among the leaders of Black Africa. His ten years in America (1935–1945) had been a long, often grueling, preparation in the skills required for leadership. Nkrumah earned a B.A. degree in 1939 from Lincoln University, and needing to maintain his student status in order to remain in the country, he took a master's in education and another master's in philosophy, both at the University of Pennsylvania. He taught Negro history and philosophy at Lincoln, where the student magazine voted him "the most outstanding professor of the year." During much of this time he had to earn his living, when away from campus, at various menial jobs, as he relates in the accompanying excerpts from his autobiography. He polished his oratorical talents by frequent preaching in Negro churches, and developed his social insights by his contacts with hundreds of Negro families while doing a survey in the Philadelphia area.

His political activities began with his organizing the African Students' Association of America and Canada, and with his early recognition of the uses of a West African and Pan-African approach to the nationalist liberation struggles. His studies of the methods used by various American political organizations and Negro associations, like his study of Marxist-Leninist writings, were part of his single-minded preparation for his return to the Gold Coast and his destined role there.

But first he was to spend another two and a half years in Britain. Arriving in London in June, 1945, he soon became the close friend and coworker of the West Indian George Padmore, the outstanding Pan-African ideologue and former functionary of the Communist International. Before long Nkrumah had established ascendancy in the leadership of West Africans living in England, and had become the general secretary of the West African National Secretariat. In his autobiography Nkrumah saw fit to reproduce a colorful bit of documentation entitled "The Circle," which was the constitution of a secret inner coterie of leaders who, at the right moment, would "come out as a political party embracing the whole of West Africa, whose policy shall be to maintain the Union of African Socialist Republics." In addition to oath and rituals, the document details seven articles of faith, of which article seven reads, "I accept the leadership of Kwame Nkrumah." While this West African Union never materialized, Nkrumah did, of course, become prime minister of an independent Ghana in 1957. The spirit of "personality cult" inherent in Nkrumah's "Circle" document was to blossom grotesquely within a decade into a totalitarian regime, borrowing from Leninist theory and Stalinist practice, forcing upon Ghanaians the omnipresent image of Osagyefo ("Redeemer") Nkrumah, throwing hundreds of political opponents into jail without trial, and running an original $400-million reserve into a debt of $600 million. Nkrumah was overthrown by an army coup in 1966 while he was visiting Peking. He went into exile in Guinea. He died in April, 1972, in Rumania, where he had gone for medical treatment. In July, 1972, his body was returned for burial in the small town of Nkroful, where he was born.

In the excerpted chapter given here, Nkrumah credits Marcus Garvey with having had the greatest influence on him. This may have been so while he was still in America, but Dr. Ali Mazrui, the East African political scientist, makes this comment: " . . . I would argue that the mature Nkrumah was far more Leninist than he was Garveyite. The most important part of Marcus Garvey's thought was the glorification of *blackness*.

And yet Nkrumah abandoned quite early this commitment to colour and embraced instead a commitment to the African *continent.*"[1] The aura of this commitment and the charismatic force of his personality inspired many black Americans. Elsewhere in the present volume[2] other accounts are given of Nkrumah's influence on Afro-Americans. His voice was, indeed, as Professor Mazrui has characterized it, "the golden voice of solidarity." His oppressive hand, however, drastically weakened that solidarity.

Hard Times in America

My ten years in America had been happy and eventful, but at the same time they had been remarkably strenuous. Life would have been so much easier if I could have devoted all my time to study. As things were, however, I was always in need of money and had to work out ways and means of earning my livelihood.

When the first summer vacation came round at Lincoln I was at a loss to know what to do because it was a rule that no student could remain on the campus after term had ended. I went to New York and stayed with a Sierra Leonean friend in Harlem. He was in no better straits than I was and so we immediately set about planning how to get a job. We thought we had a brainwave and went to the fish and poultry market early each morning, bought fish at wholesale prices and spent the rest of the day trying to sell it on a street corner. This job was particularly uncomfortable for me as I seemed to have some kind of an allergy towards fish. Although both my arms and eventually my body became covered in the most irritating rash, I would willingly have stuck it out if the job had shown the least bit of profit. After a fortnight of this, however, it was clear that I was losing what

---

[1] *Transition,* No. 32, Kampala, Uganda.
[2] See the selections from Horace Mann Bond, Richard Wright, Leslie A. Lacy, and Ali A. Mazrui.

little money I had and so I decided to pack it up. This caused a row between us, which was a pity, for it meant that I was not only without a job but also without a place to stay.

I was wandering down Seventh Avenue in Harlem wondering where I could turn next when I suddenly ran into a fellow student from Lincoln who came from Demerara in British Guiana. I told him of my difficulties: no money, no job and nowhere to go. "Don't worry, old chap," he said encouragingly, "I think I can solve the accommodation problem as a start." He explained that he knew a West Indian family who were extremely kind and sympathetic and that if he went along and put my case before them, he felt they might help me out. Sure enough, by the time I had told my story, tears were in the eyes of the womenfolk who offered me their small spare room, and added that I was not to worry about the payment until I managed to find a job.

It was through a doctor friend of this family that I was introduced to my first girl friend in America. This was Edith, a nurse in Harlem Hospital. I must have been a great disappointment to her. I was quite penniless, so, apart from taking her for walks and gazing into shop windows, I could not offer her much in the way of entertainment. And I must have been a bit of a bore because my favourite amusement at that time was to stand and listen to the soap-box orators at the street corners. I was quite happy to spend my evenings there either quietly listening or, as was more often the case, provoking arguments with them. Poor Edith! She was crazy about dancing, the movies and the gayer things of life. It was not surprising, therefore, that she slowly drifted away from me.

It was round about this time that I found a job in a soap factory. I had imagined that I would leave work each day exuding the scent of roses or honeysuckle but this was far from the case. It turned out to be by far the filthiest and most unsavoury job that I ever had. All the rotting entrails and lumps of fat of animals were dumped by lorries into a yard. Armed with a fork I had to load as much as I could of this reeking and utterly repulsive cargo into a wheelbarrow and then transport it, load after load, to the processing plant. As the days went by, instead of being steadily toughened, I had the greatest difficulty in trying not to vomit the whole time.

At the end of two weeks I was almost fit to be transformed

into a bar of soap myself. My limbs ached so much at the day's end that I had to rub myself nightly with liniment before I could hope to get any sleep and build up enough energy to tackle the next day. A doctor friend of mine advised me strongly to leave the job. If I did not, he said, I would certainly never complete my education in America.

Taking his advice, I began to look for other work. Job hunting in America at that time was most difficult because the country was just emerging from the depression. Life was so hard on some people that sometimes I would see men and women picking scraps of food from out of the dustbins. In fact, had it not been for the generosity of my landlady, I should have been doing the same thing.

As I seemed to have no luck in finding a job I decided to go to sea. In order to do this I became a member of the National Maritime Union, a body affiliated to the Congress of Industrial Organizations, which was at that time one of the most active trade union organizations in the United States. As the competition for employment was so great in New York, I went to Philadelphia where the demand was less. There I was lucky in getting a job aboard the *Shawnee,* a ship of the Clyde Mallory Line plying between New York and Vera Cruz in Mexico.

Every summer thereafter, until the outbreak of the second world war in September 1939, I managed to get employment at sea. When I first applied for a job, the official of the shipping line asked me brusquely, "Can you wait, boy?" At first I thought he was asking me to postpone my application and when I hesitated, he raised his voice and said: "Well, come on! Can you wait at table?" Terrified of being turned down, I assured him that I could wait. So I was sent to sea as a waiter.

I was dressed up smartly in clothes to suit my new position and the time for the first meal approached. The dining room started to fill up and the head waiter told me to "Get along, then!" I felt like a frightened rabbit as I looked helplessly around the kitchen for somebody to give me a lead. And I had said I could wait! The head waiter glared at me and shouted—"Well, take in the soup!" I mumbled, "The soup," as I looked round for it. When I found it I betrayed myself completely by pouring it into, or rather on to, a flat plate. This was not discovered until I had carried it carefully into the dining room and placed what little there was left of it before the first passenger I saw with nothing in front of him. I was in too much of a hurry to get back to the kitchen and crawl in with the next plate to notice the strange looks that were appearing on the faces of the passengers. When I got into the kitchen, however, I found the head waiter almost ready to throw a fit. He got hold of my collar and started to shake me. How dare I say that I could wait, he demanded. When I could get my breath back I apologized profusely and pleaded with him not to be too hard on me because I was so desperately in need of the job. Luckily, underneath his stiffly starched exterior he had a very soft heart. He hastily put another man into my uniform and told me that I could wash pots for the rest of the trip. This was a soul-destroying job, but at least it did not require experience. Later I was promoted to dish washing. I was extremely careful with dishes but one day as I was taking them out of the huge steam contraption through which they passed, one broke and cut my hand so deeply that I still have the scar to-day.

For the next trip, having learnt a little about dining room routine and the names of various foods, I was promoted to Mess Room Waiter. The officers were not quite so tricky as the passengers and after being chivvied around a bit, I soon got into the way of things. Eventually I managed to get the cream of jobs, that of bell-hop. This was most sought after as the tips were good and a smart uniform was provided, complete with a pill-box hat. It had embarrassing moments, however. One day, a bell rang from one of the cabins. I knocked on the door and a lady's voice told me to enter. The next moment I beheld a most attractive woman reclining on her bunk almost completely naked. I was so taken aback that I rushed out again before she had time to speak. The bell went again, and with cheeks aflame under my dark skin, I once again knocked on the door. The voice, full of laughter, called out that I could come in, that all was safe and I had no need to worry. I went in with my eyes respectfully on the ground and took her order. When I looked at her, at her request, she was quite covered up.

This kind of life was a new experience to me. I had no knowledge of the ways of sailors and I was sometimes pretty shocked at their topics of conversation and the pornographic literature that used to be handed round among them. They used to try to persuade me to go ashore in the various South American ports where we docked. Sometimes I would join them, just for the fun of it and because I didn't want to be thought of as something unusual, but after my experience in Las Palmas, I was always a little wary of such pastimes. I did meet a French woman, however, who seemed to be of a rather better sort and I used to visit her every time the boat went to Mexico. But somehow or other she got the idea that I had promised to marry her. Perhaps it was the language difficulty; anyhow, rather than argue the point, I said that I would be back the following trip to stay. I had not lived with sailors for nothing!

I was really sorry when war broke out and my sailor days came to an end, for apart from the lighter side of it, the pay was reasonably good and we were always assured of three good meals a day.

On the other hand, except for the camaraderie which existed among the crew boys, there was always a most haunting feeling of loneliness, not just being without companions, but of being nobody's concern. Many times as I walked in the streets of Vera Cruz or in other foreign ports the thought struck me that anybody could have set upon and killed me and nobody would have missed me unduly. I don't suppose any steps would have been taken to discover even my identity.

I learned too, that to sleep under the stars in my native Africa was, in spite of the raiding mosquitoes, a far happier prospect than sleeping out in the cities of America. When I first visited Philadelphia with a fellow student neither of us had any money for lodgings and, as we had nowhere else to go, we walked back to the railway station and sat on one of the benches intending to pass the night there. We had not reckoned with the ubiquitous American police. At about midnight we were rudely shaken out of our doze and greeted by a firm but not unkind voice saying, "Move on, chums, you can't sleep here."

With aching limbs and eyes almost blind for want of sleep, we felt that it was the most cruel thing that had yet been done to us. We shuffled out of the station and wandered into the nearby park. Luckily, unlike the London parks, the gates were not locked against us, and we managed to find a couple of benches where we thought we could spend the rest of the night undisturbed. Again fate was unkind for no sooner had we closed our eyes than the rain started. It came down so heavily that we were forced to abandon our makeshift beds and spent the remaining few hours of darkness standing about in doorways with other tramps, trying to keep dry.

For wet nights thereafter I devised another plan. The idea came to me in New York one night after I had been ejected from my room and had nothing in my pockets except twenty-five cents. During the day the problem of shelter had not seemed so acute, but when night came and I found that the streets had been taken over by stray cats and down-and-outs like myself, it was a very different picture altogether. Suddenly I got an idea. For a nickel I bought a subway ticket and boarded a train plying between Harlem and Brooklyn. With this ticket I travelled backwards and forwards on the train the whole night, getting what sleep I could. It was, of course, a very disturbed night, for every time the subway reached its destination I got out and changed coaches in case the guard became curious about me being in the same coach for so long.

Poverty and need drive one to surprising ends. For want of something better to do and because it provided me with an evening's free entertainment, I used to go round quite a lot to various Negro religious gatherings and revivalist meetings. The only one that I gave much attention to was a movement headed by Father Divine, and then only because of the privileges attached to membership. By being a follower of Father Divine I discovered that it was possible to obtain a good chicken meal for half a dollar, instead of the usual two or three dollars charged at other restaurants, and also a hair-cut at a certain barber's shop for only ten cents instead of a dollar. To an impoverished student this was quite enough to attract him to any sort of movement and as long as I could be fed and shown at cut prices by merely raising my arm above my head and whispering "Peace," I fear I did not concern myself with the motives of Father Divine's group.

One thought did cross my mind, though. It was a condition of membership that no one should be married, because they were "married" to the church. If a couple were legally married before they entered Father Divine's mission, then the union was in name only. I wondered whether this was not a movement backed financially by some white Americans to exterminate the Negroes, for, apart from the marriage ban, as far as I could see nobody ever paid anything towards the movement and yet it never lacked funds. Anyhow, I was truly grateful at the time for the benevolence of Father Divine.

While I was studying theology at Lincoln Seminary I spent much of my free time preaching in Negro churches. Almost every Sunday I was booked to preach at some church or other and I really enjoyed doing it. I had made many friends, for the Negro churches play the part of community centres more than most places of worship. It was after I had been preaching in a Baptist Church in Philadelphia that I was introduced to Portia and her sister Romana. They invited me back to their house for dinner and from that time on a strong friendship existed among the three of us. It was Portia, however, who became my special friend. She was extremely generous and many times provided me with pocket money when I was out of funds. It was she who taught me the meaning of a "Dutch treat," when we shared the expenses on an outing. I was really not worthy of such a devoted girl friend for, as usual, I neglected her shamefully. I was always pleased to see her but I never wanted anything permanent to develop from our friendship. It often amazed me how Portia stuck by me so long. Probably she believed that with patience even the most stubborn of men will give in in the end. I remember one day thinking that she must be psychic. I had struck up a mild friendship with some girl or other and the second time I saw her I had to go on to Portia's house for dinner. When I arrived looking, as I hoped, innocent and composed, Portia took one look at me and accused me of two-timing her, as she put it. I denied it but she insisted and she said that she would go as far as to say that that very night I had embraced another girl. I felt it was impossible to hold out against anybody with second sight and I confessed that some girl had in fact kissed me but that there was nothing in it, which was quite true. Then she said smugly, "It might be a good idea if you washed the lipstick off your collar before you do anything else."

Unfortunately, the fact that I enjoy women's company has led to a great deal of misunderstanding from those who look at my life from outside. I have never wanted to become too entangled with a woman because I know that I would never be able to devote enough attention to her, that sooner or later whether she was married to me or not, she would begin to wander away from me.

I was afraid too, that if I allowed a woman to play too important a part in my life I would gradually lose sight of my goal. Few people have been able to understand this attitude of mine and I have been described by various people as a Don Juan, an impotent man and even a eunuch! Those who know me, however, regard me as a very normal man with probably more than average self-discipline.

When I was in Philadelphia I carried out an intensive survey of the Negro from a religious, social and economic standpoint. This work, which was given to me by the Presbyterian Church, took me to over six hundred Negro homes in Philadelphia alone, as well as many others in Germantown and Reading. I enjoyed the work immensely and it was certainly an eye-opener to the racial problem in the United States which, particularly in the Southern part, was acute. When I compared this racial segregation with the modernity and advancement of the country it made my heart sink.

I well remember my first experience of active racialism below the Mason-Dixon line. I was travelling by bus on one of my lecture tours from Philadelphia to Washington and the bus stopped en route at Baltimore for the passengers to refresh themselves. I was parched from thirst and I entered the refreshment room at the terminal and asked the white American waiter if I could have a drink of water. He frowned and looked down his nose at me as if I was something unclean. "The place for you, my man, is the spittoon outside," he declared as he dismissed me from his sight. I was so shocked that I could not move. I just stood and stared at him for I could not bring myself to believe that anyone could refuse a man a drink of water because his skin happened to be a different colour. I had already experienced racial segregation in the buses and in restaurants and other public places, but this seemed to me to be stretching it rather far. However, I said nothing but merely bowed my head and walked out in as dignified a manner as I knew how.

While at the University of Pennsylvania I helped to set up an African Studies Section there. It was there also that I began to organize the African Students' Association of America and Canada. This was actually the beginning of my political activities in the United States. When I first arrived this Association was only a small gathering of African students who used to meet occasionally but who, because of lack of organization were not strong enough to achieve anything effective. I arranged things so that the organization took in not only the students but also Africans engaged in other types of work in the country. By this means I was able to bring them all together, At the first conference I was elected president, a position I held until the day I left for England.

With the assistance of fellow African students, in particular Ako Adjei (now Minister of the Interior in my Government) and Jones Quartey (now in the Institute of Extra-Mural Studies at the University College, Achimota), I arranged for the publication of the Association's official newspaper which was called the *African Interpreter*. Through the medium of this newspaper we tried to revive a spirit of nationalism.

It was not easy going by any means for we were continually coming up against internal conflict between the Nigerian and Gold Coast elements. The Nigerians claimed that there was no question of considering African or West African unity at the existing stage of colonial dependency and insisted that we should leave these colonial territories to struggle for themselves, each one working out its own salvation as best it could, without any link or co-operation with the other territories. I and the Gold Coast students, on the other hand, felt strongly that the question of territorial solidarity—that is to say, each territory mapping out and planning its own liberation—could not hope for ultimate success until it was linked up with the other movements in West Africa. We believed that unless territorial freedom was ultimately linked up with the Pan African movement for the liberation of the whole African continent, there would be no hope of freedom and equality for the African and for people of African descent in any part of the world.

The idea of West African unity, which, of course, I strongly supported, became the accepted philosophy of the African Students' Association and we directed the students that when they returned to their respective territories they should work hard politically to organize particular areas, but that in so doing they should maintain close contact with the political activities of their territories. By this means they would maintain not only unity within their own territories, but would pave the way for unity among all the territories in West Africa.

At that time I was interested in two sociological schools of thought in the States, one represented by the Howard sociologists

led by Professor Frazier, and the other led by Dr. M. J. Herskovits, Professor of Anthropology at Northwestern University. The
Howard school of thought maintained that the Negro in America
had completely lost his cultural contract with Africa and the other
school, represented by Herskovits, maintained that there were
still African survivals in the United States and that the Negro of
America had in no way lost his cultural contact with the African
continent. I supported, and still support, the latter view and I
went on one occasion to Howard University to defend it.

Apart from all my academic work and the various activities
that I have mentioned, I made time to acquaint myself with as
many political organizations in the United States as I could. These
included the Republicans, the Democrats, the Communists and the
Trotskyites. It was in connection with the last movement that I
met one of its leading members, Mr. C. L. R. James, and through
him I learned how an underground movement worked. I was also
brought into contact with organizations such as the Council on
African Affairs, the Committee on Africa, the Committee on War
and Peace Aims, the Committee on African Students, the Special
Research Council of the National Association for the Advancement of Coloured People and the Urban League. My aim was to
learn the technique of organization. I knew that when I eventually returned to the Gold Coast I was going to be faced with this
problem. I knew that whatever the programme for the solution of
the colonial question might be, success would depend upon the
organization adopted. I concentrated on finding a formula by which
the whole colonial question and the problem of imperialism could
be solved. I read Hegel, Karl Marx, Engels, Lenin and Mazzini.
The writings of these men did much to influence me in my revolutionary ideas and activities, and Karl Marx and Lenin particularly impressed me as I felt sure that their philosophy was capable
of solving these problems. But I think that of all the literature that
I studied, the book that did more than any other to fire my enthusiasm was *Philosophy and Opinions of Marcus Garvey* published
in 1923. Garvey, with his philosophy of "Africa for the Africans"
and his "Back to Africa" movement, did much to inspire the
Negroes of America in the 1920s. It is somewhat ironical that the
white Americans in the South supported Garvey in these movements of his. They did this not because they were interested in the
emancipation of the Negro as such, but because they wanted to

get rid of the black man from the South and felt that this would solve the Negro problem. It was unfortunate that I was never able to meet Garvey as he had been deported from the country before I arrived, in connection with some kind of alleged fraud that he had got involved in. He eventually went to England where he died in 1940.

E. U. ESSIEN-UDOM

One of the most penetrating views of the Afro-American situation is the work of the Nigerian scholar E. U. Essien-Udom. Now of the political science faculty of the University of Ibadan, Professor Essien-Udom spent over a dozen years in the United States. For most of those years, beginning in 1952, he lived in the Black Belt of Chicago, studied at Oberlin College, Ohio, and took his postgraduate degrees at the University of Chicago. He has also taught at Brown and Harvard Universities. His book *Black Nationalism: A Search for an Identity in America* (1962) is the result of two years of sympathetic close study of the Nation of Islam (Black Muslims)—its leaders, members, history, beliefs, and practices.

Dr. Essien-Udom points out that although "suspicion, fear and the apparent atmosphere of secrecy which surrounds the movement" sealed him off from certain data and lines of inquiry, he was able to have frequent and cordial meetings with Elijah Muhammad and some of his top subordinates, including Malcolm X, and acknowledges "with deep feelings of kinship and friendship their courtesies and regard" for him. Obviously, his genuine tact and compassion were of vital help to his research, during which, he tells us, he "participated continuously in the religious, social, and, to a limited extent, business activities of the Muslims in Chicago . . . attended two Muslim Annual Conventions in Chicago and interviewed ministers and lay Muslims from other cities on

197

many occasions . . . observed the meetings of other black nationalists organizations in Chicago and New York City, and discussed
their objectives and programs with members."

The present selection, the final chapter in the book (there entitled "Conclusions and Trends"), seeks to sum up the inner core
of the Negro American dilemma, as revealed in the author's study
of the Black Muslims.

The agitation of the Black Muslims and other black nationalists
projects "voices from within the veil"—voices of estrangement,
not only of blacks from whites, but of blacks from other blacks.
The tensions and despairs of urban Negroes—so many of whom
migrated from rural areas—are similar to those suffered by urban
whites, but exacerbated by far greater psychological problems.
The rise of a substantial black middle class has only made the
lower-class black feel more abandoned and powerless—and this
impotence induces a mood of withdrawal and separation. Thus
the dream of a homeland becomes for many a desperately desired
escapist compensation. This was true of the Garveyite masses in
the twenties and is true of the Black Muslims today. (And yet
Muslim mystique and rhetoric often confuse Negro auditors as to
the exact nature of their origins and identity: as Essien-Udom
tells us, "Muhammad tries to circumvent the Negroes' aversion
to Africa by asserting they are Asiatics, of whom Africans form
only a part.")

Strange as it may seem in view of the virulent antiwhite and
antiestablishment rhetoric of the Muslims, one of their major
achievements, according to the author, is that "the nation [of
Islam] assists its members to strive for traditional American
middle-class values while maintaining their identity with the
Negro community."

Dr. Essien-Udom sums up his own perspective in this way:

In communal-oriented activities, presently woefully lacking, Negroes
would discover their identity and would best reflect what is good about
America through self-assertion. It might enable them to develop their
potential, a greater sense of the "public interest" and to participate
more constructively in the society. The Negro is unquestionably an
American, "reluctantly" at times, even as the deviant doctrines of Mr.
Muhammad show; yet he is a member of a group with four centuries
of unique experiences and traditions that cannot easily be wished
away. Besides, the Negro, though removed by centuries from Africa,
has never been, and cannot now be expected to be, indifferent to the
land of his forebears. This remote heritage, no matter how insignifi-

cant its content may be, is part and parcel of the Negro's being. This too, like his Americanism, should be understood. In these circumstances, sentimentality toward assimilation or toward chauvinistic nationalism is blatantly wishful, unrealistic, and contrary to fact, in so far as the masses of Negroes are concerned.

In Search of a Saving Identity

In the preceding chapters, those themes were singled out that seemed important for understanding the character of black nationalism in the United States. It would be foolish, however, to suppose that explanations have been exhausted concerning the behavior of the black nationalists. There is risk involved in any explanation of the behavior of human beings and, especially, of social groups. This caution applies equally to the subject of this study—a controversial, vocal, but numerically an insignificant minority of American Negroes, looking for a saving identity with which to transcend the social, psychological, and spiritual barriers of the "invisible ghetto."

Broadly, the study of black nationalism is a case study of the social and psychological consequences of what Gunnar Myrdal aptly summed up as "An American Dilemma" on the personal and group life of American Negroes. The sum total of these consequences—psychological constraints, institutional weaknesses, contradictory "value systems" of the subculture, and the absence of an ethos—is what we described as the Negro dilemma, dramatized in the doctrines of black nationalism. These constraints are deeply rooted in the subculture although they depend on and are supported by the white society. The Negro dilemma, in a subtle and profound way, exercises a constraint, which is by no means easy to specify, on the social advancement of the masses of Negroes, especially in the northern United States. Although the study points to a possible relationship between these constraints and the obstacles imposed on Negroes by the white society, it does not, however, tell us much about the relative weight to be attached to one or the other on the advancement of the masses of Negroes. Common sense suggests, however, that the attitudes and actions of the white society are more decisive. Nevertheless, both are inextricably interwoven and, analytically, they are difficult to disentangle. The uneasy coexistence between them is not adequately understood or appreciated. Black nationalism, especially the Muslim movement, is an attempt to "break through" the vicious circle which emerges from this relationship.

Furthermore, the study underscores the Negroes' ambivalence toward assimilation, i.e., the loss of their identity, cultural traits, and history. Black nationalism, the Muslim movement in particular, raises such questions: Can the majority of Negroes be assimilated into American society? Do they really want to be assimilated? What "price" will they have to pay for assimilation or non-assimilation? If they want to be assimilated, what are they themselves doing to facilitate this process? If not, are there discernible attitudes among Negroes which impede this process? Were there a rational choice, can the Negro subculture successfully resist the pressure for conformity exerted upon it by the dominant culture? Can they (Negroes) revitalize and regenerate the subculture?

Negroes will argue, and often glibly, that they are not concerned with assimilation but with integration (i.e., total acceptance without discrimination) and that the prospects for the former are very remote. Hence, they dismiss the question as academic. Although the probability of assimilation is remote, the question is not psychologically insignificant for the Negroes. It is significant, in part, because one's attitude toward assimilation may or may not foster the feeling of separateness and will determine the intensity of one's effort to merge into the larger culture and society. However, the question is particularly important during this period of rapid improvement in the Negro's status and the trend toward integration. These changes, in themselves, are sources of anxiety to many Negroes.[1] Although Negroes do not

---

[1] It is interesting to note that a report of a two-year study of Negro and white attitudes toward integration, prepared for the State Commission on Civil Rights in Connecticut by Elmo Roper, revealed that although 90 per cent of Negroes questioned hoped for integration and favored it (in most phases of activities), 37 per cent voiced some misgivings for racial mixing in purely social affairs, especially, "parties," 46 per cent whites questioned objected to racial mixing in purely social affairs. "Connecticut Ends Study of Integration" by David Anderson, *New York Times,* April 14, 1961, p. 21.

express their concern publicly, the writer found that it was widely, but privately, voiced in and outside the Muslim movement. This concern and their ambivalent attitudes—be it at the level of conscious or unconscious awareness—explain, in part, why so many Negroes pay attention to black nationalism but do not actively support the Muslim movement, which is only a specific manifestation of their uncertainties. This question involves the "destiny" of the Negro people in America. We should seek to understand it; we should not explain it away. The price for assimilation is clear; the price for non-assimilation is not obvious. If, however, the sense of separateness and ethnic consciousness, now developing, were to dominate, society at large will have to pay a price for minority exclusiveness, especially for the kind now fostered by the Muslim movement.

Ideologically and culturally, however, the assimilationist strand has been stronger among Negroes. The dominance of this strand is already discernible and much stronger among the middle- and upper-class Negroes and intellectuals.[2] But this strand is somewhat weaker among the lower classes because the realities of their social situation do not support the assimilationist mentality. Consequently, the sense of separateness and ethnic consciousness actually dominates their lives. This feeling has always been present but it lacked positive articulation. The intensification of these feelings is one of the most important developments in the contemporary social situation of American Negroes.

Perhaps, the black nationalists' agitation is the loudest expression of a "manifesto of identity"—the Negroes' conscious, though slow, awakening to their heritage of abuse and degradation, and, especially, to their possible destiny as human beings. It may well signal the beginning of the end of the Negroes' aimless and vain desire to hide their dark skins behind a white mask. The manifesto of identity is a subjectivity: its voice reflects the past and the present and perhaps the future as well. It requires no real objects and relationships for its expression; yet in a significant way, the manifesto brings to public attention "voices from within

---

[2] Elmo Roper, the chairman of the Connecticut Civil Rights Commission report, referred to previously, explains that Negroes harboring racial prejudice against white people are either well-educated Negroes who have come up from the South and are resentful of their treatment there, or else are northern Negroes of poor education. *Christian Science Monitor*, April 14, 1961, p. 6.

the veil" and subtle and imperceptible changes which are occurring among the black masses. They are voices heralding perhaps the psychological and spiritual liberation of the black masses from the shackles of a past that still haunts the present. The manifesto announces their "presence" in America and their impatience and disaffection with the limitations imposed upon their "equality in opportunity." Their impatience and disaffection cannot be disassociated from the important changes (most contributing significantly to the general improvement of the Negroes) in the United States as a whole and in the Negro community or from the rising protest of millions in the non-white world against discrimination and exploitation based solely on racial or religious distinctions.

The "voices from within the veil" and the manifesto of identity do not deny the Negro's Americanism. Indeed, they affirm what is commonly known: that the Negro is American in heart, loyalties, and in everything else. In its mild forms the manifesto of identity is best expressed in the "Negro History Week" and by such organizations as the American Society of African Culture or the Afro-American Heritage Association. Its voice is a reaffirmation of the Negroes' faith in the possibilities offered by the pluralistic character of American society for their cultural, intellectual, and spiritual development. In its extreme form, the Muslim movement is the best example; it reveals how deeply the cancer of American racism has infected all its parts, making the oppressed and the oppressor mutually depraved.

The study of black nationalism illustrates the desperate character of the social situation of the lower-class Negroes in the large northern cities and the tensions which arise from this situation. We tried to show that their life is devoid of meaning and purpose. They are estranged from the larger society which they seek to enter, but which rejects them. Similarly, they are estranged from their own group which they despise. The result of this feeling of dual alienation is apathy, futility, and emptiness of purpose. In a psychological sense, many are lonesome within and outside their own group. They are rootless and restless. They are without an identity, i.e., a sense of belonging and membership in society. In this situation, there is neither hope nor optimism. In fact, most lower-class Negroes in these large cities see little or no "future" for themselves and posterity. This is partly because they have no faith in themselves or in their potential as black men in America and especially because important decisions which shape their lives appear entirely beyond their control. We should stress, however, that the sense of social estrangement and alienation is not limited to the Negroes. In fact, it is a problem common to urban dwellers. The consequence for a meaningful life is, in varying degrees, the same for Negroes as well as others in comparable social situations. The point, however, is that the impact of contemporary urban tensions and anxieties on an already marginal and despised group is dramatic and paralyzing. It corrupts the personality of its victims, depriving them of any sense of human worth and dignity.

Three more factors in the contemporary social situation of Negroes help to explain the growing sense of separateness and ethnic consciousness among the Negro masses: the bifurcation of the Negro caste, i.e., the emergence of a real Negro middle class and the Negro's re-definition of himself not only in terms of the whites but in relation to this "new" class; his re-definition of himself in relation to Africa; and his reactions to the traditional Negro institutions and leadership groups in terms of these new definitions.

The bifurcation of the caste, especially in the North, is an important development of which the implications are not generally recognized. Nevertheless, the emergence of a Negro middle-class may have serious consequences for the Negro masses, creating an "imbalance" within the Negro community. One obvious consequence is that lower-class Negroes are beginning to re-define themselves not only in relation to the white society but also to the Negro middle- and upper-class "society." For this reason, they resent middle-class Negroes whose social situation is incomparably better than theirs. This situation is important for understanding the character of race relations in the North. First, the position of the middle-class Negroes tends to obscure the problems of the lower-class Negroes, in part because Negro "progress" (with some justification) is defined largely in middle-class terms; it is measured by the conspicuous consumption of the middle- and upper-class Negroes, who, in fact, have found their identity with the white middle-class. As individuals, they can escape the open contempt which Northern whites have for the less fortunate of their race. They, too, display haughtiness toward the lower-class Negroes. The "bonds of solidarity in chains" which previously characterized the relationship between them is no longer apparent, i.e., the fact that in the past middle- and upper-class Negroes were able to identify with the struggles and aspirations of lower-class Negroes. The interests of the middle-class are different and, in some measure, lower-class Negroes are estranged from them. But, like middle-classes every- where, the essentially middle-class Negro leadership takes for granted that its strivings represent unquestionably the interest of the masses. This may well be, but the estrangement between the two classes is incontestable. The important point is that precisely because lower-class Negroes are beginning to define themselves in relation to the Negro "image" portrayed by the middle-class and are attracted to it, they are also repelled by it because their actual conditions do not permit genuine identifica- tion with the middle-class Negroes. As it is in their relations with the white society, lower-class Negroes tend to withdraw and disassociate themselves from the middle- and upper-class Negroes. This estrangement suggests the beginning of class con- sciousness and conflict among the Negro masses, directed not against whites, but against the Negro middle and upper classes. This development aggravates tensions in the Negro community and produces distrust of the middle-class leadership among the lower-class Negroes.

These Negroes feel powerless not only in relation to the white- power complex but also to what appears to them as the monopoly of power by Negro middle-class leadership. Black nationalism, especially the Muslim movement, reflects this sense of dual mar- ginality and impotence in both power centers. But an important distinction should be made here: Although black nationalism is a general reaction against whites as "possessors" of vital social, economic, and political power, the nationalists do not question, except in utopian and religious terms, the legitimacy of the white- power monopoly, nor have they sought to alter it. Instead, their sense of impotence produces a need for withdrawal and racial separation (a desire for a homeland) as the means by which Negroes might become masters of their destiny. However, the Muslim movement reflects the increasing class consciousness and conflict[3] among the lower-class Negroes and questions, specifically,

---

[3] That this conflict has not found widespread organized expression is not important for our analysis.

the legitimacy of the Negro middle-class leadership. In other words, the movement questions the "monopoly" of power by the middle-class leadership in defining both the "needs" and "destiny" of the Negro people in America. It questions the trend toward integration which its leaders see as a trend toward assimilation. Furthermore, its leaders question the "balance" between the ideal of integration and the definition of lower-class Negro "needs" in practical terms. The Muslim movement, in a real sense, is an attempt to alter the power relationship within the Negro community. The concerns now voiced by the black nationalists may well determine the character and style of future Negro leadership in their communities.

Another defect in the contemporary social situation of the urban Negro masses is the impotence of traditional Negro institutions in dealing with either the psychological or practical needs of their community. For a long time, these institutions and leadership groups have been the interpreters of the social scene for the masses of Negroes. Of these, the Negro church is the most important. There is evidence that the Negro church has lost its significance for the urban proletarian who seeks to define his situation in terms of the church. However, where its influence is still felt, the Negro church is particularly culpable for its general lack of concern for the moral and social problems of the community. Rather than face the problem of the degradation of its people and take positive action for moral, cultural, and economic reconstruction, it has been accommodatory. Fostering indulgence in religious sentimentality, and riveting the attention of the masses on the bounties of a hereafter, the Negro church remains a refuge, an escape from the cruel realities of the here and now. Furthermore, evidence abounds of the misuse of the pulpit for furthering personal ambitions at the expense of the already harshly exploited masses. The grim fact is that the pulpit, with exceptions spread far and wide, has become during the present century and especially in the large cities of the North, a route to social mobility for the charlatans in the Negro community. There is some evidence, however, of growing realization of their social responsibilities among many Negro church leaders. The most important evidence is the Southern Christian Leadership Conference, led by the Rev. Dr. Martin Luther King, Jr.[4] The same concern was shown by Dr. Joseph H. Jackson, President of the five-million-member National Baptist Convention, who recently announced the purchase of 600 acres of farmland for resettlement of Negro tenant and sharecropper families dispossessed of any means of livelihood by whites in Fayette and Haywood Counties as reprisals for their attempt to exercise the right to vote.[5] In large measure, however, both the Negro Church and other traditional leadership groups do not seem to appreciate how debased the life of the urban lower-class Negro is, nor the magnitude of effort in thought and action required for the reconstruction of the "Souls of Black Folk."

Lastly, the liberation movements and the emergence of the independent African states have had a significant impact on the Negro's total redefinition of himself, in relation to both his situation in America and to Africa. These events have not only awakened an unprecedented interest in Africa but have led, in a limited way at least, to what may be called "an African orientation." This does not mean that their effort to re-define themselves in relation to Africa is an expression of their desire to emigrate there. The practical importance of their African orientation should not be exaggerated. It should be balanced against the strong integration and assimilationist trends. We may observe, however, that recent developments in Africa have led a great many Negroes to identify with the struggles and aspirations of the African people. This, together with the domestic developments and changes, appears to create a psychological situation fostering and intensifying the sense of separateness and ethnic consciousness among the masses. This psychological situation fosters among Negroes a new self-image, pride, and an impatient and urgent desire for equality, personal dignity and self-assertion. In some measure, the consequences of their "new" psychology are evident in the confidence shown by southern Negro student "sit-in" demonstrations. Similarly, the emotional appeal, though otherwise limited, of black nationalism to the Northern urban Negro

---

[4] See Martin Luther King, Jr., *Stride Toward Freedom: The Montgomery Story* (New York, Harper, 1958).

[5] *The New York Courier,* March 25, 1961, sec. 2, p. 18. The *Courier* editorially described Dr. Jackson's action as "Statesmanship in the Pulpit."

masses suggests the same psychological changes.[6] We might add, qualifiedly, that the Negro's need for an identity and his desire for equality and dignity lead him increasingly to merge his aspirations with those of millions throughout the non-white world who are protesting against discrimination and exploitation. They, too, are caught in the "revolution of rising expectations!"

Elijah Muhammad, then, emerges against this background of tensions, change, and of neglect by the traditional Negro institutions and leaders; the failure of the white society to extend "equality in opportunity" to the Negro people, the Negro's dual sense of alienation and marginality; and the increasing sensitivity of the masses to their lowly material fortunes and the anxieties about their "destiny" in America. Keeping this background in mind, and disregarding but not condoning the excesses of Muhammad's ideological concoctions or racial mysticism, it is clear that his is a unique effort to reconstruct the Negro soul, by providing a "world" (*a mystique*) in which one could be black and unashamed, and by regenerating the Negro's moral and social values. So far as the writer knows, no Negro has ever dared to tackle the bewildering problems of the "Negro in the mud" with equal vigor and such obdurate determination as Mr. Muhammad. Seen in this light, and in the light of the limited alternatives open to these Negroes, the Nation of Islam, with its moral and economic reforms, provides a way out for these Negroes. The ideological and racialist excesses are more symptomatic and symbolic than crucial in themselves. They reflect the harsh cruelties, discontent, and the grave social malaise which afflict millions of Negroes in America. Stated simply, the message of the Nation of Islam is this: Despite important, though slow, changes which have occurred in the Negro's formal status as citizen, the lot of the masses of Negroes in the North has not changed in

---

[6] It is interesting to note that Dr. Joseph H. Jackson announced recently that the National Baptist Convention has sent a three-man commission to Liberia with a view to arranging for purchase of five thousand acres of land for young Negroes interested in resettling there. Although Dr. Jackson stressed that his project was not a "Back-to-Africa" movement, it is significant that this is the first commission of this nature sent to Africa since the abortive effort of Garvey in the twenties (*Courier,* p. 18). For our analysis, what we describe as "an African Orientation" is important because for the first time in recent history, some Negroes are beginning to look to Africa as a possible alternative to the United States. Some are interested in business and cultural ties, but there are many who are interested in emigration.

substance. Evidence of pauperization, cultural disorientation, and moral degradation persists in spite of, and perhaps because of, the facade of public progress. These, Muhammad asserts, exist in spite of the fact that inequalities between blacks and whites are not legislated in the North; that the subordination of the masses of Negroes in the North reveals a few stubborn facts of social life which no amount of declarations of good intentions or wishful optimism can obviate. The first, he says, is the unequal distribution of political and economic power between blacks and whites. The possibility of an equalization of this distribution of vital social power is too remote to warrant speculation; but for a long time, there will exist Negro communities, and the position of Negroes is likely to remain marginal. Thus, Negro striving for advancement, Mr. Muhammad says, is fundamentally circumscribed by their awareness of this fact. Their formal freedom is concomitantly limited by the substantive limitations as well as by their perception of the limitations. Yet within these restrictions, Negroes can give meaning to their freedom.

Formal freedom, insists Muhammad, without a substantive basis is, in effect, meaningless. Substantive freedom, a people's style of life—material, cultural, moral and a sense of human dignity—cannot be bestowed upon people who do not want it, and if they do, are not prepared to help themselves and make the sacrifice necessary for its attainment; they must help create the conditions for it. Thus, if the masses of Negroes are to rise in the social scale, if they are to gain respect from others, if they are to be regarded as human beings rather than social outcasts, they must become consciously aware of their predicament, their degradation which is the bond of their common identity. They must also become conscious of their opportunities, however limited, and must take advantage of them. It is pointless to indulge in the fantasy that through some biological miracle black Americans will be transformed into white Americans or that the Negro communities will disappear in the foreseeable future.

Muhammad is convinced that the chief obstacle to be overcome is the "mentality" of the masses of Negroes. This is the true enemy of their advancement and progress. The result of centuries of oppression, it has helped to produce the moral and material conditions in which the Negro masses now find themselves. The enemy of the Negro people, he maintains, is not simply white people, but also the "value system" of the subculture.

The writer is convinced that Muhammad's ideological pronouncements, which are popularly termed "black supremacy," are aimed at purging lower-class Negroes of their inferiority complex. The "real" rather than the "ostensible" enemy of the Nation of Islam or of the Negro masses in general, is not the white people *per se*, but the Negro himself—his subculture, his image of himself and of his "place" in society, his attitude toward white people, and his idealization of all that is white. For the point of view of all black nationalists, the Negro can never be really free until he has purged from his mind all notions of white superiority and Negro inferiority and thus ceases to despise himself and his group. In doing so, he may have to shed the outward appearances of white culture and, most importantly, the "old time" religion. Indeed, they insist that Negroes should proudly accept rather than deny any contrasts between them and whites. Thus, it seems, the mission of the Nation of Islam is to reverse the process toward assimilation by means of militant separatism.

The process by which whites have been able to create and sustain the Negro's image of his own inferiority is known in common parlance as "brainwashing." In Muhammad's teaching, this process is known as "tricknowledgy." It would appear to the observer that it takes another kind of "tricknowledgy" to undo the former. This in the writer's view, is in part the significance of the racial doctrines, especially the eschatology emphasizing the eventual "supremacy" of the Black Nation. If, indeed, Muhammad is aware that whites used "tricks" to "fool" the Negro, then it is plausible that his eschatology or other doctrines of "racial supremacy" are gimmicks meant for the consumption of his followers and for combatting the "enemy within"—the Negro's "mentality." If this is correct, the frequent comparison of the Muslim movement with the Ku Klux Klan or with the White Citizens Council misses the point and has only a superficial relevance. Although alike in the crudity of their racial diatribes, they differ significantly in their objectives—for instance, the Muslims do not seek to deprive their fellow citizens of their political rights.

The Nation of Islam represents an esoteric, in-group struggle to provide standards by which the social, cultural, and moral life of the Negro masses can be raised to a meaningful community fabric. It seeks an outlet for Negro striving and performance. The movement combines the attractions of religion, nationalism, and political "pies in the sky" with a peculiar sense of belonging and achievement, and proposes the possibility of "greater" achievement for its members. The Nation assists its members to strive for traditional American middle-class values while maintaining their identity with the Negro community.

However, these values are interpreted for the members via the dogma of Islam, which in a direct and uncompromising way, assists them to overcome lower-class values which are held to impede the advancement of the Negro masses. Religious and nationalistic symbols, combined with a mutilated version of western eschatology, endow the practical and moral concerns of the members with meaning and a strong sense of purpose and destiny. However, these ideological strands seem to dominate the "community" fabric and conceal the socially relevant aspects of Mr. Muhammad's teachings, the primary concern of which is the "quality" of life of the urban lower-class Negroes. Although the ideological strands give the Nation of Islam an appearance of a wholly anti-white movement, properly conceived, it is uncompromisingly anti-lower-class Negro values, anti-white paternalism and injustice. Perhaps, more than the movement has been credited, it is far more opposed to the entire "way of life" of the lower-class Negro and the "dependence" mentality of their leaders than it appears.

The Nation of Islam is important not because it tells whites how bitterly Negroes feel about their present conditions, but for showing the Negro masses "why" they feel the way they do, "how" they may get out of their degradation, and "how" they may become self-respecting citizens. The Nation sets standards of achievement and excellence for its members and interprets for them standards of morality and economic norms generally cherished by middle-class Americans. (Of course there are some deviations.) The Nation recognizes the needs of Negroes, like other human beings, for membership and identity in some community. It insists that Negroes have the capacity to redeem themselves and recover their sense of human worth; that they must take the initiative in their struggle for human dignity. The alternative to these admonitions, says Muhammad, is continued complacency, moral deterioration, cultural degradation, crime, juvenile delinquency, and social and cultural stagnation.

Negro middle-class leadership being what it is and white attitudes being essentially unchanged in the vital areas of housing, equal opportunities in employment, etc., even in the Northern cities—what logical type of leadership can one envisage emerging from the deplorable conditions of the northern ghettos? What alternatives exist for meeting the urgent needs of the Negro communities except through an appeal to Negro initiative? It seems conceivable that if the masses of Negroes were in the *mood* for the Nation of Islam or for something akin to it, under the right kind of conditions and leadership, communal initiative (call it nationalism or what you will), not chauvinism, holds some promise as a way out for them. If this should happen, then it would be tragic if the white society did not understand it. The white society may even encourage it. In fact it promises to be for the good of society. In communal-oriented activities, presently woefully lacking, Negroes would discover their identity and would best reflect what is good about America through self-assertion. It might enable them to develop their potential, a greater sense of the "public interest," and to participate more constructively in the society. The Negro is unquestionably an American, "reluctantly" at times, even as the deviant doctrines of Mr. Muhammad show; yet he is a member of a group with four centuries of unique experiences and traditions that cannot be easily wished away. Besides, the Negro, though removed by centuries from Africa, has never been, and cannot now be expected to be, indifferent to the land of his forebears. This remote heritage, no matter how insignificant its content may be, is part and parcel of the Negro's being. This too, like his Americanism, should be understood. In these circumstances, sentimentality toward assimilation or toward chauvinistic nationalism is blatantly wishful, unrealistic, and contrary to fact, in so far as the masses of Negroes are concerned.

American Negroes have contributed to American culture not by denying their identity (or contrasts) but by asserting it through music, folklore, etc., in spite of the harsh circumstances in which they found themselves. Indeed, they stand to contribute more to the culture and welfare of their society by recognizing and appreciating their own identity, rather than by despising themselves. Until most have been assimilated, the desire for ethnic self-assertion will continue to manifest itself in their social and cultural life, in private as well as in public matters, though taking various forms.

The Muslim movement is a grand reaction to the American scene and especially the Negro's position in it; yet the scenery (the stage set) shackles and delimits the drama—the potential for meaningful political or social action. Herein lie the factors which limit its social usefulness. It is handicapped by its very "style of life," i.e., the mentality, the social and moral values and economic habit of the group which it seeks to redeem. Its separatist ideology is irreconcilably in conflict with the dominant assimilationist thinking of the vast majority of Negroes. On the other hand, it is limited by its anti-white ideology which strikes deep at the Negroes' fears as well as those of whites—their fear of a possibility of a "Black Revenge." The stark reality is that there can be no substantial or disruptive political action by the Nation of Islam other than that akin to the campus gadfly —a nuisance, mildly frightening, but actually not as deadly as the tsetse fly. Yet a frightened public or civic authorities, incensed by a sensationalist press, may well be led in such a way as to precipitate the fulfillment of alarmist prophecies.

JOHN PEPPER CLARK

Over the years—and especially in the past decade—many thousands of African students have come to American schools and colleges on scholarships from the United States government or funded from private sources. So too have come hundreds of government officials, educators, journalists, technical and cultural personnel, to perfect their knowledge and skills and return to do more effective jobs for their countries. How one of these programs (and, indeed, the host country itself) looked to one visiting scholar is revealed in a provocative book, *America, Their America* (London, 1964; New York, 1969), by the Nigerian poet and playwright John Pepper Clark.

Born in 1935 and educated at the University of Ibadan, Clark worked initially as a journalist with the *Daily Express* in Lagos and later as a lecturer in English at the University of Lagos. He has published two books of verse and three verse plays. His talents as a writer having been widely recognized, and with African and American friends ready to help, his securing of a coveted one-year Parvin Fellowship at Princeton was not difficult. In fact, Clark was not sure he wanted it, and his friend Langston Hughes had even advised him not to take up the Parvin with its full year commitment, and to accept instead a short visit "on a State Department ticket" for which he could easily qualify, and which would leave him more fancy-free as befits a poet. But it seems that Clark opted for something more

213

ambitious and journalistic—the Parvin with its rich choice of courses at Princeton, opportunities for extensive travel, and almost unlimited access to editorial sanctums and other seats of influence and power. The result was his report *America, Their America*—certainly a virtuoso outpouring of contempt for practically everything and everybody in America, although, undeniably, he encountered provocation in what seemed to him chauvinist smugness and vulgarity in many places.

For our present purpose Clark's reports on his involvement with the Afro-Americans are the relevant ones. The selection given is composed of three distinctly significant passages. In the first Clark shows himself in a Negro bar in Princeton intruding a censorious note into the cozy chaffing and camaraderie of the place. In the second he flays the black bourgeoisie and the intellectual organization AMSAC—the now defunct American Society of African Culture (see pp. 7 and 99)—for their effete isolation from the struggles of the masses. In the last passage he tells us of two black couples who befriended him and opened their homes and hearts to him, and he concludes, typically, "It seemed a simple and straight natural relationship could not exist for long between my American Negro friends and myself without their wanting me to do something or another to help them."

The disgusted Afro-American in the Princeton bar who exclaims about Clark, "There he goes! . . . The fellow's come from Africa to do our fighting for us," has shrewdly perceived one of Clark's underlying notions, the condescending idea that American Negroes have been supine victims who need prodding and tactical lessons from Africans who have had the experience of "kicking out the colonial masters." This is the obverse of a certain condescension in some black Americans who think they can go to Africa and shape policy for developing nations.

Mr. Clark's displeasure with the Negro middle-class is based on heavy borrowing from E. Franklin Frazier's famous study *Black Bourgeoisie* (1957). In Clark's hands sociological categories become weapons of petty-minded castigation instead of tools of understanding. Of course, he is hardly original in this kind of abuse. "Middle-class values" have long been a hissing-term, and, in fact, especially so in the intraclass struggles of the middle-class itself. Mr. Frazier was himself a member of the "black bourgeoisie"; Mr. Clark obviously belongs to the equivalent class in Nigeria (his brother, he tells us, is a member of his country's diplomatic service, posted to India). Why, one wonders, does Mr. Clark find AMSAC's acceptance of money from foundations so suspect when he himself calmly weighs whether to take a grant from the Parvin Foundation or from the State Department?

Mr. Clark's performance, as he candidly reports it in his book, illustrates in striking fashion some of the ideas and attitudes that militate against fruitful relations between Africans and Afro-Americans.

The Garment of Damnation

"Hey, honey," he motioned to Becky, "let that drink be on me. No, no," he brushed off my half-hearted protests. "You come from Africa, don't you?"

"That's right," I said.

"Then we are brothers," he announced. I took his offer and there in the glare of eyes stronger than all the neon lights dancing in the mist of the place I ventured to ask whether he was a Black Muslim.

"I ain't nothing of the sort," he stayed me with one hand as the other ferreted in his overcoat pocket for loose dollar bills and change to pay for the beer he was standing me, his brother from Africa. "No, I ain't nothing like what you call a Black Muslim," he underlined his point. "I do my job at the post office and when I feel like it, I come over here for my scotch and soda."

"That's right," said Sam from the corner into which he had sunk. "That's right, son. A man's got no right not to serve you a pint some, after a day in yonder salt mines. Now, look here, honey, pour me out the poison. Will you?"

"I knew we were heading for that." A daughter kicked the counter. Everybody laughed.

"I don't need no excuse to have me booze," Sam dismissed it all.

Somebody had put another dime or quarter in the jukebox, and now a big raucous voice was belting away at a number which instantly got everyone there clapping and swaying on their seats. A few even joined in the singing, swinging to the beat, snapping their fingers at no one in particular, and before long, they were shouting, eyes shut tight, as lustily as the local star in the slot, only being much more bodily there, their combined voice filled out the place more than the smoke cloud from their cigarettes.

"Not so loud, folks," Becky appealed to them.

"Hell," one said, "is there a damned place a man can blow his top without some kind of cop showing up?"

"What do you want to blow your top for anyway?" Sam smirked, "When the goddam bottom of it stays solid from the light of day?"

"Those of the Black Muslims don't like such music, nor drink," I said, again very tactless. "They say both make you sleep."

"You pity us very much, don't you?" the young man who had bought me a drink pinned me down.

"Why do you say that?" I asked.

"He should hev a long time ago, young man," an elderly woman came in. "I been hearing all that's said here this night, and don't you go away thinking I don't. We brothers and daughters meet here as one family. But it don't look you like our ways, least of all, our drinking and singing habits." I made to say something but there again was Sam.

"Don't say nothing," he raised his balmy palm. "Every sinner got a right to get boozed before the moon turns round. Don't they in Africa—or ain't that the country you from?"

I said yes. "Then, let's drink all together as one family," he held up my hand. "None of us, not with all the blessed Indian and African tribes behind us, can push the Kennedys off their high seat, can we?"

"Why not?" I asked.

"There he goes!" someone said in disgust. "The fellow's come from Africa to do our fighting for us."

* * *

Of the large body of professionals, artists, and intellectuals whose shady colouring assigns them to a sort of limbo in the American hierarchy, I saw very little to win me over from the unsparing views of the late Professor Frazier in his *Black Bourgeoisie*, although much to enlist for them sympathy and understanding. Daubed in a white society as Negro lawyers, Negro doctors, Negro professors and Negro writers or entertainers, and therefore not quite belonging to the civilized and prosperous professional guilds and cults, this class of the blacks in America struck me as falling into two main groups. The first, much embarrassed that they stand out at all, would rather, like members of the middle class anywhere, that they were left alone to pursue their slow pension schemes in peace. When not worrying about the rent or mortgage on the house, or what brand of car to open new installment payments on now the Joneses have changed their own, and whether Jack Jr. is smart enough to get into college and play football, they spend the little that is left of their time in pottering about, adding gadgets to the house, or better still, behind the closed doors of the club or fraternity lodge, safe away from wives who are for ever reminding them of the next rung to climb on the ladder of success. At house parties, they sit close by the bar, and especially if the hosts are white liberals and that kind, they conscientiously try to talk shop and swap stale jokes and wise-cracks carried over from another party no less wet and dreary, while all the time the women are together head to head like hens, scratching up this gossip about some neighbours out of hearing, or ruffling their own proud feathers and tempers with remembrance of gorgeous holidays past, and with hopes and plans of those still to come in some outlying state or far-off country in Europe and elsewhere.

"Oh, John and I took the family to California last time."

"Yes, wasn't that real wonderful!"

"Everybody ought to do the United States from coast to coast."

"And did you drive all the way?"

"Arthur made all of us fly, you know."

"But, Sue, I still think a month or so in Europe is the best."
Such often is the small talk engaging the entire mind of those
of this special sub-class of Negroes. All of which helps them
like drug and drink to forget there is a strange destiny that has
consigned their kind to a social limbo that neither touches the
hell of the unemployed, uneducated and desperate of their race
nor the heaven of the lowest of the whites to whose heights they
aspire but cannot get assumption. Yet it is not uncommon to run
into some, like the vivacious and formidable lady I met at a
New Year party in Princeton, who when pricked briefly out of
her cocoon and emphasis, swore something to the effect and in
the hearing of her white hosts that whoever feels persecuted and
oppressed under the sacred Constitution of the United States,
the most democratic country on earth, deserves to remain so!

Members of the other sub-group, far from being faceless and
forgetful of the garment of damnation in which America has
for long invested the black in their midst, make a profession of
their identity, and indeed a booming business out of it. Its
members, like birds of the same feather, which in fact they are,
very much move and associate in groups, societies and organizations. These sprout all over the land and are as diverse among
themselves as one species of mushroom is edible and other fatal.
Apparently, the one strain common to all these groups is their
frenetic strife in one form or another to improve the lot of the
black and make it possible for weed and wheat to survive together in the fabulous garden that is America. And they nearly
all enjoy the backing of strong influential private donors, benefactors and foundations, several of them discreetly anonymous
and not showing their hands. In fact, the patronage in some cases
appears so lavish and guided that one or two uncharitable and
ungrateful critics have spotted behind them some very muscular
arm of state or corporate power with a great deal up its sleeves
of lace and gold.

Typical and at once unique is the American Society of African
Culture all very well set up in down-town New York. As is evident from its name, the society does not present a broad front
in the fight to attain for the Negro an equal place, taken for
granted in his native American society. Rather, the big point

those in it make is the home they have found anew in Africa. Thus its sponsors, most of them Lincoln alumni, would shut out even those whites with genuine interest and perhaps better knowledge of Africa, a restriction and reverse bias that should stand the society in good stead if ever it comes out for sit-ins, freedom-rides, street demonstrations, and popular expressions of that kind, as the very respectable and gouty NAACP has had to do recently. But fortunately for AMSAC, it is always in better company and far removed from the bad breath and sweat of the man uptown in Harlem. Like some bored old lady with a lot of money and who is always scared to be alone by herself, the society is for ever thinking up some party or platform. And it has a nose that smells out an honoured guest from abroad even before he has set foot on U.S. soil. Every leader of any delegation from Africa, preferably in sumptuous agbada or kente, is sedulously scouted out, courted and asked over by AMSAC to a party for which he pays with an address, often with only very little to do with culture except in the widest sense of the word. And of course no artist from Africa, on a grant the society knows little of or cares little about emulating, is ever missed on the list of notables the society constantly compiles to its credit, comfort and complacency.

In such circumstances, it matters very little if the religious and social significance of an original Bambara head-piece copied and proudly hung up on the wall of the AMSAC centre is completely lost and forgotten there. Perhaps it had not even been recognized to begin with. Indeed the mix-up and masquerade could be most crushing. The story goes that on one occasion the proud AMSAC host actually slapped on the back the honourable gentleman from Gabon and asked in great cheer how the old capital city of all the Congos was doing after the maverick Lumumba!

Most symptomatic of the social-climbing and status-seeking habits that probably provide the strongest driving force behind the AMSAC was that grand ball it gave last Christmas for all African ambassadors to the United Nations. Like the great festival of folly with which the society had earlier sought fame in Lagos, the gala affairs featured luminaries and debutantes but gave little or no room to undiscovered stars and ordinary folks teeming in the ghettos of Harlem, perhaps for fear they might darken the gleaming hall and gates of the Hotel Americana. All was white ties and tails and mink stoles, and the fabulous Duke Ellington himself was there with his band to serenade everybody into dreamland. But not much dancing was done that night since everybody who was anybody or as likely as not part of that bleak stratum of society starved of high cocktail occasions, made sure of a place on the floor so as not to lose for another season or life this one chance of rubbing shoulders with the great of the land. With me that night was my friend James Ward, an old boy of Princeton only now beginning to put his weight behind the lever to upturn for once and all the oppressive burden his black people have had to bear all these many years. And between us sat in dazzling dress his old girl friend of schooldays in Philadelphia. They seemed quite overwhelmed with all the pomp and circumstance of the occasion, especially during the pompous roll-call of honoured guests present. First of them all, it turned out amid great cheers, was the distinguished United States Ambassador to the UN, Mr. Adlai Stevenson. The great man was even prevailed upon to make a speech and was walked to the rostrum by the super-host of the occasion Dr. John A. Davis, all beaming and sweating with satisfaction. Later, when Duke struck up another tune well-remembered with tears by many, and when hosts and guests began shuffling on their feet and basking in all the limelight, Dr. Davis and the partner in his arms stopped graciously in front of me.

"Meet my wife," he said. We exchanged how-do-you-do, after which he kindly added: "Have a dance with her." I shook my head, and he asked why not. Without thought, I told him there and then I was disappointed in the whole show. Both husband and wife looked appropriately shocked, and appeared not to understand. So that in quick succession I asked: Why the build-up for the American Stevenson? How was it not one of his excellent friends from Africa had been given a similar opportunity of saying a word or two, or wasn't the party for them after all, but in fact for Ambassador Stevenson? And if he had to speak at all as the home representative, should that not be after the doyen among the African guests of honour had had the floor? Or was it simply giving the great man a big hand, which he needed somewhat, after being mauled and daubed a dove and an appeaser in the Cuba eyeball-to-eyeball aftermath? Undoubtedly I had goofed, but the Davis couple took it all very politely, and as they resumed dancing and fell back among the convivial crowd on the floor, the man suddenly brightened up and said laughingly over his wife's fair shoulders that I might probably be correct about the tail-end of my query.

From the upper middle-class club of AMSAC to the "Family" night gathering that branches of the New York Public Library in Harlem sponsor in a sort of healthy rivalry among themselves, it is not really a long walk. These occasions, usually ones of friendly encounter, sometimes between local writers and their readers, and at other times on a triangular level with visiting African authors brought in, provide a "culture" doses for those of the lower income brackets herded in Harlem as junkets downtown cater for the dilettanti whose one distinction, to quote Frazier, is an indisputable capacity for conspicuous consumption. Apart from that, the taste and indeed the fare are the same between both circles. Each asked me over as a speaking guest, and on each "at home" host and guest were happy to part, never to cultivate each other's company again. Such was the unpleasantness and nausea felt on both sides, a professional hostess, who floats promotion parties for upcoming artists of all kinds, called for her smelling salts, took a sniff or two as my grandmother would her snuff, and turning to an equally embarrassed friend at one of these affairs, said in everybody's hearing: "Of course, the young man may be a genius. But how can I possibly ask friends over to meet him when he shows such a penchant for making enemies?"

There was so much that was wrong with the house of the blacks in America, even among themselves and on the level of artists, that the most well-mannered cousin calling from abroad could not help but be openly critical—unless of course a primitive pride in the family and an equally primitive urge to clean it out and make the place better for all were lacking. It was a unique and rich experience sharing with the black citizens of America their growing excitement and sense of discovery towards Africa, a place only vaguely remembered by them before, and that with absolute shame and horror, from memories of an irrevocable fall, as Christians years ago recalled the doings in the Garden of Eden. Now, not only has this place they had been taught all their lives to look upon as a jungle full of fatal fruits and serpents turned out to be a rich and open plantation farmed all along by foreign squatters for their own benefit, but the black sons of the soil have at last actually risen and driven the exploiters back across the seas from where they came. And it was no mean or distant performances that could be kept out or distorted for the ears of the people. Today, even the bum on Harlem's 125th Street, although he may not be able to read the *New York Times* that prints all the news that is fit to print, and although he may not own a TV set to tune to community-minded stations, can see with his own eyes all the black diplomats at the UN.

Going from one independent country in Africa to another still burning to have its turn, I had observed a similar sense of vicarious satisfaction and feeling of elation that the enemy is at least out of the city gates, although other than those one is defending. In the United States, however, the joy appears even more intense among the emergent Negroes. Their goal, though, is not the African one of expelling the host, but that of kitchenmen, laundry-hands, motor-boys and noncoms, all of them long restricted to the lowest ranks in the armed forces for no just and legitimate cause, demanding at long last a fair share in the victory and spoils with colleagues really having no special abilities and merits to set them up and apart in permanent positions of privilege.

Out of this new emotional response to Africa among the Negroes in America has come a great love for everything African. It is all very heart-warming that a Negro can now get up today and declare the roots of his origin even if he cannot be as definite or far-reaching as President Kennedy disclosing his Irish ancestry to Newark voters also of that extraction. But when he goes collecting masks, and imitations at that, without knowing their religious and social symbols and observance; when he goes sporting drums, called over there tom-toms, in blissful belief that anybody can beat on them, however different in kind and intention, and produce the famous talk for all to grin at; if he goes collecting music from Africa and proclaiming each piece "simple" and "folksy"; then such an "Afro-American," making a profession of his faith among the uninitiated, more silly than cynical, must be called to order before he misleads himself and others into total perdition.

A greater danger still is the habit of identifying this phoney, rushing business partly or wholly with the genuine historical stand of Negritude as established by Aimé Césaire and Léopold Senghor, or with the African Personality, to use Kwame Nkrumah's flamboyant slogan, which is better known in the States. There is an interesting feed-back here. The idea of the African Personality, especially in its political context, derived of course from the Pan-African Movement of Marcus Garvey and Dr. Du Bois, and although both prophets naturally were never ones to listen to each other, it was to the lost black people of America they preached their sermons of Africa that must be redeemed, of an exodus back there, and of the glory and splendour that were its past. It is an irony of fate that today the black educated of America should be falling back upon the very doctrine they rejected and pooh-poohed half a century or so back. That they helped to hurl stones at both wisemen and still would deride them today should the two appear in Alabama or New York City may seem overstating the point. But both men are hardly ever remembered except by a few doubtful faithful squabbling on the fringe of Harlem's murky streets and slums. And more still, the spirit of union which has consecrated for better, for worse several heroes and leaders in Africa, providing for each of their people a pivotal point, has apparently either by-passed America or presented her with so many candidates that they confound themselves.

*   *   *

Surprisingly, the one thing I missed in the U.S. and which I still regret very much was the break-up of my ties with a couple of Negroes out in their comfortable ghettoes and lone posts. I visited my folks of St. John's Street, as I came to call them, quite frequently for a time.

The man had been a Captain in the Army during the War but now he was quite contented with being an attendant by day in some Women's Club in Princeton. His wife worked at night as companion and watch for an old invalid widow or spinster with a lot of money. Together they made a jolly, bustling couple with their jobs, home, and children, the first of which had long since begun earning his own keep. The man used to say to me:

"Look at your friend who went to college, and to Princeton at that, how much dollar do you think he makes in a week with all his education? Of course, I regret not going to college or continuing with my commission, but look here, my wife and I here comb up quite a bit between us. Which is more than you can say for some people with all their libraries and airs."

It was hard arguing this when examples abounded everywhere, depicting the ugly and unbelievable phenomenon in the American firmament of opportunity and plenty which makes many a cleaner and porter, with his odd shifts and spare-time jobs (called moonlighting), as well off as, if not better than, graduate teachers and trained technicians. So although college, they say, is America's best friend, why shouldn't there be drop-outs, and a very heavy rate too among the Negroes, when the unskilled and uneducated can perfectly well afford to marry the girls of their dreams, and both spouses can settle happily ever after in the regular home plus the automobile that are their combined dreams? The only snag is that the unskilled man might perhaps be more exposed to the dangers of settling down in a rut or getting rattled about in shallow grooves, whereas his compatriots with developed brains and skills may make a better fight of it, against automation, perhaps, and so move up the social scale with a fair degree of acceleration. Yes, this probably was so, agreed my Mt. John's folks, and it certainly has been one of the cruel factors that have kept the black man down and out in America for so long. "But things will sure change" they cheered themselves. "Why, look at you here drinking with us when President Goheen wants you over at the college to dine with him."

My other couple, much older and more by themselves, have a thirteen-acre home on a hill some miles outside of Princeton. From there on a clear-skied day the visitor can see New Brunswick some twenty-five miles away. Not having children of their own, and constantly harassed now by land speculators and city planners making designs on their estate, my friends have turned their property into a trust. It was their hope when their large swimming pool was complete, to license the place as a community and holiday centre for the Negroes, just as the Jews and others do for their people. To this end, they actually invited me and other Parvins, that is, the coloured ones only, to dinner one night, so that each of us in turn, being so highly spoken of in Princeton, could bring over to the opening of the centre envoys and other influential people from our countries. Only their presence and sponsorship, they said, could convince the blacks of Princeton that it was time they all got together. Corporate action, the secret of big business corporations like RCA, all very vulnerable if only the black people of the earth will boycott them for exploiting them, was what a centre like theirs would strive to foster in the heart of members. And could all of us there help?

It was a pity they seemed not to know of the wary habits of diplomats, Africans not excepted. And it was so painful that I never saw them again before being chucked out of the country of their birth and beleaguerment. It seemed simple and straight natural relation could not exist for long between my American Negro friends and myself without their wanting me to do something or another to help them. And not really being in a position to help myself, I found it a better policy keeping away, although this too was an unnatural and impossible position. In such circumstances, I often found it more congenial and convenient, while in New York, to walk on Harlem's 125th Street, to skirt Times Square, and to meander among the alleys of Greenwich Village, where for all their pimps, prostitutes, dope-peddlers, and promiscuous clients in homosexual pubs, you knew what exactly you were being solicited for, what the risks and price were, and what was more, your own capability, leaving no tender feelings of loyalty and other susceptibilities trampled behind.

But moving to neutral, commercial ground and refusing to get engaged and involved in the affairs of my embattled friends only served to isolate me more, making me most lonely when in the thick of that human mart where Broadway becomes Times Square.

ALI A. MAZRUI

An African of Moslem background, born in Mombasa, Kenya, in 1933, Ali A. Mazrui is one of Africa's most distinguished social scientists and a prolific writer combining wide-ranging perspectives with a keen Pan-African interest. Dr. Mazrui studied at Manchester, Columbia, and Oxford and was professor and head of the Department of Political Science and Public Administration at Makerere University in Kampala, Uganda. He is presently with the Hoover Institution at Stanford and also teaches at the University of Michigan.

In addition to such scholarly books as *Towards a Pax Africana*, *The Anglo-African Commonwealth*, *On Heroes and Uhuru-Worship*, and *Violence and Thought*, he has also published a provocative novel of ideas, *The Trial of Christopher Okigbo*, which is a heady brew of fantastic fiction, political philosophy, and historical fact.

Having lived and studied in the United States for extended periods, he has firsthand knowledge of the Afro-American community and its connections with African developments. In October, 1965, at the annual meeting of the African Studies Association in Philadelphia, Dr. Mazrui delivered a characteristically lively paper entitled "Borrowed Theory and Original Practice in African Politics," which analyzed the ways in which African nationalism employed in turn the rhetoric of Western liberalism when fighting to win independence from the colonial powers, and the rhetoric of socialism in its struggle to protect newly established regimes against the clamor of clashing internal interests. From that paper we give here only one section, there entitled "Liberalism from America." In this excerpt Professor Mazrui shows how the historic ideology of the American revolution as well as the actual black experience in America both helped to shape the development of nationalism in Black Africa.

He cites the example of Kwame Nkrumah, an "ex-Harlemite," coming back to Harlem as a visiting president of an African country and acting as a "good militant symbol for radical Afro-Americanism." This, says Mazrui, is a form of "recompense that African nationalism has paid to the Negro struggle in America," for Afro-Americans had played a significant part in launching Pan-Africanism on the world stage.

New World Roots of Pan-Africanism

But it was not merely from Britain that English-speaking Africa inherited the liberal ethic. It was also from the United States. By no means uniquely, Americans tend to exaggerate the favorable side of their impact on the minds of others abroad. As the United States has grown into a world power, so has this piece of her traditional vanity—perhaps always ahead of America's real stand in the world. "Everyman," wrote Thomas Jefferson "has two countries—his own and France." Everyman has two countries," echoed Max Lerner two centuries later, "his own and America."[1]

A less sweeping if still rhetorical claim was the one once made by Chester Bowles in an article in the *New York Times Magazine*. It is a claim that other Americans have made—that the

---

[1] *America as a Civilization: Life and Thought in the United States Today* (New York, Simon & Schuster, 1957).

American Revolution was "a revolution intended for all mankind."[2]

One need not accept this assertion in entirety. But in a mood of romantic hyperbole, one could indeed argue that while the French Revolution was the great explosion of democratic ideas, and the Russian Revolution was the great assertion of Marxist ideas, the American Revolution came near to being the great invention of anticolonial ideas and the kind of nationalism which springs therefrom. At any rate, this was the view of Julius Nyerere when he described the occasion of the American Declaration of Independence as "the first time in history that the principles of struggle for freedom from foreign domination had been clearly defined."[3]

Claims about something being done "for the first time" often contain an element of an exaggeration. Moreover, we can dispute Nyerere's assumption that the American struggle in the eighteenth century was really against foreign domination. The British in the eighteenth century were no more foreigners in American eyes than Harold Wilson was a foreigner to Ian Smith when the latter declared Rhodesia's independence in November, 1965. The American War of Independence was indeed a war against colonial rule. What Africans, Asians, and sometimes contemporary Americans are apt to forget is that colonial rule need not be foreign rule. The American War of Independence was much more like a civil war than a war against foreign domination. The rebels were objecting to being treated like second-class Englishmen. They were demanding the rights of first-class Englishmen—"No Taxation without Representation." When they failed to get thoses rights, they decided that, to use the words of Thomas Paine, "'tis time to part!"[4]

When all allowances have been made, however, it still remains true that the American Revolution has been of some

---

[2] See Chester Bowles, "A Revolution Intended for All Mankind," *New York Times Magazine*, December 10, 1961. For a discussion of the risks of the analogy between Afro-Asian national movements and the American War of Independence, see Herbert J. Spiro, *Politics in Africa: Prospects South of the Sahara* (Englewood Cliffs, N.J., Prentice Hall, 1962), pp. 33–35.

[3] Nyerere, "Africa's Place in the World," *Symposium on Africa* (Wellesley, Mass., Wellesley College, 1960), p. 150.

[4] This point is also discussed in my book *The Anglo-African Commonwealth: Political Friction and Cultural Fusion* (Oxford, Pergamon Press, 1967).

relevance for the growth of nationalism in Africa. Yet how could an event way back in the eighteenth century have had any influence on African militants in the twentieth?

The role of American education for Africans is one important link. As a Nigerian student dramatically put it two decades ago, "The first skirmishes in the struggle for political freedom of the 21 million people of Nigeria are being fought in the colleges of the U.S."[5] This too is a romantic exaggeration. But it is at any rate substantially true that Africans who were educated in the United States have tended to be more singleminded in their nationalism than Africans educated in, say, Great Britain. It was perhaps not accidental that the leadership in Ghana passed from British-educated personalities to the primarily American-educated Nkrumah. Nor was it entirely a coincidence that the founding father of modern Nigerian nationalism was Nnamdi Azikiwe, also a product of American education.

But what has made American-educated Africans more militant in their nationalism than British-educated ones? The factor which is directly linked to the American Revolution is, of course, the tradition of anti-imperialism which many Americans continue to subscribe to even if their government does not always do so. There is also the derivative factor that America is a more ideological and more rhetorical country in its politics than Britain usually is. *The Observer* of London might have been overstating the case when it described Communist China and the United States as "the two most ideologically inspired States of the modern world."[6] But it is certainly true that political beliefs tend to be articulated with greater passion and more hyperbole by Americans than by the British. And exposure to such a climate could make an African educated in the United States more ideological and more rhetorical in his own anti-imperialism than his fellow African educated in the British Isles.

A third factor making education in the United States conducive to African militancy is the race issue. In his book on Nigeria, James Coleman put the question in the following terms:

The special situation of the American Negro, into whose company

---

[5] Prince Okechukwu Ikejiani, "Nigeria's Made-in-America Revolution," *Magazine Digest,* January, 1946, p. 57, cited by James S. Coleman, *Nigeria:* California Press, 1960), p. 244.

[6] Editorial, the *Observer* (London), May 9, 1965.

an African student is inevitably thrown, was . . . an important conditioning factor. African students in America were perforce made acutely aware of color discrimination, in itself provocative of racial consciousness.[7]

Coleman went on to point out that West Africans did not meet in their own countries the highly institutionalized and omnipresent discrimination characteristic of Southern states, and to a degree also of Northern states, in America. Racial discrimination in Nigeria (formally outlawed in 1948) was irritating mainly as a symbol of European imperialism, but "it did not engulf the individual and plague him at every turn." Thus many Nigerians encountered racial discrimination on a large scale for the first time when they arrived in the United States.[8]

Coleman was on less solid ground when he suggested that the same sort of racialistic cultural shock, though less pronounced, hit an African student studying in England. On the contrary, a reverse type of shock was more usual. What impressed African students in England in those early days was the apparent racial broadmindedness of the British people in England as compared with the type they encountered at home. Many a student came to draw a sharp distinction between these two types of Britons , in his experience.

And so, while African students studying in the United States found themselves in a more racialistic society than they had in their colonial homes, African students studying in England found themselves in one less racialistic. This is probably one more reason why the American-educated Africans has been the more single-minded in his nationalism.

African attitudes towards the United States are sometimes colored by a feeling of having been betrayed. What then did the Declaration of Independence really mean by "All men are created equal"? Did the Founding Fathers use the argument merely as a debating flourish to justify their unilateral assumption of sovereignty? Was the word *all* in the claim *all men* no more than rhetoric?

It was in the age of Abraham Lincoln that such questions assumed critical importance in the United States. In October, 1858—one hundred years before the First Conference of Inde-

[7] *Nigeria: Background to Nationalism,* p. 245.
[8] *Ibid.*

pendent African States and the All African People's Conference held in Accra in 1958—Judge Douglas was arguing to the American electorate that the Declaration of Independence did not include Negroes when it declared all men to have been created equal. This was Judge Douglas's last joint debate with Lincoln. He accused Lincoln of construing the Declaration to include Negroes. The Judge repudiated any such suggestion as "a slander on the immortal framers of our Constitution."

It was this "slanderous" misinterpretation of the intentions of the Founding Fathers which was later to inspire Africans and Afro-Americans. The roots of Pan-Africanism do, to a certain extent, lie in the New World. West Indians like Marcus Garvey and American Negroes like W. E. B. Du Bois will remain among the founding fathers of Pan-African movements. But in those early days Africans, as well as Afro-Americans, were less stimulated by America's assertion of independence from British rule than by America's egalitarian arguments in support of that independence. In other words, African nationalism in its early days drew its inspiration from the unfulfilled part of the American revolutionary aspirations. Even as late as the Fourth Pan-African Congress in 1923 the central aspiration of Pan-Africanism was less that black men be given their independence, as the American revolutionaries had got theirs, than that "black folk be treated as men," as the American revolutionaries had implied in their words.

Curiously enough, the Fourth Pan-African Congress was held in both London and Lisbon. London as an imperial capital was later to concede to Africans the right of independence. Lisbon, another imperial capital, was to offer to Africans—too late—active racial equality and assimilation, which was all they had asked for in those early days. If the American Revolution had proclaimed "equality" in pursuit of independence, the African nationalists were now seeking full independence in pursuit of racial equality.[9]

Partly arising out of this African desire for national independence, the bonds between the Negroes of the Old World and the Negroes of the New became weaker. After all, it is not

---

[9] See also Ali A. Mazrui, "On the Concept of 'We are all Africans'," *American Political Science Review*, 57, no. 1 (March, 1963). For useful accounts of the earlier Pan-African conferences see Colin Legum, *Pan Africanism* (London, Pall Mall Press and New York, Frederick A. Praeger, 1962), and George Padmore (ed.), *History of the Pan-African Congress* (London, Hammersmith Bookshop, 1947, 1963).

colonialism that the American Negro has been up against; it is a different form of racial handicap. And this difference became important enough to entail different strategies for African nationalism and for the civil rights movement in the United States. It is true that the bonds of shared blackness have far from disappeared even now. Black Rhodesians are among the last Africans to wage a struggle for self-rule. But in spite of their own preoccupations, the one-hundredth anniversary of the Abolition of Slavery in America did not go unnoticed. In September, 1962, the *Zimbabwe News,* the international organ of a banned African nationalist party of Southern Rhodesia, carried an article entitled quite simply "Abraham Lincoln." The general thesis of the article was that the plight of the American Negro had not improved much since slavery was abolished. This was an exaggeration. But it was an exaggeration arising out of a sense of fellowship between black Rhodesians and black Americans. When all this has been said, however, it remains true that African nationalism is now more preoccupied with peculiarly African matters than with problems of the Negro race as a whole.

This situation has been aggravated by the fall of Nkrumah from power. Kwame Nkrumah might not have been a great Ghanaian, but he was, in a sense, a great Afro-American. No African leader was more conscious of his ties with the black people of America than Nkrumah. As we know, Nkrumah himself was educated in the United States. His activities among American Negroes ranged from dating Negro girls to preaching in Negro churches. The book that had the biggest impact on him in his formative years was, he tells us, the testament of Marcus Garvey, the Jamaican who captured the nationalistic imagination of black people in the United States.

At a state dinner to mark Ghana's independence many years later, Nkrumah had occasion to recall Garvey. But just before he mentioned Garvey's name to illustrate a point, he used the dramatic device of asking the band to play Ghana's national anthem. Then he made his point, saying:

Here I wish I could quote Marcus Garvey. Once upon a time, he said, he looked through the whole world to see if he could find a government of black people. He looked around, he did not find one, and he said he was going to create one. Marcus Garvey did not succeed. But here today the work of Rousseau, the work of Marcus Garvey, the work of Aggrey, the work of Caseley Hayford, the work of these illustrious men who have gone before us, has come to reality at this present moment.[10]

Earlier in the same speech Nkrumah reaffirmed the bonds of Pan-Negroism in the following terms:

There exists a firm bond of sympathy between us and the Negro peoples of the Americas. The ancestors of so many of them come from this country. Even today in the West Indies, it is possible to hear words and phrases which come from various languages of the Gold Coast.[11]

In the history of political Pan-Africanism perhaps the most important Negroes of the Americas alive in 1957 were George Padmore from the West Indies and W. E. B. Du Bois from the United States. To these historic figures Ghana opened her doors on attainment of independence. They died citizens of Ghana. The whole phenomenon was a "Back to Africa" event of unique symbolism.

A year after Ghana's independence Nkrumah visited the United States at the invitation of President Eisenhower. Being his first visit there as Prime Minister of the newly independent Ghana, Nkrumah looked upon the occasion as, in a sense, "the fulfilment of the hopes and dreams of my student days at Lincoln University." Among the places he visited during his stay in the United States was Harlem in New York City. Nkrumah has recorded that "the spectacular and spontaneous welcome given to me by the people of Harlem remains one of the happiest memories of the whole tour."

In the spring of 1961 Nkrumah once again visited Harlem, this time as President of the Republic of Ghana, and addressed a Negro rally there. He reminded his audience that Harlem had once been a home for him. As a visiting Head of State, Nkrumah was careful about what he said on civil rights in his host country. In fact, he hardly mentioned the specific Negro problem of the United States. To some extent his audience was disappointed. Yet his very presence in Harlem as President of an African country was a moment of excitement to the audience and to Nkrumah.[12]

---

[10] Nkrumah, *I Speak of Freedom* (New York, Frederick A. Praeger, 1961), p. 107. See also Ali A. Mazrui, *Towards a Pax-Africana, op. cit.,* pp. 60–61.

[11] Nkrumah, p. 91

[12] I was present at the rally.

Nkrumah has now fallen.

In their crisis of identity the Negroes of the United States sometimes feel a need for a sense of pride in their origins. They want to be proud of Africa. But which Africa? Is it just the concept of Africa? How can one be proud of a mere abstraction?

For intellectuals perhaps one can only be proud of an abstraction—a romantic abstraction. Once one comes into contact with reality, the pride receives a shock.

This might be the attitude of intellectuals. But the ordinary Negro people in the Americas often need a little more substance in their abstractions. The Africa they want to be proud of needs to have a little more meat. So they sometimes personify Africa; Africa becomes embodied in a single symbolic individual. These ordinary Negroes of the New World who feel an actual spiritual need in their identification with Africa have sometimes turned to the symbolism of Ethiopia. The Emperor of Ethiopia, visiting Jamaica in April, 1966, was overwhelmed by Jamaicans who thought of him as a god.

But sometimes the Negro of the New York needs a modern symbol of pride, an African leader who stands for modernity, for progress as well as for the dignity of the black man. No other African leader was as well qualified to capture the imagination of this kind of Afro-American as Nkrumah was. The black people of the United States in particular must have found it easy to identify with him: he was an ex-Harlemite, he was English-speaking, and he had a defiant pride when dealing with the government of the United States. He was a good militant symbol for radical Afro-Americanism.

This was perhaps the nearest thing to a recompense that African nationalism has paid to the Negro struggle in America. It was, as we have noted, American Negroes and West Indians who launched Pan-Africanism on to a world stage. They helped to strengthen the morale of African nationalists in the colonies. But now the triumph of African nationalism and the attainment of independence have in turn strengthened the morale of Negro fighters in the United States.

Behind it all is the influence of the liberal ethic, coupled with the feeling that those who had expounded that ethic were among the first to violate it in their dealings with the colored world. The sense of "liberalism betrayed" was, to a certain extent, what ignited African nationalism in the first place. In the words of Nnamdi Azikiwe, the spearhead of modern Nigerian nationalism:

Having been educated in the United States, I could be expected to be steeped in the traditions of Jeffersonian democracy. But we cannot be blind to any situation which might stunt the natural development of my people towards an independent national existence. At times I am perplexed at the role of the United States on the African continent. Is this great nation buttressing the forces of European reaction so as to manacle the people of Africa and thwart their legitimate aspirations towards nationhood?[13]

---

[13] From an address delivered in Washington, D.C., on December 27, 1949. See Zik. . . , p. 8.

LÉOPOLD SÉDAR SENGHOR

Léopold Sédar Senghor, eminent poet, and president of Senegal since 1960, is probably Africa's most literary and learned head of state. Though undeniably African by birth, background, and dedication, Senghor is, for all that, thoroughly a man of French culture. As an advocate of ideas flying the Negritude banner, he has (perhaps understandably) been mistaken, by some opponents as well as some zealous followers, as a doctrinaire of racialist obscurantism, while actually he has moved toward positions of the greatest integration consistent with affirmation of African confidence in making contributions to universal culture. This attitude is illustrated in the warmly fraternal rhetoric of his address at the Howard University centennial convocation in September, 1966, reproduced here. A man of philosophical subtlety and literary graces, he remains supremely political, in the sense that for him myth (e.g., socialism, Negritude) is the ceremony that seals a marriage with the real world.[1]

A bibliography of Senghor's writings takes up about six pages, but a summary of his political career, its advances, retreats, strategies, and objectives might well require ten times that number of pages. A single-sentence summary, however, could justly say that no head of state in black Africa has held power longer

---

[1] cf. Irving L. Markovitz, *Leopold Senghor and the Politics of Negritude* (New York, 1969).

than Senghor, and that he has managed this without violent civil strife, if not without opposition.

Léopold Sédar Senghor was born in 1906 in a small coastal village of Senegal. His father was a well-to-do merchant belonging to the Serer tribe, who are a small minority in Senegal and, moreover, profess the Catholic religion in a country which is overwhelmingly Moslem. The young Senghor, having distinguished himself at school, was sent to France on a government scholarship, where he went on to study at the Sorbonne. He won high honors there, and was the first African to qualify to teach in the French lycées, where he taught from 1935 to 1939. When the war came, he joined a Senegalese battalion of the French army, spent two years as a prisoner of the Nazis, and returned to teaching upon his release. In 1946 he married his first wife, the daughter of Felix Eboué, a Negro from French Guiana, who had been governor-general of the French equatorial colonies and had been associated with the Free French under De Gaulle. Senghor's second wife is a Frenchwoman.

From 1946 to 1958 Senghor represented colonial Senegal in the French National Assembly, holding from time to time significant positions in the French cabinet and at UNESCO. At first he had worked through the French Socialist Party affiliate in Senegal. Later having formed a new party, he found that urban politics had been preempted by a communist-controlled party, and turned his own attention to the countryside. There he made himself a popular leader among the rural masses. Apparently his position as a Catholic among Moslems only gave play to his skill in accommodation and intergroup compromise. His political experience in metropolitan France also helped, and he eventually emerged as the leader of Senegalese politics. Senghor developed his own Pan-Africanist scheme, which was to build a regional union of all French West Africa in a partnership with France. This dream failed in the collapse of the Mali Federation in 1960. Out of that collapse he salvaged the Republic of Senegal with himself as president and his close coworker Mamadou Dia as prime minister. In 1962 the latter tried a coup against Senghor, but Senghor marshaled his forces adroitly and was able to arrest and imprison Dia for attempting to overthrow the constitution. Senghor's power has not been effectively challenged since then. Whenever opposition parties appear—and there is no legal bar to them—Senghor manages to outmaneuver them or absorb them into his own party.

Senghor is an ardent propagtor of cultural Pan-Africanism, but a cautious realist about continental Pan-Africanism. On the cultural plane, he was one of the prime movers of the famous 1956 convocation in Paris (see p. 97ff). In Senegal he organized the First World Festival of Negro Arts in 1966, a few months before he spoke at Howard University. But on the idea of forming a central government for the whole of Africa, he has said: "I do not think the United States of Africa are something for tomorrow.... It would be more sensible to begin at the beginning. It would be more honest and realistic to recognize the equality of African states and at the same time to respect their frontiers, artificial as these may be. All frontiers are artificial, even in Europe. They have been drawn by history."[2]

When the acting president of Howard University awarded Senghor the honorary degree of doctor of humane letters, he spoke of the things that Afro-Americans had come to appreciate in the work of the African poet-president:

In your poetry you have sung of Africa and the Negro, of your childhood in Senegal, of your homesickness as a young student in Paris, of African Masks, of the Black Woman "clad in her color which is life, in her form which is beauty." You have eulogized the Senegalese martyrs and American Negro soldiers. You have found poetry in the mighty Congo River and in the streets of New York City.

Convinced that the Negro has made and will continue to make a significant cultural contribution to world civilization, you have become the spokesman of Negritude. Your unshakable faith in the Negro's cultural heritage and potential found its crowning justification a few months ago in the First World Festival of Negro Art, which you sponsored.[3]

Like Nkrumah, although in a quite different style, Senghor illustrates certain currents of idea and sentiment which influence the interaction of black communities in Africa and in its diaspora. While Nkrumah stirred black militants and radicals with his blend of Garveyesque charisma and Leninist concepts, Senghor, who has developed a meld of socialist politics and Negritude philosophy as a bridge between the African elite and the French establishment, is able to inspire some Afro-American intellectuals to seek

---

[2] Quoted in John Reed and Olive Wake (ed. and trans.), *Senghor Prose and Poetry* (London, Oxford University Press, 1965).

[3] Citation by Dr. Stanton L. Wormley, September 28, 1966.

a cultural role in America through a distinctive Afro-American synthesis.

The Living Values of Negritude

For some thirty-five years I have known of the existence of Howard University. For thirty-five years I have pondered over its significance, imagining it to be the temple of Negritude in the U.S.A. Is it not the university of Alain Locke, the spiritual father of the Negro Renaissance? This is why, Mr. President, I could not be more sensitive to any honor than the one you are conferring upon me today.

I am convinced that my only merit is that of having been for thirty-five years a conscious and constant militant for Negritude. In the French-speaking world I did not invent the word. It came rather from my friend, the poet and dramatist Aimé Césaire. And I surely did not invent the concept—that ideology which has enabled tens of nations, a whole race throughout the world, to recover its being, its strength, if not the taste for life.

"A tiger does not proclaim its tigritude," a Nigerian writer quipped. I was asked what I thought about that. I fear that it may indicate an inferiority complex inoculated by the former colonizer, a complex that the former "colonizee" has not yet cured.

My answer would be: The tiger does not proclaim its tigritude because it neither speaks nor thinks. It is an animal. To man alone the privilege is given to think and rethink his thought: the privilege to know himself. *Gnothi seauton,* Socrates advised.

The British speak of "Anglo-Saxon civilization" because they are men, and the French speak of "French civilization" or of "Greco-Latin civilization." We Negroes speak of Negritude, for we too are men—men who, forty thousand years ago, were the first to emerge as *Homo sapiens,* the first men to express themselves in art, the first to create the earliest agrarian civilization in the valleys of the Nile and of Mesopotamia.

Yet I must render to you, Negro Americans, what belongs to Negro Americans: the merit of having invented, before all others, perhaps not the word, but certainly, what is more important, the concept, the ideology of Negritude. To be sure, at the beginning of this century the French and Germans had made known and extolled first the artistic values, then the social and philosophical values of Negritude. The École de Paris, at the height of its triumph and while it was the pride of Western civilization had, by borrowing from us, given us a place at the universal banquet table. Without overlooking the role played by Haiti, the fact remains that you were the ones who, between the years 1920 and 1925, started the Negro Renaissance and gave birth to the New Negro, conscious of his Negritude, determined to *live* it; to defend it and make it famous.

Some years later, in the Latin Quarter of Paris, a few young men, a few students, found, on reading you, the remedy for their confusion and food to appease their hunger for dignity, or rather, an example to follow. For you were not only talking about Negritude, you were living it, you were Negritude.

I am pleased to render homage here to the pioneer thinkers who lighted our path in the years 1930–1935: Alain Locke, W. E. B. Du Bois, Marcus Garvey, Carter G. Woodson. And also to pay well-deserved tribute to the poets whose works we translated and recited, and in whose footsteps we tried to follow: Claude McKay, Jean Toomer, Countee Cullen, James Weldon Johnson, Langston Hughes, Sterling Brown. I cannot forget the two magazines that we feverishly skimmed through: *The Crisis* and *Opportunity*. That was a time of fervor. At the First World Festival of Negro Arts, I quoted a poem by Langston Hughes that I had translated thirty years before and that the poet himself no longer remembered. And how could I forget that one of those who initiated us to the New Negro Movement, along with Paulette Nardal, founder of the *Review of the Negro World,* was a Negro American, a student at the Sorbonne—Mercer Cook, who is present here today and once again a professor at Howard University.

But what is Negritude? As you may well guess, we have often been asked that question. It is neither a French engine of war, as has been charged, nor one of those brilliant abstract ideas which are so often born in Paris. Once again, though the word was coined in France—invented, moreover, by a West Indian, an

American—the thing itself, the ideology, was indeed a product of the Negroes of the U.S.A.

And yet, before being an ideology, an ideal, Negritude is first of all a fact. It was Langston Hughes who wrote, shortly after World War I: "We younger Negro artists who create now intend to express our individual dark-skinned selves without fear or shame."

Yes, that's what Negritude is first of all, "Negro personality," the fact of being a Negro among other men who are not black. For you, as you have felt and still feel, this means being Negro Americans among white Americans. For us, Negro Africans, this meant, yesterday, being the colonized among the colonizers. Today it means being underdeveloped nations among the developed nations, being poor in the midst of the rich. Thus, in reality, the fact is a *situation,* a network of relationships.

It is because we are in a situation that the fact of being Negro solicited yesterday and requires today an ideology, in other words, an ideal situation in the future. Yesterday's ideology consisted in disalienation and in the resolve to be free, the equal of other men before the law. For you, it was a matter of getting rid of slavery and segregation; for us, it was a question of getting rid of colonization. The truth of this year 1966, this year of the centennial, is that though you have transcended slavery, you have not yet completely transcended segregation; by the same token, though we have gotten rid of colonization, we have not yet completely mastered underdevelopment. Thanks to your own efforts and to men of faith among your white fellow citizens, you are walking on the road to integration. Thanks to the efforts of the Negro African peoples themselves and to the aid of rich friendly nations, we are on the road to *development.*

These are the reasons which offer us in 1966, in this centennial year of your university, a new ideology, a new ideal to be realized. On the one hand, the abolition of slavery and the beginning of integration; on the other hand, decolonization and membership in the UN have become possible only through the discovery, under the Negro fact, of the values of Negritude. As early as 1808, Abbé Grégoire, the leader of the French abolitionists, in a volume entitled *On the Literature of Negroes,* had made Europe aware of Negro culture. Let us make no mistake about it: it is because one discovered men and a civilization under the Negro fact—

under the black skin and the flat nose—that our situation has changed.

To repeat, because that situation is being normalized, we must set up a new ideal to be realized, a new world to be built. But, in truth, it has begun to be built, the new humanism of the twentieth century. It can be deeper and richer than the humanism of the Great Renaissance. For the latter, while resuscitating Roman and Greek ruins, massacred the Indians and organized the slave trade.

Twentieth century humanism will be the symbiosis of all human values if only all civilizations contribute to it. Negro civilization first and foremost. For there is, underneath the physical fact of being Negro, a mine of cultural—technical and spiritual—values, by which Negritude is defined. But why have I said "Negro civilization first and foremost?" That is what I should like to explain in my conclusion.

Forty thousand years ago, the Negroes then were the first men to create works of art, the first to give art, better than its techniques and rules, its deepest significance. It was because Western art, except during the Christian Middle Ages, had forgotten this significance that it degenerated until the twentieth century, when the values of Negritude came to reteach the West and the world not only the meaning of art, but also that of man.

But what is this meaning of art? Let us return to the first statuettes in soapstone and ivory, sculptured by the Negroids of Grimaldi. Let us remember two of them: the famous Venuses of Grimaldi and Lespugue. Their creation answers the fundamental needs of man, which the Grimaldian artist, the Negro artist, satisfies by the characteristics of his arts.

The first spiritual need of *Homo sapiens,* of the man who has crossed the thresholds of reflection and co-reflection, is to express his inner self in the form of an idea. This is what our sculptors do when they express the idea of fertility, that is to say, the idea of life everlasting. This is the very idea of the human being in all its fullness. Thus, the first characteristic of Negro art is always to turn its back to the anecdotic, to express an essential idea.

Here is its second characteristic. The idea is expressed concretely but not directly in the manner of a photograph; it is expressed by an image-symbol. Man translates his inner self by choosing the elements of his language in the dictionary of nature, the dictionary of external forms. The Grimaldian artist translates the idea of fertility by the image of a woman with rounded forms.

I should have said, by repeating curved forms. In order to acquire its strength as a symbol, the image must be rhythmic. I need not explain to Negro Americans what rhythm is. It is unity in diversity, asymmetrical parallelism, repetition in change. It is at once the most concrete and the most abstract expression of life: the most sensual because it is expressed in or by our senses; the most spiritual because it suggests rather than describes.

Starting from these characteristics of Negritude, you can guess what could be deduced from them, in the realm of thought, for a philosophy of life. Thus it is that, at the beginning of this century, without even waiting for our complete emancipation, we began to make our contribution to the civilization of the universal: in America, Europe, Africa, everywhere in this vast world.

Ever since a Negro mask appeared, like a phantom, in a Paris bistro, ever since the first muted trumpet sounded in the cemetery during the First World War, one no longer paints, sculptures, sings, or dances—I may even say one no longer thinks, at least one no longer lives—as one used to do in this world. Warmth has been communicated, dialogue has been established between man and man, who has regained the taste for life.

Mr. President, Ladies and Gentlemen:

Despite the trials which at this very moment are bearing down on the black community in the U.S.A., this is no time to be discouraged. It is, in large measure, by you and by America that the values of Negritude, that the values of life, have conquered the world. Your greatest strength lies not in material arms but in those of the spirit: the living values of Negritude.

Continue your work of humanism, and the rest—your fair share of temporal power—will be given you to boot.

TOM MBOYA

Tom Mboya, one of Africa's ablest young leaders and widely expected to be Jomo Kenyatta's successor as president of Kenya, was assassinated in Nairobi on the 5th of July, 1969, at the age of 38. Son of an illiterate sisal worker, Mboya was educated in mission schools and went to work as a sanitary inspector for the Nairobi City Council. Before long he was organizing a staff association and then a general trade union movement across the country. In 1955, while studying trade unionism on a fellowship at Ruskin College, Oxford, he also waged a vigorous crusade for colonial freedom before many British audiences. Three years later, at the age of 28, his brilliant political talents won him election as chairman of the All African People's Conference at Accra. After playing a key role in achieving independence for Kenya, he became Prime Minister Kenyatta's minister of justice and the general secretary of the ruling political party (KANU). Later he was made minister for economic planning and development.

His visits to the United States, from 1956 on, won many friends and allies in liberal and trade union circles on behalf of Kenyan independence. Aided by these friends, both white and black, he succeeded in raising funds to provide scholarships for a thousand African students in the United States.

Mboya's article *Africa and Afro-America,* reprinted here, was written for the *New York Times* shortly before his death. Earlier that year a meeting he was addressing in Harlem had been disrupted by a small faction of black separatists who challenged the Kenya government, in the person of Mboya, for its refusal to grant automatic citizenship in Kenya to any black American who wanted it. The article goes beyond this particular matter to the broader questions involved in the relationship between Africa and Afro-America. He agrees with Bayard Rustin that a separatist Back-to-Africa orientation has been historically the posture of despair and escapism. He strongly affirms the mutual benefits that can come to the Negroes here and in Africa when each population makes strides in its own society and supports the other in its efforts. The African nations, with their urgent problems of poverty, unemployment, tribal tensions, and political instability, cannot, he indicates, heedlessly swing open the doors to unlimited and indiscriminate immigration, although, on an individual basis, many Afro-Americans can and do settle in Africa. The tragic precariousness of building cohesive national societies in Africa is pointed up by such events as Mboya's assassination. His article —and indeed his life—were, in large measure, directed toward mustering realistic self-help and mutual help by the black communities of Africa and America.

Africa and Afro-America

Black Americans today are more concerned with their relationship to Africa than at any point in recent memory. The emergence of this concern at the present time is a phenomenon of great significance and a source of increasing controversy and confusion. The *nature* of the relationship between Africans and black Americans therefore merits extensive dialogue between the two groups, in the hope that issues can be clarified, illusions dispelled and a common understanding reached as to where our immediate objectives coincide and where they do not. Our struggle and goal are the same, and we need a common understanding on strategy so as not to cancel each other out.

It is precisely because communication and clarification are so important that I was deeply disturbed by an incident that occurred when I spoke in Harlem on 18th March. In my one-hour speech I explained the challenges of development in our new African nations. I discussed the difficult period of post-independence through which we are now passing. The economic and social problems we face are complex, and it is very important that those who are interested in our development understand the formidable task that now confronts us. I found the audience in Harlem highly receptive to my remarks on this subject. At the end of my speech, however, in response to some people who had approached me before the meeting, I decided to comment on the proposal for a mass movement of black Americans back to Africa. I began by rejecting the proposal, but before I had a chance to elaborate I was noisily interrupted by two or three people, one of whom projected four or five eggs in my direction. His aim was as bad as his manners.

Needless to say, I found this a rather curious and crude way of impressing African leaders with the genuine desire of black Americans to identify with Africa. By their deliberate and planned activities, a handful of people succeeded in disrupting a very important opportunity for dialogue between an African leader and black people who feel the need for closer relations with our new nations. Africans involved in the serious task of nation-building can hardly be expected to look kindly upon the discourteous and self-indulgent activities of these few individuals. They may also be led to doubt that black Americans in general have any appreciation of, or desire to understand, the problems that we must cope with. Apart from this, the enemies of the black man's struggle were given yet another excuse to justify their continued efforts to disorganize and divide and weaken us.

We must, however, be careful not to dramatize or generalize this incident. Indeed, I have received many letters from black people disassociating themselves from it. The only significance that I now attach to the incident is that it may be, by underlining certain confusions, help clarify the relationship between Africans and Afro-Americans. Thus the disrupters, who wanted to obstruct dialogue, may unwittingly have helped to foster it.

In a fundamental way, Africans and Afro-Americans today find themselves in remarkably similar political and economic situations. As I have already indicated, the new nations in Africa have passed through one stage—that of the movement to independence from colonial rule—and are now engaged in the post-independence stage of nation-building. The first stage was primarily *political,* our objective being to achieve the political goal of self-determination.

We suffered during our struggle for independence, but in many ways it was a simpler period than today. It was one of mass mobilization, dramatic demonstrations and profound nationalist emotions. The present period is less dramatic. Fewer headlines are being made; fewer heroes are emerging. Nationalist sentiment must remain powerful, but it can no longer be sustained by slogans and the excitement of independence. Rather, it must itself sustain the population during the long process of development. For development will not come immediately. It is a process that requires time, planning, sacrifice and work. Colonialism could be abolished by proclamation, but the abolition of poverty required the establishment of new institutions and the development of a modern technology and an enormously expanded educational system. We are engaged, therefore, in an economic and social revolution that must take us far beyond the condition we had achieved when we won our independence.

Our slogan during the independence struggle was "Uhuru Sasa," and I do not think it is a coincidence that its English translation, "Freedom Now," was the slogan for the civil rights movement in America. For the black American struggle in the 1950s and early 60s was very similar to our own. The objective of both was political liberty for black people. In America, black people demanded the abolition of Jim Crow segregation and the right to vote, and they won their fight through courageous and inspiring political protest. But like their African cousins who must meet the challenge of development, they now confront the more difficult task of achieving economic equality.

I have seen black ghettos in America. I have seen individuals living under degrading conditions. Black poverty is more outrageous in America than in my own country because it is surrounded by unparalleled wealth. Thus, for black America the problem of equality looms larger than the problem of develop-

ment; but they are similar in that the achievement of both requires massive institutional change.

The struggles of black people in Africa and America are related on more concrete levels. Let us not forget that the independence movement in Africa has had a great impact on the civil
rights movement in America, besides giving it a slogan. In addition, this movement for independence has posed many important
questions for white America in regard to the race problem in the
United States. For example, James Baldwin has quoted in *The
Fire Next Time* that the 1954 Brown v. Topeka Board of Education decision concerning school desegregation was largely motivated by the competition of the cold war, and the fact that Africa
was clearly liberating herself and therefore had, for political reasons, to be wooed by the descendants of her former masters. In
its supporting brief in the Brown case, the Justice Department
explained that "it is in the context of the present world struggle
between freedom and [communist] tyranny that the problem of
racial discrimination must be viewed." In other words, the United
States Government understood very well that it would have difficulty making friends in Africa so long as the black American
remained subjugated. Africans are highly conscious of the plight
of black America, and they will be suspicious of the intentions of
American foreign policy until they are convinced that the goal of
American domestic policy is social justice for all.

I believe, furthermore, that our independence movement has
also influenced the thinking of black Americans towards Africa
and towards themselves. I have returned to the United States many
times since my first visit in 1956, and have observed a remarkable
transformation in the black's attitude toward Africa. Thirteen
years ago Africa was seen as a mere curiosity, a jungle country of
primitive people. This is not surprising, since the image that *all*
Americans had of Africa was created by sensational novels and
Hollywood films that were far more indicative of American values
than of actual life in Africa. Of course, there were some exceptions,
like Dr. W. E. B. Du Bois; but the majority of black Americans
either were ashamed of their association with Africa or were entirely indifferent to her.

These attitudes changed rapidly as much of Africa gained independence. New states and leaders took their place in the world
community. African flags flew high and the national anthems of

the new nations were sung with dignity. Respected statesmen, scientists and professional men became visible representatives of Africa, thereby destroying the stereotypes that had existed for so long. Many black Americans observed these phenomena at first with disbelief, but soon their shame in their African heritage was transformed into great pride, and they began to identify with Africa with great intensity. Indeed, it can be said that some of them became, in a sense, more African than the Africans.

It is important that this new identification be understood within its proper context. Most African leaders have emphasized the *universality* of the black man's struggle for freedom and equality. Thus, we see the gains made in Africa as representing battles won in a much bigger war that must continue until total victory is achieved. It is in this spirit that African states accept as their responsibility struggles that continue in parts of our continent not yet freed from colonialism and white racist domination. Thus, the new nations of Africa will not be entirely free until the black man is liberated in South Africa, Namibia [South West Africa], Rhodesia, Angola and Mozambique.

The social movement of black people in the United States is also part of this universal struggle for equality and human dignity for all our people. We cannot survive as free nations if there is any part of the world in which people of African descent are degraded. This is the context in which African interest and aspirations extend beyond the borders of our individual nations and of our continent. This is also the basis of the long-standing collaboration between African nationalists and black leaders from other lands. The heroes of the black man's struggle include those who fought in Africa as well as in America. A. Philip Randolph and Jomo Kenyatta are universal black spokesmen, as were the late Malcolm X and Dr. Martin Luther King Jr. Africa is the birthplace of the black man, but his home is the world. To us, this is the meaning of total independence. We refuse to think of being free in Africa but treated as inferiors the moment we step out of the continent.

In this decade the black man has made enormous progress, in Africa and elsewhere. It is our political decade. Particularly in America, the society has been forced to undergo a genuine social revolution in response to the black struggle. Special note must be taken of the role of young people in this cause. Their fearlessness, resourcefulness and resolve must be recognized and encouraged. My only regret is that many of our leaders and people in Africa have not had the opportunity to visit the United States and thus do not fully appreciate the new mood of militancy and self-assurance that prevails there among black people.

African nationalism is, by its very nature, integrationist, in that its primary objective is to mould numerous tribes into a single political entity. Tribalism, in fact, was one of the major obstacles in the way of independence, and it remains a problem today, as can be seen in the Nigerian-Biafran conflict. The European colonial powers tried for a long time to build up tribal antagonisms in order to weaken nationalist opposition to their rule. Local energies that were channeled into tribal hostilities obviously could not be used to oppose colonialism, and if one tribe became hostile to the Europeans, the latter would befriend another tribes, foment tribal conflict, and then watch the fighting from the sidelines as "neutral" observers. This was the straightforward tactic of divide-and-rule.

This tactic is by no means unique either to Africa or to colonialism. In Northern Ireland, for example, conservative aristocrats have been able to maintain their power by playing on the religious hostilities between working-class Protestants and Catholics, and have thereby prevented the emergence of a broad-based opposition. A kind of religious tribalism is thus obstructing the formation of a unified and progressive political force there, and in the United States I would think that the same role is played by racial and ethnic tribalism.

Just as the African must reconcile the differences between his tribal and his national identity, so too must the black American realize to the fullest extent his potential as a black man and as an American. I find his task an extraordinarily difficult one, particularly because he has been part of an oppressed racial minority. His new assertiveness is important here. He has cast off the myth of racial inferiority, and he is demanding that he be treated with dignity. But the danger is that his racial pride may become a form of racialism that would be unfortunate not only from a moral point of view, but also from a political one, in that he would be separated from potential allies. From the African point of view, the black man's struggle in America must assert the right of equal treatment and opportunity. I have not found a single African who believes in a black demand for a separate state or for equality through isolation.

The contradiction between black nationalism and American nationalism can lead to much confusion, particularly when black nationalists, in search of a national base that they cannot find at home, turn to Africa. There is the possibility that they want to identify with Africans on a purely racial basis—which is unrealistic since they are citizens of different nations. I think it is this confusion that has led some black Americans to try to impose upon the American political situation concepts and ideologies that grew out of the African experience with colonialism and imperialism. Thus, writers like Frantz Fanon have become popular in certain black American circles, even though these very writers would be the last to want their ideas exported to other continents. Fanon, for example, wrote that "the test cases of civil liberty whereby both whites and blacks in America try to drive back racial discrimination have very little in common in principles and objectives with the heroic fight of the Angolan people against the detestable Portuguese colonialism."

Fanon, who advocated the use of violence by the oppressed, is popular among some black Americans because of their tremendous frustration with the conditions under which they must live. The fact that these black Americans would turn to an African for guidance may be an indication of why some of them are now thinking of expatriating to Africa. I think the reason is, again, their frustration, as well as their inability or unwillingness to resolve the tension between their racial and national identities.

At this point I should deal with the specific question of the Kenya Government's attitude toward a motion tabled in our Parliament last year. Reference was made to this motion at the Harlem meeting. Some of the Afro-Americans who spoke to me were angry that our Government had rejected a motion calling for automatic citizenship for any black American who wished to come to settle in Kenya. The point here is a legal one. The fact is that even Africans coming from neighbouring states cannot acquire automatic citizenship. The Constitution lays down the conditions that must be fulfilled by all persons who wish to become citizens. We could not discriminate in favour of any group without first having to amend the Constitution itself. The point must also be made that our Government has to retain the right to keep out undesirable individuals, i.e., people with criminal records, mental cases or others whose presence would create problems for our new nation.

I know that those who meet the conditions will be able to acquire citizenship as easily as have many foreigners since Kenya's independence. Kenya has a large body of non-black and non-African citizens. At the time of independence we gave all persons of non-African origin two years to become citizens by registration, and more than forty thousand Asians as well as thousands of Europeans took advantage of this. Since December, 1965, when the two-year period ended, many more have become citizens through the Naturalization Act. This method is available to foreigners even today. What is more, we now have many more foreigners in Kenya who have come as businessmen, technicians, etc., since independence, and who enjoy protection under the law without actually being citizens.

Perhaps some of our critics do not realize that we, too, have the many problems confronting black people in America. We have our slums, our unemployed and other social shortcomings. Our first responsibility must be to our own citizens. Emotional crusades cannot change this hard fact.

Perhaps the desire to return to Africa is so unrealistic because it is based upon despair. I do *not* mean by this that African states should refuse black Americans who wish to expatriate. On the contrary, those who want to make a home in Africa are free to do so. There are many opportunities in the new nations, particularly for trained and skilled persons. They could help us enormously during our period of development, and we welcome our American cousins to come and work among us.

What is unrealistic about the proposal is the ease with which some black Americans think that they can throw off their American culture and become African. For example, some think that to identify with Africa one should wear a shaggy beard or a piece of cloth on one's head or a cheap garment on one's body. I find here a complete misunderstanding of what African culture really means. An African walks barefoot or wears sandals made of old tires not because it is his culture but because he lives in poverty. We live in mud and wattle huts and buy cheap Hong Kong fabrics not because it is part of our culture, but because these are conditions imposed on us today by poverty and by limitations in technical, educational and other resources. White people have often confused the symbols of our poverty with our culture. I would hope that black people would not make the same error.

Our culture is something much deeper. It is the sum of our personality and our attitude toward life. The basic qualities that distinguish it are our extended family ties and the codes governing relations between old and young, our concept of mutual social responsibility and communal activities, our sense of humour, our belief in a supreme being and our ceremonies for birth, marriage and death. These things have a deep meaning for us, and they pervade our culture, regardless of tribe or clan. They are qualities that shape our lives, and they will influence the new institutions that we are now establishing. I think that they are things worth preserving, defending and living for.

But I should point out that there is a great debate raging in Africa today over our culture. Certain customs and traditions are being challenged by our movement toward modernization. People are asking what should be preserved and what should be left behind. They argue about the place universities should have in the society. African intellectuals and governments demand the teaching of African history, and efforts are being made to provide new school syllabuses and to encourage African writers. Some fear the breakdown of the extended family, others the emergence of a new élite removed from the people. We even argue about the use of cosmetics, hair-straighteners, mini-skirts and national dress. Thus, black people who come to Africa will find many of their questions unanswered even by us.

Our new nations are in a transitional stage, and I think we can benefit greatly from contact with our American cousins. The African needs to understand and encourage the revolution of the black people in America, while the black people in America need to understand and encourage the effort of nation-building now taking place in Africa. Communication must be strengthened between us.

I have been impressed by new enterprises and economic and social institutions organized by black Americans. There is also a movement in the universities to establish programmes in African studies. These are areas in which we could co-operate and promote our joint interests. Of course, I do not share the view of those who demand black studies and then insist that white students be barred from them. Such an attitude reflects a contradiction, and conflicts with our search for recognition and equality.

Freedom for both Africans and black Americans is not an act of withdrawal, but a major step in asserting the rights of black people and their place as equals among nations and peoples of the world. Freedom involves the full realization of our identities and potential. It is in this sense that the objective of the African must be the development of his nation and the preservation of his heritage. And the objective of the black American must be the achievement of full and unqualified equality within American society. The black American should look to Africa for guidance—and for a chance to give guidance—but not for escape. He must merge his blackness with his citizenship as an American, and the result will be dignity and liberation.

Black people in Africa and America have survived slavery, colonialism and imperialism. Today we can survive change. We have been oppressed as a people, and have been divided to the point of taking roots in different cultures. But as we struggle to achieve our full liberation, these differences should become less important. If and when we are all free and equal men, perhaps even those racial distinctions that now divide our societies and that separate one nation from the other will disappear in the face of our common humanity.

In conclusion, I note a similarity between the positions of the black American and our own people. In both cases there is impatience to see a promise kept—on the one hand is the promise of civil rights legislation, and on the other, the promise of independence. There is a crisis of confidence. The danger in America, as in Africa, is that such impatience can lead to confusion of priorities and failure to recognize the goals of the movement. Effective unity and committed national leaders are needed more now than ever before. If these elements are absent, the enthusiasm of the young people and the tremendous sympathy and support of other groups may be lost in despair.

This, in my view, is the challenge before the black people and their leaders in America. The struggle calls for even greater resolution and dedication if they are to translate past victories into a programme of action for the more difficult task of achieving actual equality—as against legal and constitutional proclamations.

Bayard Rustin has offered the best explanation I have yet read of the origins of the "Back to Africa" movement among his people:

There is a reason for this movement which has far less to do with the Negro's relation to Africa than to America. The "Back to Africa" and separatist tendencies are always strongest at the very time when the Negro is most intensely dissatisfied with his lot in America. It is when the Negro has lost hope in America—and has lost his identity as an American—that he seeks to re-establish his identity and his roots as an African.

This period of despair has historically followed hard upon a period of hope and of efforts to become integrated—on the basis of full equality—into the economic, social and political life of the United States. The present separatist mood, as we know, has come after a decade in which the Negro achieved enormous and unprecedented gains through the civil rights struggle, and it has coincided with a right-wing reaction that has obstructed further measures toward equality. The combination of progress, aroused hopes, frustration and despair has caused many Negroes to withdraw into separatism and to yearn for Africa.

Rustin goes on to observe that this syndrome has occurred three times in the past: in the early 1800s, when the African Methodist Episcopal Church was formed; in the late nineteenth century, when Booker T. Washington became famous, and in the 1920s, during the heyday of Marcus Garvey.

I have accepted the opportunity to contribute this article, not as an apology for the Harlem incident, but because of my genuine concern about the relations between Africa and the black people in America. The achievement problems they face are of great interest to us in more than one way. In the first place, they are our cousins and we share together the black man's fate in the world. His complete liberation is our joint concern because, as I have said, black people cannot be fully free if there remains any part of the globe where a black man is denied his rights. Second, the complete emancipation of America's blacks will influence the country's policies in a way that can only lead to a better understanding of and sympathy for the cause of black people everywhere. And finally, a free and vigorous black community in the United States can, within its own organization, play a much more effective and practical role in helping African and other black nations meet some of their challenges of development.

I have, since 1958, witnessed the true potential of the black American in this regard. People like Ralph Bunche, Jackie Robinson, Harry Belafonte, Sidney Poitier, Frank Montéro, Bayard

Rustin and the heads of such Negro institutions as Howard University, Tuskegee Institute and Morehouse, Morris Brown and Spelman Colleges in Atlanta played a decisive part in my campaign for a students' airlift to the United States. This programme helped to bring over one thousand students from Kenya and other parts of East and Central Africa to study in America; today, many of these students are home, and providing the backbone for our new public service.

A number of Afro-American leaders in church and community groups, like the Rev. James Robinson of New York, labour leaders like A. Philip Randolph and Maida Springer, and many black families across the United States took part in this unique experiment in people-to-people international co-operation. And there were, of course, many white Americans, like the late Senator Robert F. Kennedy and his brother, Senator Edward Kennedy; Theodore Kheel, the attorney and mediator; the distinguished statesman, Averell Harriman; Dr. Buell Gallagher, the educator; I. W. Abel, the labour leader; and white institutions and families who contributed to it.

The point I am making, however, is that black people have the scope and capacity to join in the challenge of development in Africa as free citizens in America. We need them there. I am not afraid of an exodus of black people from America to Africa because I know there will be no such exodus. I am, rather concerned that the emotion and effort needed to promote such a movement would lead to sterile debate and confusion when there is an urgent need for unity and decisive leadership.

The challenge of the black American was stated with great beauty by W. E. B. Du Bois over a half-century ago:

One ever feels this twoness—an American, a Negro; two souls, two thoughts, two unreconciled strivings; two warring ideals in one dark body, whose dogged strength alone keeps it from being torn asunder.

The history of the American Negro is the history of this strife— this longing to attain self-conscious manhood, to merge his double self into a better and truer self. In this merging he wishes neither of the older selves to be lost. He would not Africanize America, for America has too much to teach the world and Africa. He would not bleach his Negro soul in a flood of white Americanism, for he knows that Negro blood has a message for the world. He simply wishes to make it possible for a man to be both a Negro and an American, without being cursed and spit upon by his fellows, without having the doors of opportunity closed roughly in his face.

TABAN LO LIYONG

Taban lo Liyong was born in northern Uganda in 1939. At thirty he published *The Last Word,* a book of critical and controversial essays. Since most of what might be called the literary establishment of Africa is centered on the west coast (whence also most of the black diaspora came), the East African lo Liyong has a certain fresh outlander's point of view, letting icons and pieties fall where they may. He went to school and college in Uganda, and then came to the United States, where he studied at Howard University, Knoxville College, and the University of Iowa. He now teaches at the University of Kenya. His studies and extensive travels through the United States very possibly had some influence in shaping his confident, tough-minded, future-oriented outlook, which he has labeled "cultural synthesism."

The main targets in his essay "Negroes Are Not Africans" are the romanticizing of primitivism and the past, and the fetishizing of Negritude. He neither uses the term "assimilation" nor does he directly discuss the issue; but the implication of what he writes is clearly that he is not at all worried about such an eventuality. In another essay he says, "Cultures are amalgams. Present African 'cultures' are already mixtures." In the essay reproduced here he says, "If you want to be our archaeologists, fine. Meanwhile, I am sending my children to study Keynesian economics, quantum physics, existentialism, Chinese landscape painting, the classics, Danish and Swedish social welfare, as matters of priority."

Apparently he feels that the African, having mastered such European (or Asiatic) disciplines, will still remain himself, in his own milieu, serving his own African society. And so to him, assimilation is no threat. He does not grant at all that the situation in which American Negroes find themselves may call for different strategies. He counsels his Afro-American "cousins and nephews" not to rely too heavily on Africa as "a guiding spirit," audaciously revives Booker T. Washington's advice, "Lower your bucket where you are," and signs himself, "With love, Uncle Africa.'"

Negroes are not Africans

The Negro is a unique creature. He is of Africa; and yet not quite. He is of Europe; and yet not quite. He is of America; and yet not quite. But he combines these three disparate strands in his constitution. The confusion which ensues from this combination is the root of all his problems.

In these late days of race pride, he has just awakened to the search for racial, cultural, and historical roots. Hastily, he is likely to pounce on Africa. If he sticks to that, and that only, he is mistaken. For, although African slaves were transported to America three or four hundred years ago, the moment they left the African coast, they were no longer African entirely. Europe, America and the seas determined their fates.

I have travelled far and wide in America. I have been to Atlanta, to New York, to Boston, to Buffalo, to Minneapolis, Minnesota, to Chicago, to Philadelphia, to Washington, D.C.; but I have never come across a Negro who looks, talks, behaves, thinks like a full African. Apparently, there are no more Africans left among the Negroes. What we have are "coloured"—in the South African sense of the word—meaning descendants of black African parents and white parents. Hence the Negro is the joint product of Africa and Europe, in America. If he calls Africa "motherland," he must also call Europe "motherland"—or more appropriately, "fatherland." He has the right to be proud of the old African empires of Ghana and Songai. Equally, he must take pride in French civilization, in English empire, in German greatness, in the Spanish Golden Age, in classical Italy and classical Greece. Those are the homes of his other parents. Culturally, he is sub-American, and extremely little African.

There was an act of deception. It went like this: Whites called Negroes blacks. Negroes agreed they were blacks, no matter the amount of black and white pigmentation in their skin. Whites said Negroes came from Africa. Negroes agreed that they came from Africa. The Negro's fate thus placed in my hand, I, in my African humanitarianness, have welcomed him. But the Negro is merely my nephew and cousin. Most of the mothers were my sisters, a few of the fathers were my brothers. But the greater number of the fathers were my "brothers-in-law"—the white man in America. Old man, it was too bad you sowed your wild oats. You must now take care of my nephews and cousins running about in your compound, as I have taken care of the descendants of African slaves resulting from the internal slave trade.

The act of self-deception continued. Whites have not been claiming rapport with the white-skinned Negroes. Never have Negroes claimed their places in the white world on the basis of the whiteness of skin, sharpness of nose, length of hair, and a common culture. Instead they come asking me whether "I live in trees over there," or have I a tail. It is mostly my cousins who are inquisitive. I don't know what most of the boys think.

The persistence of this myth of Negro origin—that he is the descendant of Africa, alone, has placed the Negro in a four hundred year political, cultural and philosophical jungle. Consequently he has not been able to establish a solid American base for functioning as a full-fledged American. When most parts of Africa were under European tutelage, he (convinced that his home was Africa only) felt ashamed of his country of origin, of the cannibalism, of the nakedness, of the backwardness found there. Shame for Africa agitated the black Muslims so much that they left Africa altogether and embraced Arabia as the point of origin of the Negro. And Black Muslim is not yet thirty years old.

In history, it resulted in the creation of Liberia. Liberia as a home for free slaves, yes; but Liberia as a home for returned

Africans, no. Later, Marcus Garvey's Back to Africa Movement, supported not surprisingly by the Ku Klux Klan, was still another act of flight, of despair in hostile circumstances, among half-brothers and half-sisters, all the same.

In those old days of Washington, Du Bois and Garvey, and their ideological war, the person who emerged with the best record is Booker T. Washington. Washington, realizing that the cards he held in his hands were worth so much if dealt right, showed a political astuteness which his detractors cannot efface completely. If a politician is one who gets the most for his own people—prevailing conditions taken into consideration—Washington's project of co-operation between Negroes and whites paid dividends, and would have paid more if it continued, since it operated under sympathetic conditions. It is a fact of life that—short of a revolution—you cannot emancipate serfs overnight, you can't make all (or most) slaves professors overnight. So, one had to go stage by stage, equip the uneducated with skills that can make them earn now, and strengthen their houses, the houses from which would come the future professionals and intellectuals. (In the American social strata, the Negro is in the lower caste. Therefore, when thinking about his improvement or uplifting, bear in mind that you have a low caste problem, compounded by a visible colour.)

I do not think the Washington project would have kept the Negroes "hewers of wood" forever. He was an achiever. But Dr. William Du Bois upset the whole thing in his haste for making intellectuals, elites. Part (perhaps the greater part) of the blame for the present poverty and ignorance of the Southern Negro (and those who ran North) should be laid squarely at Dr. Du Bois's door. Du Bois's elites are doing relatively well for themselves. Not so the poor whose lot Washington would have raised.

The confusion of identity still continued. The Black Muslims look forward to the day when the United States will give them a land, part of the Union, rich in mineral, agricultural potential, etc., where they may worship and live as they think best, undisturbed by Uncle Sam.

And the Black Power advocates want to have exclusive areas where they can do things the truly Negro way without the white man's interference or help.

Americans have pride in their European countries of origin. Apart from the sense of identity this provides, the ethnic (and consequently "social") solidarity pays political dividends through political machines and winning elective posts. The outsiders have been Negroes and Red Indians. Feeling excluded, the Negro has had to set up his own exclusive clubs, counter clubs.

In these post-Hitler years, it may be wondered whether ethnic and racial prides are worthy of perpetuation at all. White Americans, Negroes and South African whites should wonder.

But, ethnically, the Negro is one better than the African and the European or white American. He has another source of pride none of the others has. The Negro doesn't have to wait till Africa is dotted with skyscrapers before he acknowledges his African origin. He doesn't have to wait till Europe or white America has claimed him for one of their sons in order for him to realize that the name Mahoney he carries is his passport for an Irish-American club; if he is called Baldwin, he is Anglo-Saxon as well.

Consequently, he should have got into line long ago and marched along with other whites to receive his western legacy as well as to acknowledge his indebtedness to it. He is a European too. The whole European civilization (which began, er, er, from Africa and flourished in Asia before going West) is as solidly behind him as it is behind any white in this country.

Not only that. Negro women should have applied for memberships in the Daughters of the American Revolution. After all, you were here even before the *Mayflower,* and you have English blood in you. Others should apply as Jews to Bennington College. Others should hold private talks with Senator Edward Kennedy and ask him a typical Irish question: "Ey Man, you ain't gonna leave me out when our next kingdom come, air you?"

But so far, Negroes have been playing at being Negroes, with little profit and much hurt to themselves: with horizons which are poor and mediocre. Their *raison d'etre* has been to be a Negro. A Negro hamstrung by looking at dark Africa and groping for life in the lower levels of America, albeit.

And the bulk of the Negroes have remained penned up in Negro reserves by the New Slave Dealers—the Negro professional politicians. The Negro politicians, the Negro ministers and churches and mosques and gangs are all on equal footings; all are vampires. (Politicians and churches are exploiters everywhere, no doubt. The point is the Negro counterparts have little to offer to their clients.) And for easier manipulation, the Negro has to be kept low and in one place where he can be reached instantly. And he must know he is a Negro, a descendant of dark Africa who has no share in the present dispensation, except if these middlemen deliver it to him. And the middlemen? They are also exploited. Negro artists and sportsmen are the only people who know where they want to go and how to get there directly.

Actually, Africa and Europe have been struggling for the possession of the Negro soul. And Europe has the greater part. That is as it should be. The Negroes are only Africa's cousins and nephews, in a patriarchal world. Europe, settled in America, dominates the landscape.

The wearing of a moustache is a success for White Power: moustaches mask thick Negroid lips. The use of hair straighteners is a success for White Power: removal of kink. Crew-cut hair is a success for White Power.

A pertinent question could be asked at this juncture: Must one have a racial pride before one can live successfully in this our twentieth century? Must the Negro go to excavate all the old tombs in Africa in order to catch the life spirit to make him function as a human being? As an African, my answer is simple. If you want to be our archaeologists, fine. Meanwhile, I am sending my children to study Keynesian economics, quantum physics, existentialism, Chinese landscape painting, the classics, Danish and Swedish social welfare, as matters of priority.

Rather than go to the Moorland Library, New York City Library, the Library of Congress, in order to look for your African parentage (invariably ending up somewhere in a West African royal family) is it not more worthwhile for you to find out who your European foreparents were? There might be a family legacy lying somewhere for you, or one the state took away on grounds of intestacy.

For some twenty years now, African and West Indian intellectuals have been debating the relevancy and irrelevancy of Negritude as a guide for the future ordering of African affairs. Negritude is a philosophy which states, among other things, that the Negro (and African) have certain unique characteristics, and these make him function in a virtuous way, establish relationships with the human aspects of things before the scientific ones; that these peculiarities need be preserved, and need also be placed on the pedestal among the other twentieth century world contributions, guiding lines for ordering of matters; and that the Negro (and African) must function in the peculiar ways the exponents of the philosophy have laid down. Stated in the Negritudist way, it is very confusing because the Negritudists are confused and have shifted ground so much that they are at a loss about the cardinal and immutable canons of Negritude. We shall cut the Gordian knot and say Negritude says: "Negroes and Africans of the world, since you have been rejected and kicked about and your shrines abused, refuse to move any more and declare that you are satisfied with what you have. You have no bombs: that is a virtue; you have no industries; that is a virtue; you had witch-doctors; that is a virtue," etc., *ad absurdum.*

And Negritude is an American philosophy—it was imported into Africa by default, by Du Bois of the United States and Aimé Césaire of the French West Indies. President Léopold Sédar Senghor of Senegal and the former President of Ghana, Dr. Kwame Nkrumah, were the African representatives of this alien and dismal philosophy. It burnt Nkrumah out, and it almost did Senghor in, except that he has recanted.

American Negroes have just received Negritude dressed piping hot by Stokeley Carmichael. So American Negroes (late as Americans always are) are re-enacting scenes from African politics of ten years back. Then Negritude (Francophone Africa) and the African Personality (its version in the English-speaking parts of Africa) were in great demand to arouse the blacks from stupor and political apathy—to arouse them into political activism. In their heydays, Negritude and African Personality worked wonders. After independence was won, we had to roll up our sleeves and get to work—no more luxurious talks. Doing, that is, working to achieve lasting results, is not easy.

Now, when American Negroes woke up to the fact that their plights were not getting any better than those of West Indians and Africans, hysterically they revived Negritude—and named Negritude—and named it Black Power. Black Power, used as an *ad hoc* program, works well in arousing people to political consciousness. But it can only be used as a short-term project—before it turns sour, or worse, poisonous—in the service of a long-term project.

Black Power has no healthy future, just as Negritude hadn't. It will sizzle out sooner or later. The big question is: What, after Black Power? After knocking his head in the *cul de sac* of cultures, Negritude came back and spoke in a new voice and started marching in the direction to the future. "For the future—and this conviction guides a chief of state—" (it is the President of Senegal, and the leader of Negritude in Africa, M. Léopold Sédar Senghor, speaking) "the future belongs to a hybrid civilization." And that is where everybody who knows where he is going—and even who doesn't know where he is going—is going.

False starts—and quite a few of them—have been made in Africa. We may be failing in doing certain things, but most of us know the direction we are going—straight into the twenty-first century. And to arrive there we are not going to go the way our grandparents would have gone—on foot and by canoe—we shall fly, we shall go by missiles, we shall go with the white man, we shall go with the yellow man. And, we shall go—by all means.

Now, you Negroes who want something peculiarly and authentically African in order to identify with and feel manly, what peculiarly African characteristics will you find in the Africa of the 21st century?

Part of your trouble is that you don't know Africa that well. White America knows more, Negro America knows less. White America is the government and white American officials meet with African government officials. Those Negroes who romanticize Africa that much should take compulsory courses on Africa, read Richard Wright and Frantz Fanon and René Dumont for enlightenment.

And when we reach the 21st century we shall arrive there without our kings and aristocrats (isn't that why Nkrumah demoted feudal lords?), we shall arrive there without serfs (isn't that why Uganda kings had to go?); we shall arrive there without tribes (isn't that the test going on in Nigeria, Kenya, Sudan, now?). By the time the 21st century comes—that century of the man of equal privileges—Africa might offer more to each individual citizen while the white Appalachian poor might still roam the hillsides, migrant farmers might still be underpaid. Ghetto Negroes might still room with rats.

The Negro subculture is a culture. But it is essentially sub. Institutionalize it and you have formed a permanent sub-American culture. Pride in it is essentially an act of despair—and Negritude, or Black Power, if you like—is an act one resorts to when the grapes are slightly above one's reach. But must one be content with a half? Shouldn't one try for more—shouldn't one's reach exceed one's grasp, however elusive that grasp might be? In the mythologies we learn that Proteus will give you his "true" character after all false poses.

I have toured Atlanta (suburb slums, and all), lived in Knoxville, Tennessee, for a year, lived in South-East Washington, D.C., for three years, roamed Harlem at night and during the day, seen what Philly has to offer, I have walked Boston's Roxbury Negro ghetto—and I have walked with my eyes open, my nose functioning, my ears sharp. Seriously, will any educated (no, that word may not apply very well here)—will any enlightened—Negro come forward and tell me that that is the type of life the Negro must be proud of, the one the white man is not to desecrate? All those week-end drinking bouts? All those fights? All that vegetating? Mental rotting? All that squalor? God forbid! Are these the repertoires the Negro college students want to nourish and fondle in their exclusive "Soul Tables"?

If I were a Negro, I would go to school in order to place a long distance between me and the ghetto. If I develop complexes in the process, I wouldn't mind. That will be the price to be paid in pursuit of higher ideals. The rise of the coloured world is part and parcel of the rise of the world's workers. Chitterlings are delicious, no doubt. Steak is even better and more nourishing. I would work my way into the American middle class, get myself a house in the suburbs and say: "Ghetto, adieu!"

There will be others who will be active in raising the standards of the poor. There always are. They get their pleasure out of it. Well and good. God bless them if they have convictions and integrity. God bless them if they are Negroes. God bless them if they are Whites. God bless them—the twelve just people.

In most countries revolutions are led by members of the enlightened upper and middle classes who know the best things the establishment could offer but are disenchanted by the amount it gives, the pace it is taking, and the inequality of distribution. These are the people who normally change the systems, or some parts of it.

In India, it had to be the high caste Gandhi to lift up the untouchables. Rome had its Gracchi brothers to try to alleviate the problems of the plebeians. In Cuba, it had to be Fidel Castro. Only in America do trade unions fight for their own betterments.

Only in America do Negroes have to try to emancipate Negroes. Only in America are Puerto Ricans supposed to solve their own problems. In America people want to dodge the "drafts"—and let the devil take the hindmost—nobody wants to remove the "drafts" completely. Those who are afflicted by these scourges are to try to extricate themselves as best they can, through self-help projects. Self-help projects by the poor? the ignorant? the wild? and manned by the poor and ignorant? If they burn their way out, who can blame them? We the enlightened ones, teachers, journalists, politicians, who always knew better but never lifted a finger in aid?

In India, Gandhi changed the minds of the upper castes towards the acceptance of the untouchables. Here, there is no idealist Gandhi no dedicated Gandhi, available to soften the hearts of White Power and change White Intellect.

While there have been few Negro visionaries to solve American problems, there have been fewer white visionaries. The only truly dedicated ones are three, three Southern ladies—Harriet Beecher Stowe, Lillian Smith, and Carson McCullers. In South Africa Alan Paton fights with dedication. Here I can't think of an imposing name of conscience.

It is a fact of life in our 20th century that we are our brothers' keepers—regardless of whether they descended from monkeys or were created on the sixth day, or how they got into their fixes. We want to uproot disease, ignorance, hunger, poverty, fear, from the surface of the earth. The hungry have always cried out for bread, not stones. In order to do this, we must develop a permanent idealism, an idealism incorrosible by nationalism, racialism, wealth, practicality, political manipulation—in a word, an idealism between hearts.

Harlem is not a Negro problem—not a *particularly* Negro problem. Harlem is the problem of New York City, the State of New York, the government of the United States, the citizens of the United States. It is not for the Negro to raise Harlem up. They may help just as any concerned American would help. If the people of the States consider it "beautiful," why, then, let them make it more beautiful. If they feel it is an eyesore, they will uproot it.

Minorities everywhere—in Iowa City, or Lumbumbashi in the Congo—have their peculiar problems. And minorities are of all sorts. Left alone, they cannot solve their own problems. The enlightened members of the majority groups have simply to help.

Uncle Africa wrote a letter to his Nephews and Cousins in America once. That letter fell in the wrong hands—my hands. I will share it with you:

My dear Cousins and Nephews (it read):
Greetings,

I have learnt lately that you want to install me as a guiding spirit. Naturally, I am flattered. But I have changed a lot since your fathers and mothers left here some time ago. And now I am changing faster and faster. I don't know which "spirit" of mine can act very well as your guiding spirit. Perhaps keep as much (or little) of me as you can and get more and more into the ways of your new home.

I am currently engaged in putting up a modern permanent house. The old one was falling apart and we pulled it down in order to have the site for the sturdy one now being built.

Next time you stop by you will be surprised at the amount of progress we have made away from the dark ages. Those ages were really dark—that's a fact of history; it can't be denied. But we don't celebrate the skull-hunting days any more, just as Hawthorne would not like to see the witch-burning days at Salem glorified.

From time to time, I shall be coming to discuss matters of state with your chief: Chief Plenty. I have more mouths which need feeding, and I would like to plant enough food for them. I need better hoes, and hope Chief Plenty will spare me a few.

In your last letter, you complained that you were poorly housed and fed, more poorly than your other brothers and sisters. Too bad. To live in the palace of Chief Plenty and yet starve to death! When I come there, I shall suggest tactfully to my host that you could receive better at his hands. Beyond deploring the fact, and wishing my host had done more, I can't do more. Remember, I shall be a guest.

I understand you want to use Black Power in order to knock certain obstacles down. I thought your Black Power was used up in the cotton fields, civil rights marches, working on the railroads. Don't you think it is high time you used your White Power? After all, you have White Power too.

You see, Black Power, used as a ram for battering down certain fortifications, works. But there comes a time when the knight has to alight from his horse, sheath his sword, in order to embrace his beloved. And again, some doors open easier with keys, others await a mere push, others are already ajar, and some are always open. Your wisdom will be measured by the means you adopt in each particular case.

When you are thirsty, lower your bucket where you are. That estuary has fresh water also. I am sure, by now, my in-laws know the looks of a thirsty man, and can give him drinking water without waiting till he has prostrated himself before them.

Remember, the problem you are fighting is the inhumanity of man to man, of nature to man. If any man comes forward and asks if you need any help, tell him to join in. If any man rolls up his sleeves and comes to lighten your burden without asking you, let him indulge himself. You need every available hand, maximum cooperation, in order to score a resounding victory, a victory over problems, not over man. This is not the type of war to be fought single-handed.

The darkest night is not that dark. Your grandmothers and grandfathers saw darkness compared to which you see now is morning light. They had hope. Revive that hope and you will cross the remaining rivers towards Jerusalem in a shorter time.

With love,
Uncle Africa

P.S.

Cousins and Nephews,
We do not go skull-hunting any more. In our new dispensation, we have not set up memorials for everything we did in the days past. About some of them, the less said the better. I am saying this so that you don't go re-introducing defunct rites. For, we now play soccer, participate in boxing, and win long distance races. I hope to see you in Mexico City next year when I come to compete in the Olympic Games. If you win more glory this time, I won't let you do that again. In coming Olympics we shall carry all the medals back to Africa.

Bye,
Africa